Palgrave Studies in Workplace Spirituality and Fulfillment

Series Editors
Satinder Dhiman, School of Business, Woodbury University, Burbank, CA, USA
Gary E. Roberts, Robertson School of Government, Regent University, Virginia Beach, VA, USA
Joanna Crossman, University of South Australia, Adelaide, SA, Australia

Satinder Dhiman, *Editor-in-Chief*
Gary Roberts and Joanna Crossman, *Associate Editors*

By way of primary go-to-platform, this Series precisely maps the terrain of the twin fields of *Workplace Spirituality and Fulfillment* in the disciplines of business, psychology, health care, education, and various other allied fields. It reclaims the sacredness of work—work that is mind-enriching, heart-fulfilling, soul-satisfying and financially-rewarding. It fills the gap in scholarship in the allied disciplines of Workplace Spirituality and Flourishing. Using a comprehensive schema, it invites contributions from foremost scholars and practitioners that reflect insightful research, practices, and latest trends on the theme of workplace spirituality and fulfillment. The uniqueness of this *Series* lies in its anchorage in the moral and spiritual dimension of various positive forms of leadership—such as Authentic Leadership, Servant Leadership, Transformational Leadership, and Values-Based Leadership.

We welcome research monographs and multi-authored edited volumes representing myriad thought-positions on topics such as: Past, Present and Future Directions in Workplace Spirituality; Workplace Spirituality and World Wisdom/Spiritual Traditions; Culture Studies and Workplace Spirituality; Spiritual, Social and Emotional intelligence; Nature of Work; Mindfulness at Work; Personal Fulfillment and Workplace Flourishing; Workplace Spirituality and Organizational Performance; Inner Identity, Interconnectedness, Community and Transcendence; Managing Spiritual and Religious Diversity at Work; Spirituality and World Peace Imperative; Sustainability and Spirituality; Spirituality and Creativity; and Applied Workplace Spirituality in Health Care, Education, Faith-based Organizations, et al.

Thomas Thakadipuram

Leadership Wholeness, Volume 1

A Model of Spiritual Intelligence

palgrave
macmillan

Thomas Thakadipuram
University of St. Thomas
Minneapolis, MN, USA

ISSN 2662-3668 ISSN 2662-3676 (electronic)
Palgrave Studies in Workplace Spirituality and Fulfillment
ISBN 978-3-031-08052-4 ISBN 978-3-031-08053-1 (eBook)
https://doi.org/10.1007/978-3-031-08053-1

Cover credit: Kotenko Oleksandr shutterstock

This Palgrave Macmillan imprint is published by the registered company Springer Nature Switzerland AG
The registered company address is: Gewerbestrasse 11, 6330 Cham, Switzerland

Thomas would like to dedicate this book
to his beloved Mother Annamma Thomas and family

To
my mother
Who embodies hidden wholeness
From her being comes goodness
From her goodness comes love
From her love comes infinite faith
From her faith comes undying hope
From her hope comes radiant joy
From her joy comes loving sacrifice
From her sacrifice comes endurance
From her endurance comes humility
From her humility comes greatness
From her greatness comes simplicity
From her simplicity comes brokenness
From her brokenness comes empathy
From her empathy comes acceptance
From her acceptance comes trust
From her trust comes resilience
From her resilience comes peace
From her peace comes grace
From her grace comes beauty
From her beauty comes bliss
From her bliss comes hidden wholeness

Preface

With the unprecedented time of the global pandemic setback, increasing climate disasters, and escalating volatility in business and social-political environments, new ways of managing and leading are inevitable. Faced with extraordinary complexity, vulnerability, and uncertainty, the old ways of leading and managing are ineffective in bringing about sustainable holistic development. As such, leaders are challenged to find a new way to navigate organizations in the complex global arena—based on sense of wholeness, authentic engagement, and organic sustainable growth. The development of shared global values, spirituality, and virtues in organizations is necessary to build a humane world of peace, prosperity, and progress in the twenty-first century with a wholesome thriving future. Humanity and world civilizations today experience challenges not only in the political, economic, and environmental domains but also in ethical, moral, and spiritual realms resulting in existential crises and longing for a breakthrough. Focusing on wholeness allows us to radically reconnect with each other, with our planet, and with our evolving human consciousness in order to heal the existential crisis of our time which is essentially the spiritual crisis of humanity that is reflected not only in the ecological, the social, and ethical crises but also in the crises of identity, values, and meaning. Therefore, a new awakening and holistic movement that calls for the pursuit of wholeness and spiritual values is currently needed in leaders and organizations. "The real voyage of discovery consists not in seeking new lands, but in seeing with new eyes" (Proust, 2006: 657).

This book project, based on phenomenological research, investigates the journey of influential spiritual and business leaders' quests for wholeness in the contemporary world. The need for transforming the global turbulence and embracing uncertainty in organizations with the leadership requires a deeper quest for meaning, awareness, and wholeness today. Although there are number of studies done on workplace spirituality and other leadership styles such as servant, ethical, and transformational, little is known about how prominent leaders across cultures, religions, and businesses experience the journey towards wholeness in the post-modern society. While there are a few preliminary reflections on wholeness in business, systematic research on the concept of "wholeness" as a unique and necessary leadership construct has never been conducted with in-depth interviews of top leaders.

Wholeness is defined as "living an undivided life." To be whole means to envision the reality of individuals, organizations, society, and nature as interconnected phenomena designed for the purpose of common well-being, progress, and greater happiness. In order to gain deeper insight into the lived experience of twenty-three top executive leaders from both profit and not-for-profit organizations, cultures across the globe are engaged with in-depth interviews to describe their profound experience of the quest. The selection criteria for participants included leaders who are known for their integrity, compassion, and successful impact on organizations, communities, and society. Four essential themes emerged from the original study: (1) sensing crisis, (2) embracing crisis, (3) awakening hidden wholeness, and (4) serving the greater good. The initial themes were confirmed by the data gathered from the in-depth interviews with top leaders. Analysis of the themes led to the development of a new leadership model, Wholeness: A Model of Spiritual Intelligence. The leadership wholeness model portrays the interior dimensions of leaders' quest for wholeness penetrating through their existential, learning, ethical, and spiritual levels of being, and exterior dimensions of wholeness permeating through the personal, organizational, social, global, and environmental spheres of life.

The findings of the research presented in this book provide valuable insights into the leaders' quest for wholeness and confirm the classic and emerging research on wholeness and workplace spirituality. The leadership wholeness model developed through research and phenomenological analysis of the in-depth interviews, first presented in my doctoral dissertation and later in an article published in *Human Resource Development International* (Thakadipuram, 2010), has already gained the attention of other scholars and graduate students across the globe for further application and research. These key practical insights and perspectives of wholeness from the lived experience of leaders will provide a great resource for any current and aspiring scholars, students, and leaders who strive to lead and guide teams, and organizations, to greater transformation, fulfillment, and wholeness in the contemporary world.

The research literature on spiritual leadership published in the last decade has mainly focused on personal and ethical dimensions without exploring the deeper spiritual and social dimensions of wholeness and our global responsibility for all beings on the planet in the wake of global crises. This book explores the essential themes of the quest for wholeness of contemporary spiritual and business leaders from a multidimensional perspective. This phenomenological research study about the experience of prominent spiritual and ethical business leaders' quest for wholeness uncovers the profound themes, dynamics, and deep structures of the phenomena of the quest for wholeness. This current study identifies and presents essential themes that expand the existing body of research on spiritual leadership and adds a new paradigm of wholeness based on the lived experience of influential leaders. As very little research on top leaders' quest for wholeness presently exists, the discovery of essential themes of wholeness paves the way for enhanced understanding of spiritual leadership and will benefit researchers and academics, and inspire leaders to fathom deeper dimensions of wholeness in the workplace and beyond.

This book aims to satisfy the need for a new paradigm of wholeness in leadership with higher intelligence in the context of workplace spirituality and fulfillment that will help scholars, academics, and leaders to design wholesome environments in the workplace based on the key insights presented in the book. This authentic engagement of spirit and mind in contemporary leadership, enhancing the whole self, will in turn result in advancing the long-term health, success, and sustainable development of businesses and organizations.

Minneapolis, MN, USA Thomas Thakadipuram

References

Proust, M. (2006). *Remembrance of things past* (S. Moncrieff, Trans.). Wordsworth Limited.

Thakadipuram, T. (2010). Leadership Wholeness: A human resource development model. *Human Resource Development International, 13*(4), 463–475.

Acknowledgments

I would like to thank Alexander Ardichvilli and Father David Pollich for their support and guidance in reviewing the book manuscript, Celia Bloom, Father Litto Thomas, and John Paul McMonagle for digital graphics, Marcus Ballenger, Supraja Yengaraman, and Melvin Lourdes and team for the editorial support and production of this book. I would like to thank the prominent leaders who participated in the interviews by providing their expertise and experiential wisdom towards this book: Sri Sri Ravishankar, Swami Veda Bharathi, Ambassador Susan Johnson, Ingrid Vandelveldt, Corinna Lim, Larry Zimpleman, Parker Palmer, John Abbate, Reverend Greg McBrayer, Gary Zelman, Carolyn Washburn, Nick Nissley, Archbishop Harry J. Flynn, Immaculi Illibagiza, Abbot Phab Son, Abbess Pema Kuang, Sister Rosalind Gefre, Lesli Temple Thurston, Steve Lacey, Tom Mahoney, Andy Anderson, William Jarema, and Credo Mutua. Thankful to all my friends and wellwishers. I invoke divine blessings of true peace, wise counsel, and spiritual comfort upon all those who journey towards wholeness of life.

Praise for *Leadership Wholeness, Volume 1*

"The author captures a holistic (macro) view of the elements of effective leadership, explaining that however one learns, there are commonalities. Rev. Dr. Thakadipuram draws on boundless sources, both contemporary and ancient, including wholeness in the Upanishads centuries before the holistic construct. It's underscored that the essential core is one's values. Whether derived from organized religion, philosophy, humanism, or one's parents, leaders must incorporate values to be successful. The emphasis on ESG is heartening, but a key for leaders is to not succumb to short-termism. I recommend this book and hope that those who need it most will take advantage of its wisdom."
—Howard Fluhr, *Chairman Emeritus of Segal Group, USA and Canada*

"This book presents a new leadership model enshrined in ancient wisdom and contemporary discourse that is particularly apt for our turbulent times. Addressing major spiritual crisis we face in the form of identity, values, social, and ecological crisis; at its core an argument for the essentiality of spiritual intelligence development as a tool and a framework for wise leadership conduct in this day and age.

The call of Dr. Thakadipuram is both timely and compelling. I urge you to read this book and heed its message that benefit your soul's journey to wholeness."
—Prof. Dr. Yochanan Altman, *Chair, International Association of Management Spirituality & Religion, Vienna, Austria*

"The concept of Leadership Wholeness and Spiritual Intelligence is very timely refreshing research into a variety of top leaders from across the globe. It would certainly help building a new category of leaders in facing crisis and create a new and balanced world of peace and prosperity integrated with sustainable nature.

I like the excellent way the author has integrated the experiences of the 23 leaders to build a refreshing model and approach to leadership for the future."

—T. V. Rao, *Chairman TVRLS and Founder President, National HRD Network, India*

Contents

List of Figures

CHAPTER 1

Introduction

The introduction presents why this book focuses on the concept of wholeness based on the lived experience of the top spiritual and business leaders in the context of workplace spirituality and fulfillment. Raising the problem of the lack of empirical data into spiritual and business leaders' quest for wholeness, this section will explain how this research, based on in-depth interviews, will provide a resource for scholars and academics. "If you wish to converse with me," said Voltaire, "define your terms" (quoted in Durant 1961: 48). Thus, the definitions of wholeness, spirituality, and workplace spirituality and spiritual leadership are discussed in order to engage in the full discourse of this book that explores leadership wholeness: A Model of Spiritual Intelligence.

The history of humanity can be seen as an unfolding story of the quest for wholeness. Starting from the Eastern sages' call to "Realize the Self," the *Atma sakshatkara (Self-realization)*, and from the Greek philosopher Socrates' clarion call to "Know thyself," humanity has been on a perennial quest to find true meaning and experience the wholeness of life. This perennial search for wholeness has been an integral part of beliefs and practices of many cultures and traditions until modern times. However, despite modern advancements, it is widely acknowledged by contemporary thinkers that, with the start of modern philosophy, Descartes' dualism of mind and body took a strong hold on modern scientific thinking.

T. Thakadipuram, *Leadership Wholeness, Volume 1*,
Palgrave Studies in Workplace Spirituality and Fulfillment,
https://doi.org/10.1007/978-3-031-08053-1_1

Although dualistic thinking is beneficial to functioning in practical life, it has resulted in a fragmented and compartmentalized view of life bereft of holistic perspective (Hammond et al., 1991; Robinson, 2016). It is said that we are born as whole human beings, but we are socialized to lead fragmented lives resulting in ethical, ecological, and social crises which emerge from the deeper spiritual crisis (Gwiazdon, 2020). A call for an inner awakening to wholeness, in the context of the global post-pandemic world, would pave the way for new global consciousness, wholesome leadership, and sustainable future. In the post-modern world, there is an emerging quest to rediscover the ancient roots of holistic thinking and spirituality to find answers to the challenges of divisiveness and polarization in these chaotic, complex, and turbulent times (Harvie & Guarneri, 2020). Albert Einstein articulated this new urge for holistic thinking quite succinctly early on when he said:

> A human being is part of the whole...he experiences himself, his thoughts and feelings, as something separated from the rest; a kind of optical delusion of his consciousness. This delusion is a kind of prison for us, restricting us to our personal desires and to affection for a few persons nearest us. Our task must be to free ourselves from this prison by widening our circle of compassion to embrace all living creatures and the whole of nature in its beauty.... We shall require a substantially new manner of thinking if mankind is to survive. (Einstein, 1950: 5)

Aurobindo (1985) claimed, in the similar vein, that this new manner of thinking could emerge from a holistic spiritual perspective when he noted, "The most vital issue of the age is whether the future progress of humanity is to be governed by the modern economic and materialistic mind of the West or by a nobler pragmatism guided, uplifted and enlightened by spiritual culture and knowledge" (1159). Kant advocated a new mindset and ability to see the "whole" first in order to make sense of the parts. For peace to reign on earth, humans must evolve into new beings who have learned to see the whole first (Teehankee, 2020). The survival and sustainability of life are not counted by the speedy progress we make but by what we are able to sustain and thrive in a wholesome manner.

With the unprecedented onset of escalating global environmental crisis, growing recession in world economy, and turbulent crises in business environments that lead to the growing stresses of the workplace, new ways of leading and guiding are inevitable (Tafoya, 2020). Faced with extraordinary levels of complexity, vulnerability, and uncertainly, the old ways of leading and managing are ineffective. As such, the previous generation of command-and-control leadership needs to give way to a new way of leading and managing organizations—a new way that is based on collective authentic engagement, holistic intelligence, and sustainable development. The development of shared global values and virtues in organizations is necessary to build a humane world of peace and progress in the twenty-first century as we continue to advance with the fast-growing technology, innovation, and massive disruptions (Askeland et al., 2020; Schein, 2017).

Humanity and world civilizations today experience problems, not only in the economic, environmental, and public health domains but also in ethical, moral, and spiritual realms resulting in brokenness and longing for breakthrough. Scharmer (2021) identified the three big divides of our time: the divide between self and nature resulting in ecological crises; the divide between the self and other self-contributing to social crisis; and the divide between the self and the higher self-resulting in spiritual crises. Therefore, the call for the pursuit of wholeness is the need of the hour currently echoing throughout every land transforming the pain into new possibilities and brokenness to wholeness.

This phenomenological research/book project investigates the journey of influential spiritual and business leaders' quest for wholeness in the contemporary world. Although there are number of studies done on workplace spirituality and fullfilment, little is known about how prominent leaders across cultures, religions, and businesses experience this journey in the post-modern society. In order to gain deeper insight into the lived experience, top leaders from different organizational contexts, cultures, and businesses around the globe engaged in in-depth interviews to describe their profound experience of the quest for wholeness.

Definition of Wholeness

The word "wholeness" is derived from the root word "hal," or whole, which means state of being healthy, happy, and undivided (Chamber's Dictionary of Etymology, 2022). The word "integrity" is evolved from the Latin adjective *integer*, meaning whole or complete. In this context, integrity is the inner sense of "wholeness" deriving from qualities such as honesty and consistency of character, values, and principles. The Greek equivalent of "whole" is "*holos*" which means totality, unbroken, and complete. Palmer (2009a: 5) defined wholeness as "living an undivided life." Living an undivided life does not necessarily mean living face to face with others; rather, it means never losing the awareness that we are connected to each other in the entire cosmos, and that we live for the universe through our choices and actions. To be whole means to envision the reality of individuals, organizations, society, and nature as interconnected phenomena designed for the purpose of common well-being, progress, and greater happiness. Griffith emphasized this interconnectedness with the individual and cosmos when he noted, "The root and ground of consciousness of being, is one with the root and ground of the whole creation" (Griffith, 1992: 61).

Palmer (2009a) reiterated that we are born with a seed of selfhood that contains the spiritual DNA of our uniqueness, the encoded birthright knowledge of who we are, why we are here, and how we are related to others. This spiritual DNA is a pure potentiality that can be actualized through the vicissitudes of life. Teilhard de Chardin noted, "We are not human beings having spiritual experiences; we are spiritual beings having human experiences" (quoted in Covey, 1989: 319). He continued to assert that "Everything is animated with a flow of presence and love-the spirit which, emanating from the supreme will penetrate for the first time into the environment which is biologically requisite for the wholeness of its task" (Chardin, 2004: 51). This holistic and non-dual perspective is offered to help one to transcend the limitations imposed by the material and the cultural universe, and emphasized the understanding that, as spiritual beings, we are organically connected to all other beings in the web of life.

Maslow (2005: 1) asserted, "What is necessary to change a person is to change the awareness of him." Self-awareness is about being fully open to the reality being in relationship whether we are alone or not. "When Buddha was asked to sum up his teaching in a single word, he said, "awareness," being awake, alert, in touch with what is actually happening" (Hagen, 2011: 3). Being deeply aware of our interdependent and ever-changing nature on this planet brings about deep difference in the way we experience and engage the world from holistic perspective. Palmer (2004: 54–55) advocated that, "We need the interior intimacy that comes with solitude and the otherness that comes with community. Together, solitude and community make us whole, like breathing in and breathing out" as one human family. The experience of wholeness is identified not as an event as such but as a process; the experience of transcendence makes us whole. It is a movement from external to the internal and vice versa. To be whole is a process of being and becoming (Aurobindo, 1972a). Palmer (2004: 2) clarified that, "Wholeness does not mean perfection: it means embracing the brokenness as an integral part of life." As such, wholeness is a journey through the process of praise and criticism, success and failure, solitude and community leading towards greater integration of life. I consider the quest for wholeness as an ongoing aspiration for harmony in life. The journey towards wholeness is a process of cultivating inner and outer harmony despite the chaos and complexities of life.

Definition of Spirituality

The word "spirituality" originated from the Latin world "spiritus" which means, breath, vigor, or consciousness. *Spiritus* is translated in Greek as *Pneuma (breath or soul)* and Hebrew *Ruach (spirit)*. The term "spirit" means "animating or vital principle in human beings and every living being. The Greek word *enthousiasmos* means enthusiasm or possessed by "divine essence" implying a sense of sacred or higher consciousness transcending the four dimensions of the material world" (Reese, 1997: 29). Spirituality is the quality of being deeply aware of the consciousness within and beyond. Kriger and Seng (2005: 772) defined spirituality as "the quest for self-transcendence and the attendant feeling of interconnectedness with all things in the universe." In modern times, spirituality pertains to deepest human experience, universal values, and virtues. Indian spiritual traditions define spirituality as *adhaÿtma*, meaning that which pertains to the inner self or higher *consciousness*. Spirituality refers to a basic perspective of being connected with one's whole self, others, and the entire universe. It is an expression of people's profound need for coherent meaning, love, well-being, and fulfillment.

Spirituality and Religion

Every religion has spiritual and mystical roots with immanent and transcendental experiences. If we look into any major religions of today, Hinduism, Buddhism, Islam, Christianity, and Judaism, they all have a basis of myths and stories, rituals, scriptures, and prayers, philosophy and theology and mystical literature. The spirituality is contained in the basic universal values and transcendental experiences. There is higher sense ontological unity and harmony at the mystical dimensions of religion and spiritualities whereas there are differences in the way stories are developed and practices have emerged based on culture and civilizations. When religion mixed with politics takes hold of the culture, it is divisive and fundamentalistic perspectives emerge resulting in conflicts, and polarizations and divisions. It is no longer a question of a Christian or Hindu or Muslim or any religious sects going about to convert others to the faith, but of each one being ready to listen to the other and so to grow together in mutual understanding and appreciation of the uniqueness and rich spiritualities of one another. Teasdale (2003) noted that Bede Griffiths, a pioneer in inter-spirituality which is a process and activity of exploring various religious traditions from a spiritual perspective, paved the way for appreciation of the religious diversity to enhance mutual understanding and cultivation of the mystical heart in the pursuit of wholeness. In fact, to be religious is to be interreligious just as to be human is to be interhuman. Although there are epistemological and ontological claims for each religion that seems to keep it separate, the mystical spiritual dimensions keep them united at the core. The uniqueness and universality of each religious traditions and spiritualties enhance the experience of diversity and differences that makes difference in the world. From an organic point of view, more integrative and mutual enriching perspective of religion and spirituality needs to be enhanced. The world civilization with a heart of Christian love, mind of Buddhist compassion, body of Islamic brotherhood, universal spirit of Hinduism, and the indomitable will of Judaism and the indigenous conscience of closeness to nature pave the way of universal harmony and co-existence of the planet. In this way, spirituality is not opposed to religion, but it transcends and integrates religious perspectives of life.

Workplace Spirituality

A review of current management, workplace spirituality, and organization literature over the last two decades shows that there is growing interest for business in spirituality, yet the concept of wholeness in workplace is understudied and under-explored (Dhiman, 2017; Gull & Doh, 2004; Kovács, 2020; Marques et al., 2007; Mitroff & Denton, 1999; Neal, 2018; Singh & Singh, 2022; Zsolnai, 2004). It's good to do away with the misconception that a spiritual workplace is a religious workplace, although the roots of spirituality are inextricably connected to religious experience. A spiritual workplace is a place of wholeness: enhancing the culture of fulfillment, friendliness, and productivity while embracing challenges with a positive and realistic attitude. Vaill noted that, in the business context, “Hunger to nourish the spirit indeed seems to be driving the movement to finding greater meaning in work” (quoted in Rigoglioso, 1999: 1).

Some of the major economic and cultural stresses that have spurred this trend for wholeness and meaning include destabilization of employment in corporations, global volatility, corresponding reductions in the workforce, increased transitions of management and employees, environmental turbulence, cross-cultural complexities, and the breakdown of families and school systems. As the context of life and work changes dramatically adding complexity and chaos, there is a deeper yearning for meaning, harmony, and search for wholeness.

In this environment of “permanent whitewater,” a phrase coined by Vaill, he noted, “We are searching for new ways of grounding to sustain us through turbulent times” (quoted in Rigoglioso, 1999: 1). The search for new ways of grounding leads to the exploration of the spiritual dimensions of management. Gull and Doh (2004: 128) alerted us about this need for grounding when they stated, “Despite an extensive set of critiques and criticisms offered by scholars and practitioners, most modern organizations remain devoid of a spiritual foundation and deny their employees the opportunity for spiritual expression through their work.” The search for meaning amidst resistance calls for creative ways to address the imbalance, growing stress, and fragmentation in the workplace. Biberman and Marques (2014) identified five ways in which spirituality in the workplace and organizations manifested: firstly, the spiritual and religious practices which are implemented in the business settings such as meditation, yoga, and prayers. Secondly, the spiritual values and beliefs held by the leaders in an organization or the spiritual behaviors manifested in spiritual leadership. Thirdly, the ways in which the mission and the vision of the organization manifest the spiritual values. Fourthly, the ways in which the spiritual perspectives are reflected in the organizational structures and policies, and finally, the spiritual and religious practices manifested in the working culture of the people.

Although talking about spirituality in the workplace context feels risky and awkward, because some people may tend to question the motivation behind it, companies around the world are becoming more tuned to the path of spirituality and growing as religiously friendly workplace to respond to their employees’ deeper yearnings (Biberman & Whitty, 2007; Singh & Singh, 2022). Considering the wisdom and resources of faith traditions and spiritualities might connect with the meaning of work and the greater purpose of life. These wisdom traditions remind us that corporate life is not about programs but people. Miller (2022: 3) stated, "It's about cultivating a covenantal mindset instead of a contractual one; about relationships not transactions." And faith and spiritual traditions emphasize individual and societal transformation for the greater good, not just what's best for me or my company. "Faith traditions also remind us of the profound stewardship responsibilities given to humanity to tend to the garden in sustainable and generative ways, i.e., to be responsible trustees of the resources and environment entrusted to us" (Miller, 2022: 2). Expressing spirituality in the workplace through career calling, ethical practices of justice and fairness, personal spiritual practices of tolerance and understanding, and dialogue showed evidence of reduced absenteeism, decreased turnover, and work place chaplaincy, increased employee satisfaction and wellness (Claude-Hélène & Dirk, 2019).

Neal (2018) identified three workplace spirituality "movements": the spirit at work movement, the faith at work movement, and the conscious capitalism movement. The spirit at work movement is primarily nonreligious and is influenced mostly by Eastern spiritual practices such as meditation and yoga, and its members tend to be coaches, consultants, and scholars (Reb et al., 2020). The faith at work movement is primarily a Protestant movement (Miller et al., 2019) and is influenced by religious values of gratitude, charity, stewardship, and justice, and its members tend to be Christian business leaders and Christian scholars. The conscious capitalism movement was founded by John Mackey, CEO of Whole Foods, and Raj Sisodia, a marketing professor at Babson College (Mackey & Sisodia, 2014). The four guiding principles behind conscious capitalism include higher purpose, stake holder orientation, conscious leadership, and socially responsible culture. Its members are primarily business leaders, CEOs, and consultants.

A number of studies have found that the long-term health and success of an organization are directly related to its values and cultivation of a spiritual environment (Ashar & Lane-Maher, 2004; Fairholm, 2000; Kovács, 2020). Leaders of corporate organizations including Jack Welch, William George, and others, who cultivated spirituality in the workplace, have noted the advantages of partnering with communities and taking on greater social responsibility while achieving sustainable growth and long-term market value (Askeland et al., 2020; George, 2007; Stephen, 2002).

While some scholars believe that spirituality and pursuit of wholeness is a new trend in line with the previous movements, others consider this growing attention on the deeper meaning of work to be part of a significant change occurring in the way work is being perceived and structured (Bella et al., 2021; Csikszentmihalyi, 2003; Stevens, 2006; Vaill, 2000; Williams, 2003). Hicks (2003: 47) stated this point of view in a striking way, "The commitment to treat workers as whole persons, and not merely as inputs to a production process, can lead to genuine and beneficial progress toward creating a humane workplace." This spiritual approach to the workplace creates a climate of respect, inclusion, and appreciation so that workplace becomes meaningful, engaging, and conducive for the human spirit to flourish as an antidote to stress and workplace anxiety today. Alonzo McDonald, a consultant engaged in leading dialogue on the "re-spiriting" of the workplace, notes, "The more they [leaders] strengthen the spiritual dimension in their own lives, the more they will enrich their own quality of life and their relationships with family, friends, and employees" (as cited in Rigoglioso, 1999: 3). The workplaces that introduce spiritual practices such as meditation, yoga, relaxation, silence, and reflection, along with positive dialogue, celebrations of religious feasts and festivals, and friendly relationships, enhance the human spirit and energy in the workplace. Employers now recognize it is essential to establish a work environment where differences are treated with respect and inclusion. In the globalized work environment where workers come from diverse backgrounds, cultures, and religions, it is important to create an inclusive atmosphere to avoid the negative impact of bias, prejudice, and discrimination. Diversity, equity, and inclusion programs, including employee training, should include religious differences along with other dimensions of diversity. Make it clear that it is the responsibility of every employee to be aware, knowledgeable, and respectful of a wide range of religious and nonreligious beliefs. These practices help increase the productivity not only of individual employees, but also of the organization as a whole (Guillory, 2000). In researching companies for his book, *A Spiritual Audit of Corporate America*, Mitroff and Denton (1999: i) asserted, "spirituality could be the ultimate competitive advantage."

The interest in spirituality and wholeness in the workplace is ever growing with new studies and practices (Bella et al., 2021; Driscoll & McKee, 2007; Harrington, 1998; Roberts & Crossman, 2018; Rocha & Pinheiro, 2021; Young, 2002; Zsolnai, 2004). Lee and Zemke (1993) reported early on the quest of baby-boomers for a spiritual home.

Tinder (1989: 51) remarked of professionals and institutions that, "Good customs and habits need a spiritual base; and if it is lacking, they will gradually in some crisis disappear." World-renowned spiritual leader, Ravi Shankar (2006: 1) states, "Trust is the breath of business, ethics its limbs, to uplift the spirit its goal." Thus, spirituality has become of primary concern in the life of the workplace rather than an epiphenomenon or simply an irrelevant factor. Spirituality in the workplace is a growing paradigm in contemporary corporations.

The burgeoning workplace spirituality literature has been mainly influenced by developments in the fields of religious studies, psychology, and biology (Fairholm, 2000; Foster & Wall, 2020; Fry, 2005a; Giacalone & Jurkiewicz, 2003; Gibbons, 2000). Giacalone and Jurkiewicz (2003: 13) defined workplace spirituality as "a framework of organizational values evidenced in the culture that promotes employees' experience of transcendence through the work process, facilitating their sense of being connected to others in a way that provides feelings of completeness and joy." Altman, Neal and Mayrhofer (2022) identified three emerging trends such as workplace spirituality and global consciousness, workplace spirituality and new technologies, and workplace spirituality and confronting dark spiritualities such as anti-semitism, religious exclusion, and diversity biases and prejudices. In addition, these authors also identified six macro-trends in the field of workplace spirituality, (a) the maturing filed of workplace spirituality, (b) the levels of analysis from individual to organizations systems, (c) resistance to the workplace spirituality movement, (d) evolution of language, (e) scholar/practitioner orientation, and (f) the impact of workplace spirituality and how it is making a difference in organizations and marketplace.

There are other emerging Employee Resource Groups initiated by Religious Freedom and Business Foundation networks such Faith Force at Sales Force to bring the whole self to work including religious diversity and faith (Warnke, 2022). Obregon et al. (2022) identified the contributions in workplace spirituality and religiosity that encompass four approaches: (i) measurement scales of spirituality and religiosity; (ii) behavioral benefits of religiosity in individuals; (iii) insertion of religiosity and spirituality in social service practice; and (iv) research directions. This research presents technical and managerial implications to provide theoretical support for the creation of programs and/or practices of spirituality and religion in the workplace as an effective strategy, towards ethical attitudes.

In summary, workplace spirituality is based on transcendent vision, religious diversity, universal ethical values of integrity, and authenticity and can promote meaning and harmony in the workplace creating an inclusive holistic environment. Pluralistic spiritual practices enhance the whole-person in the workplace, unleashing creativity, sustainability, and a positive climate in organizations.

Spiritual Leadership

Many researchers and practitioners have developed consensus that the progression of thinking over the years has developed the understanding that leadership is a flexible developmental process with each new piece of research building on to the previous theories. Main leadership theories that emerged during the twentieth century include Trait, Process Leadership, Style and Behavioral, Transformational, Transactional, and Laissez-Faire Leadership theory (Khan et al., 2016). Spiritual leadership flows from leadership theories and models that emphasize transformational, principle-centered leadership and workplace spirituality (Connie, 2017; Duchon & Plowman, 2005; Jihye & Wang, 2020; Kouzes & Posner, 2007). George (2003: 5) advocated, "We need authentic leaders, people of high integrity, committed to building organizations: We need leaders who have a deep sense of purpose and are true to their own core values." The qualities of openness, truthfulness, trust, integrity, hope, and self-confidence have been noted to be integral to spiritual leadership and wholeness (Cha & Edmondson, 2006; George, 2007; Luthans & Avolio, 2003).

Greenleaf and Spears (1998: 6), the pioneering champions of servant leadership which is based on spiritual and transcendental values of service and greater good of the society, acknowledged, "There is something subtle communicated to one who is being served and led, if implicit in the compact between servant leader and the led is the understanding that the search for wholeness is something they share." Roberts and Crossman (2018) noted the universality of the concept of servant leadership and its five attributes such as servanthood, stewardship, virtues, vision, and transcendental dimensions. It is based on the metaphor of service which is common to all major religions and spiritualities. The quest for wholeness is recognized here as integral to servant leadership although its impact on leaders and organizations has not been explored. The aspect of servant leadership and its significance in work place spirituality will be explored further in the upcoming second volume of this book project.

Whereas the conventional view of leadership emphasizes positional power and conspicuous accomplishment, spiritual leadership, which is based on wholeness, is about creating a domain in which both the leaders and the followers continually learn and become more capable of participating in the unfolding of the future. Crossman and Crossman (2018: 2) emphasized the spirituality of followership and its significance in leadership practice. "Spiritual followership functions as a process, most notably operating in its teaching and learning relationship with leadership. The spiritual follower is emancipated, empowered, and courageous." They have presented four clusters of spiritual followership theories, being leader-centric, leader-follower, multiple leadership, and follower-centric theories. Detailed discussion on this topic of spiritual followership will be done in the Vol 2 of this book.

Jaworski and Flowers (1996: 192), emphasizing the holistic dimension of leadership, stated:

> A true leader thus sets the stage on which predictable miracles, synchronistic in nature, can and do occur. The capacity to discover and participate in our unfolding future has more to do with our being - our total orientation of character and consciousness than with what we do.

The deep territory of leadership which focuses on wholeness—personally and collectively "listening" to what is emerging in the world, and then having the courage to do what is required—cannot neglect the spiritual dimension of life (Jaworski & Flowers, 1996). Fry (2003) held the view that spiritual leadership expands current models of leadership because of its focus on values, attitudes, and behaviors of leaders as well as the cultivation of the spiritual environment in organizations. Based on spiritual perspectives, a prominent leader's vision and charisma can provide new direction, build a vibrant culture based on altruistic love, and help followers create teams based on shared values and virtues.

Fry (2005a) made a distinction between spirituality and religion in the sense that spirituality is an awareness and sense of closeness to a higher being, whereas religion is defined as formal beliefs and practices that can impede an organization's spiritual development through sectarian approaches. Spiritual values and practices envisioned from an open and universal perspective can enliven the spirit and soul of the organization and its members. Such spiritual perspectives will help develop attitudes of tolerance and respect towards different point of views and can create a positive environment to unleash the creative potential of the employees, contributing towards the integral development of the organization. Although the distinction between religion and spirituality in the workplace is articulated rather clearly, the influence of one on the other cannot be denied (Kriger & Seng, 2005).

Benefiel (2005) considered spiritual leadership as the influence a leader has on followers and on the environment, and how the spiritual dynamism transforms the leader, followers, and the entire organization. Personal spiritual practices, such as reflective listening, yogic relaxation, and working towards personal integration along with collective spiritual practices, including open dialogue and communal discernment regarding their role and responsibility in society, help leaders and followers explore the unfolding future of the organization. The cultivation of such spiritual leadership practices in the workplace facilitates the quest for personal and organizational wholeness. Fairholm (2000) conducted a study on intellectual roots of business leadership beginning with scientific management, and traced the evolution of leadership ideas through the quality movement on to values, culture, and trust-based leadership models, and concluded with an emphasis on spirit in the workplace. The study suggested that the leaders in the twenty-first century need to embrace a leadership style based on the main premise of each model, along with a focus on ethics, community, service, and spirituality.

In a nutshell, spiritual leadership, which emphasizes higher consciousness, ethical values, service, and a cultivation of spiritual environment in the workplace, has been gaining momentum in recent decades. A new perspective of leadership is studied in this research using the framework of wholeness emphasizing personal and collective spiritual practices based on ancient roots of holistic thinking, interconnectedness, and collective consciousness. Studying top spiritual and business leaders' lived experience of the quest for wholeness will lend important and needed insight into the impact of the phenomenon of spirituality in current organizational life.

Phenemenological Research Methodology

Phenomenological research methodology used in this study is based on an interpretive epistemology. Interpretive epistemology has its ontological roots in social constructivism, which holds that reality is socially constructed and does not exist independently of the mind of the actors involved in the social world (Burrell & Morgan, 1979). The nature of reality in the interpretive epistemology is multiple and context dependent, whereas reality in positivist thought is singular and reductionist (van Manen, 1997). Interpretive researchers, in general, are interested in deciphering individual meanings, whereas positivistic researchers are interested in norms that can be generalized and statistical significance (Creswell, 1998). The most influential theorists who have made significant contributions to the interpretive study of knowledge through phenomenology are Edmund Husserl, Maurice Merleau-Ponty, and Martin Heidegger (Ehrich, 2005). van Manen (1983: 9) provides a description of the qualitative method that resonates clearly with the objectives of phenomenological inquiry:

> It is at best an umbrella term covering an array of interpretive techniques which seek to describe, decode, translate, and otherwise come to terms with the meaning, not the frequency, of certain more or less naturally occurring phenomena in the social world.

The epistemology of interpretive research is inductive wherein the inquiry moves from the particular to the universal. As such, phenomenological research is inherently inductive rather than deductive, as theoretical propositions *emerge* from the descriptions of experience given by individuals under investigation (Giorgi, 2002). Thompson et al. (1989: 137) explained the phenomenological focus of research as follows:

> The research focus is on experience as described from a first-person view, where researchers seek to apprehend a pattern as it emerges. The research strategy is *holistic* and seeks to relate descriptions of specific experiences to each other and to the overall context of the life-world. The research goal is to give a *thematic description* of experience.

Rather than trying to confirm or disprove existing theories, the aim of phenomenological research is to develop "bottom-up" interpretive theories that are inextricably "grounded" in the lived world (van Manen,

1997). The philosophical foundations of phenomenology rest on four key components: (1) intentionality, (2) inter-subjectivity, (3) lifeworld (*Lebenswelt*), and (4) embodied consciousness (van Manen, 1997). These four components aptly describe how a researcher uses phenomenology to interpret the world and the lived experience of a phenomenon. In addition, the five key concepts of openness, encounter, immediacy, uniqueness, and meaning (Dahlberg & Drew, 1997) support the philosophical foundations of phenomenology by moving from theory to practice so the researcher is actively conscious of his or her interactions with participants.

Method

Phenomenology is considered a human science method, a profoundly reflective inquiry into human meaning (van Manen, 1997). Kvale (1996) explains that, in phenomenological research, interviewing relevant participants is the primary data-gathering method. The interview, supported by direct observation, is employed to deeply and fully mine the lived experience of the phenomenon. The most important step in the research process is to define the research question based on the methodology to establish the focus of the inquiry. The research question, which I formulated in this study, is: *What is the lived experience of leaders' quest for wholeness?* Based on this focus question, I established the participant criteria and located relevant participants from across cultures, religions, and various continents for the study. The interviews were in-depth and open-ended conversations through which I investigated the lived experience of the phenomenon under study. The interviews were tape recorded and transcribed so that I had the auditory and written data to analyze. I then analyzed the transcribed data to discover the essential themes of the phenomenon of wholeness (van Manen, 1997).

The following section describes the participant selection including the criteria for selecting participants, identifying the participants that met the criteria, how I contacted them, and the participants' profiles. A detailed account of the interview method and research process used in this study includes my interviewing process, creating openness in the interview process, the strategies for bracketing pre-understandings, and the analysis of essential themes. This section concludes with a discussion on the validity and the objectivity of the phenomenological research.

In order to gain deep insight into the phenomenon of the quest for wholeness for spiritual and business leaders, I sought information-rich participants establishing the criteria for selecting and accessing these participants. I included the profiles of the top spiritual leader participants (Appendix 1). I sought originally ten participants who are considered to be top spiritual and business leaders and who are known nationally or internationally as having unique journeys towards wholeness. After the initial discovery of the theme of wholeness and spiritual intelligence, I did another round of thirteen interviews of mostly business leaders to confirm the findings and to validate the research process further. The criteria for participation were based on the understanding that leaders in this study are not only accepted and respected in their own spiritual or religious tradition, but have a reputation beyond the boundaries of their own tradition, culture, and organization. In selecting participants, I made a distinction between spiritual leaders and religious leaders. For this study, spiritual leadership is defined as the values, attitudes, and behaviors that are necessary to intrinsically motivate one's own self and others so that they have a sense of spiritual excellence (Fleischman, 1994; Maddock & Fulton, 1998) through calling and membership. Fry (2007) proposes that spiritual leadership is a source of ethical and spiritual well-being and social responsibility. Spiritual leaders are those who demonstrate influence across traditions and cultures regardless of whether they hold a position within a particular religious tradition or organization. In comparison, religious leaders are those whose influence is confined to their own respective traditions. I sought recommendations from well-known spiritual leaders and various global not-for-profit organizations to identify potential candidates who fit the criteria. I specifically choose spiritual leaders who are known for their quest for wholeness, for at least the last 15 years, and who are known nationally or internationally through their publications, activities, and/or organizations. This selection process enabled me to be confident in their ability to give information-rich descriptions on the phenomenon of interest.

In summary, the prominent spiritual and business leaders can be described as having the following characteristics:

- Leaders who are known nationally or internationally for their spiritual and business leadership;
- Leaders who are rooted in a particular religious or spiritual tradition but are respected across traditions, cultures, and organizations;

- Leaders who are known for their ethical-spiritual well-being and social responsibility;
- Leaders who are known for their personal integrity, and humanitarian outreach, and ecological concern;
- Leaders who are known for their quest for wholeness for at least the last 10–15 years and are able to give information-rich description of the phenomena of wholeness.

It was established that each leader participant recommendation had to be confirmed by at least two sources. These two sources were reputed organizations and publications or other prominent leaders who have knowledge of these spiritual leaders. Having two sources confirming increased the credibility of their eligibility to be a participant for this research.

Seeking twenty-three information-rich participants who are known for their sense of wholeness helped me fathom the phenomenon in its depth and entirety. Some phenomenologists, including Boyd (2001), consider two to ten participants or research subjects as sufficient to reach saturation and Creswell (1998: 113) recommends "long interviews with up to 10 people" for a systematic and rigorous phenomenological study. By interviewing 23 participants, I felt that sufficient saturation was not only achieved but also allowed me to explicate themes and validate them from the data.

After obtaining the necessary approval from the Institutional Review Board (IRB) of the University of St. Thomas for the use of the human subjects in this study (Appendix A), I sought referrals from both international and national spiritual organizations and networks for potential participants who fit the criteria of selection. In searching for recommendations, I asked for possible candidates without suggesting names. This helped me to build the potential participant pool (Seidman, 2004) of 55 top leaders. I sent introductory letters and emails to potential candidates inviting them to take part in the research if they were keenly interested in such a study.

After identifying the possible interview candidates, I accessed them through the gatekeepers and contacted them to assess their interest and their eventual participation in the study (Moustakas, 1994; Seidman, 2004). For many of the identified prominent leader candidates, a full schedule precluded their participation in the study. Since direct contact with the prominent leaders is very rare and hardly possible, I made contact with their assistants to initiate conversations about the availability of the candidate. I created an introduction letter and an overview of the research study to be mailed to each participant. In follow-up communications with the assistant and the candidate, I gained consent to interview the leader and scheduled the face-to-face interview. When the time and place for the interview was scheduled, I sent a confirmation letter to each participant of the research study.

There was no conversation with the participant about the theory of spiritual leadership or the concept of wholeness during any previous interaction. The focus of the inquiry was purely on the lived experience (van Manen, 1997) of the quest for wholeness. After an introduction and brief casual conversation, I began the interview, asking the spiritual leaders to tell their stories regarding the journey towards wholeness. My experience of being a spiritual leader and a religious leader for the last 25 years and my own search for wholeness were resources for me to engage the participants with questions that helped mine the lived experience of the quest for wholeness. My diverse background in philosophy, comparative religion, psychology, and management and my experience in spiritual counseling and organizational consulting have influenced my understanding of the phenomenon of wholeness under study. I took conscious steps to bracket my pre-understandings, especially through journaling, to reduce their effect on my study. My personal practice of meditation and self-reflection helped me to be personally detached and be truly present to the participant and to help them fully enter their lived experience of the phenomena (van Manen, 1997).

Maintaining a skeptical attitude helped me to probe deeper into the stories and to seek concrete description of the phenomena from the participants. I remained open to learning something new in each interview, with each revision of the transcript, with each visit to a new country where the participants lived, and from what I observed in participant's organizational environment. I understood the difficulty of gaining access to the top leaders as they maintain high visibility and have very busy schedules, but with persistent efforts and good networking, I managed to gain access and interview them. Some of them invited me to stay overnight in their residence so that I could experience their hospitality and observe their living environments. I spent time recording my emotions and excitement about the rich information and the wisdom each participant shared with me. I established new connections across the globe to identify participants and thereby learned new perspectives from each culture and nations from Africa, Asia, Europe, and Americas. I was skeptical whether I would be able to find consistent essential themes of the quest for wholeness from such a culturally and geographically diverse participant group and concerned that the data might not get saturated from only 23 interviews. When I began to do the data analysis by reading and re-reading the texts over and over, I noticed the themes emerging spontaneously from their accounts of their lived experience in spite of their uniquely different backgrounds.

The above-stated assumptions and decisions came from my experience, learning, and pre-understandings. As I worked through the literature review, interviews, and theme analysis process, I documented my thoughts and feelings, and remained alert to discover other emerging assumptions to enhance the entire study. I maintained this single focus on researching and understanding the phenomenon of leaders' quest for wholeness. The results of the research were shared with the participants and they reviewed the findings and validated it.

The second chapter of this book presents Wholeness: A Model of Spiritual Intelligence. This model was constructed from the key findings from the research on leaders' quest for wholeness, explicating the interior dynamics of the quest for wholeness that moves the leader from sensing existential crises to embracing the strengths and shadows and awakening of hidden wholeness towards living an ethic of co-responsibility. The exterior dynamics explains the leadership practice of co-responsibility serving the greater good with the followers, organization, community, and the larger world. How other scholars and academics find this model useful in their research and course of study, and teaching are also described.

The third chapter presents the first theme, "Sensing Crisis" from the lived experience of the top leaders in various organizations across the globe. The five aspects of the core spiritual crisis: identity crisis, value crisis, meaning crisis, social crisis, and ecological crisis, are discussed. This section will help the reader to get in touch with their own struggles and name and claim the challenges to pave the way for their own journey from brokenness to wholeness.

The fourth chapter explains the second theme of the study, "Embracing Crisis," exploring the inner transformation leaders undergo in their quest for wholeness. The five aspects of this "Embracing": awareness of the strengths and shadows, self-acceptance, *growing in authenticity*, matching soul, and role, are discussed. This section will help the readers to identify their pathway to their own inner work of transformation towards meaning and wholeness.

This fifth chapter explains the third theme, "Awakening Hidden Wholeness," that uncovers insights of leaders regarding their spiritual awakening and its five aspects: cultivating regular spiritual practice, inner silence, inner transformation, moving towards the light, and discovering inner harmony, are discussed. This intense journey unfolds the pure potentiality within and opens up the deeper and greater dimensions of being. This section will in a special way inspire and challenge readers to fathom deeper dimensions of their own being and hopefully inspire them embark on their own awakening journey towards wholeness.

The sixth chapter examines the fourth theme, "Serving the Greater Good" and how leaders lived and promoted the ethic of highest good through their own flourishing organizations, which emerged from the challenging crises experiences. The five aspects of serving the greater good: circle of trust, circle of responsibility, circle of compassion, and circle of stewardship, are discussed. The question, "Are we not our brothers' and sisters' keeper?", is explored practically from an understanding of the interdependent nature of reality and how leaders created personal trust, organization responsibility, global compassion, and environmental stewardship are described. From a deeper awareness of the interconnectedness of reality, a stronger ethic of co-responsibility is fostered throughout their life and organizations deeply respecting the differences that make the difference. The leaders have modeled their way for others to emulate and engage in a life of service and fulfillment.

The seventh and final chapter gives a summary of the new paradigm of leadership wholeness and spiritual intelligence model and the benefits of this book for scholars, academics, and practitioners at a broader level. This project adds new contemporary frame work of spirituality from the perspective of leadership wholeness and the spiritual intelligence model that will help the scholars, academics, and leaders to explore their own journey towards wholeness and help create wholesome environment in the workplace today. The authentic engagement of spirit and mind in leadership will in turn result in enhancing the long-term health, success, and sustainable development of businesses and organizations.

References

Altman, M. (2014). *Kant and applied ethics: The uses and limits of Kant's practical philosophy*. Wiley.

Altman, Y., Neal, J., & Mayrhofer, W. (Eds.). (2022). *Workplace spirituality*. Walter de Gruyter GmbH. This book is published by open access at www.degruyter.com

Ashar, H., & Lane-Maher, M. (2004). Success and spirituality in the new business paradigm. *Journal of Management Inquiry, 13*(3), 249–260.

Askeland, H., Espedal, G., Jelstad Løvaas, B., & Sirris, S. (2020). Understanding values work in organizations and leadership. In H. Askeland, G. Espedal, B. Jelstad Løvaas, & S. Sirris (Eds.), *Understanding values work*. Palgrave Macmillan. https://doi.org/10.1007/978-3-030-37748-9_1

Aurobindo, G. S. (1972a). *Synthesis of yoga*. Sri Aurobindo Society.

Aurobindo, G. S. (1972b). Involution and evolution. *Sabda, 16*, 241–242.

Aurobindo, G. S. (1985). *The Life divine*. Sri Aurobindo Ashram Press.

Bella, R. L. F., Quelhas, O. L. G., Ferraz, F. T., Barboza, D. V., & França, S. L. B. (2021). An initial approach to increase job satisfaction through workplace spirituality. *Frontiers in Psychology, 12*, 768290. https://doi.org/10.3389/fpsyg.2021.768290

Benefiel, M. (2005). The second half of the journey: Spiritual leadership for organizational transformation. *The Leadership Quarterly, 16*(6), 723–747.

Biberman, J., & Marques, J. (2014). Influences of religion on spirituality in the workplace. In J. Marques & S. Dhiman (Eds.), *Leading spiritually*. Palgrave Macmillan. https://doi.org/10.1057/9781137455635_10

Biberman, J., & Whitty, M. (2007). *At work: Spirituality matter*. University of Scranton Press.

Boyd, C. O. (2001). Phenomenology method. In P. L. Munhall (Ed.), *Nursing research: A qualitative perspective* (3rd ed., pp. 93–122). Jones and Bartlett.

Brummit, L. (2013). *Leadership wholeness in Jamaica: An exploratory case study* (Masters' thesis). Retrieved from North Carolina State University Electronic thesis and dissertation data base. http://www.lib.ncsu.edu/resolver/1840/16/8559

Burrell, G., & Morgan, G. (1979). *Sociological paradigms and organizational analysis*. Ashgate Publishing Limited.

Buller, J. (2019). *Mindful leadership: An insight-based approach to college administration*. Rowman & LittleField Publishers.

Cha, E., & Edmondson, A. C. (2006). When values backfire: Leadership, attribution, and disenchantment in a values-driven organization. *Leadership Quarterly, 17*(1), 57–68.

Champers Dictionary of Etymology. (2022, June). https://chambers.co.uk/search/

Chardin, T. (2004). *The future of man* (N. Denny, Trans.). Image Books, Double Day.

Claude-Hélène, M., & Dirk, G. (2019, March 11). Workplace spirituality and wellness. In J. Marques (Ed.), *The Routledge companion to management and workplace spirituality*. Routledge. Accessed 9 June 2021, Routledge Handbooks Online.

Connie, J. (2017). Spiritual leadership in the learning organization: How spiritual leadership enhances the learning organization's effectiveness. *Geraziadio Business Review, 20*(3). https://gbr.pepperdine.edu

Covey, R. S. (1989). *The Seven habits of highly effective people*. Simon & Shuster.

Creswell, J. W. (1998). *Qualitative inquiry and research design: Choosing among five traditions*. Sage.

Crossman, B., & Crossman, J. (2011). Conceptualizing followership: A review of the literature. *Leadership, 7*, 481–497.

Crossman, B., & Crossman, J. (2018). Spiritual followership: Emerging conceptualizations. In S. Dhiman, G. Roberts, & J. Crossman (Eds.), *The Palgrave handbook of workplace spirituality and fulfillment*. https://doi.org/10.1007/978-3-319-61929-3_30-3

Csikszentmihalyi, M. (2003). *Good business: Leadership, flow, and the making of meaning*. Penguin Group.

Dahlberg, K., & Drew, N. (1997). A lifeworld paradigm for nursing research. *Journal of Holistic Nursing, 15*(3), 303–317.

Dhiman, S. (2017). *Holistic leadership: A new paradigm for today's leaders*. Palgrave Macmillan.

Driscoll, C., & McKee, M. (2007). Re-storying a culture of ethical and spiritual values: A role for leader storytelling. *Journal of Business Ethics, 73*(2), 205–217.

Duchon, D., & Plowman, D. A. (2005). Nurturing the spirit at work: Impact on work unit performance. *Leadership Quarterly, 16*(5), 807–833.

Durant, W. (1961). *Story of philosophy*. Simon and Schuster.

Ehrich, L. (2005). Revisiting phenomenology: Its potential for management research. In *Proceedings challenges or organizations in global markets, British Academy of Management Conference* (pp. 1–13). Said Business School, Oxford University.

Einstein, A. (1950). *The Einstein papers. A man of many parts*. Retrieved June 10, 2021 from http://nytimes.com

Fairholm, G. W. (2000). *Perspectives on leadership: From the science of management to its spiritual heart*. Praeger.

Fleischman, P. R. (1994). *The healing spirit: Explorations in religion & psychotherapy*. Bonne Chance Press.

Foster, S., & Wall, T. (2020) Spirituality and wellbeing in the workplace. In W. Leal Filho, T. Wall, A. M. Azul, L. Brandli, & P. G. Özuyar (Eds.), *Good health and well-being. Encyclopedia of the UN Sustainable Development Goals.* Springer. https://doi.org/10.1007/978-3-319-95681-7_92

Fourie, M. (2014). Spirituality in the workplace: An introductory overview. *In die Skriflig, 48*(1), Art. #1769, 8 pages. http://dx.doi.org/10.4102/ids.v48i1.1769

Fry, L. W. (2003). Towards a theory of spiritual leadership. *The Leadership Quarterly, 14*(6), 693–727.

Fry, L. W. (2005a). Introduction to The Leadership Quarterly, special issue: Towards a paradigm of spiritual leadership. *The Leadership Quarterly, 16*(6), 612–622.

Fry, L. W. (2007). Spiritual leadership: State-of-the-art and future directions for theory, research, and practice. In J. Biberman & L. Tishman (Eds.), *Spirituality in business: Theory, practice, and future directions* (pp. 133–140). Palgrave Publishers.

Fry, L. W. (2008). *Workplace spirituality.* Retrieved November 2020, from http://www.iispiritualleadership.com/index_files/workplace_spirituality.htm

Fry, L. W., Egel, E., & Neal, J. (2017). *The Handbook of personal and organizational transformation.* Springer International Publishing.

George, B. (2003). *Authentic leadership.* Jossey-Bass

George, B. (2007). *True north.* Jossey-Bass.

Giacalone, R. A., & Jurkiewicz, C. L. (2003). Toward a science of workplace spirituality. In R. A. Giacalone & C. L. Jurkiewicz (Eds.), *Handbook of workplace spirituality and organizational performance* (pp. 3–28). M. E. Sharpe.

Gibbons, P. (2000). Spirituality at work: Definitions, measures, assumptions, and validity claims. *Work and spirit, a reader of new spiritual paradigms for organizations* (pp. 111–131).

Giorgi, A. (2002). The question of validity in qualitative research. *Journal of Phenomenological Psychology, 33*(1), 1–18.

Giri, A. (Ed.). (2021). *Pragmatism, spirituality, and society: Border crossing, transformation, planetary realizations.* Palgrave Macmillan.

Goodpaster, K. E. (2007). *Conscience and corporate culture.* Blackwell.

Greenleaf, R. K., & Spears, L. C. (1998). *The power of servant-leadership essays.* Berrett-Koehler.

Griffith, B. (1992). *New creation in Christ.* Temple Gate.

Guillory, W. A. (2000). *Spirituality in the workplace.* Innovations International.

Gull, G. A., & Doh, J. (2004). The transmutation of the organization: Toward a more spiritual workplace. *Journal of Management Inquiry, 13*(2), 128–140.

Gwiazdon, K. A. (2020). State's global responsibility for environmental crises: The ethical and legal implications of a state's failure to protect human rights. In L. Westra, K. Bosselmann, & M. Fermeglia (Eds.), *Ecological integrity in science and law.* Springer. https://doi.org/10.1007/978-3030-46259-8_10

Hagen, Steve. (2011). *Buddhism plain and simple: The practice of being aware right now, every day*. Tuttle Publishing.

Hammond, M., Howarth, J., & Keat, R. (1991). *Understanding phenomenology*. Blackwell.

Harrington, D. (1998). What is the place of spirituality in business? *Review of Business, 20*(1), 4–10.

Harvie, J., & Guarneri, E. (2020). Healthy people, healthy planet: Holistic thinking. In W. Al-Delaimy, V. Ramanathan, & M. Sánchez Sorondo (Eds.), *Health of people, health of planet and our responsibility*. Springer. https://doi.org/10.1007/978-3-030-31125-4_16

Helminiak, D., (2008). *Spirituality for our global community: Beyond traditional religion to a world at peace*. Rowman & Littlefield Publishers.

Hicks, D. A. (2003). *Religion and the workplace: Pluralism, spirituality, leadership*. University Press.

Høffding, S., & Martiny, K. (2016). Framing a phenomenological interview: What, why and how. *Phenomenology and the Cognitive Sciences, 15*, 539–564. https://doi.org/10.1007/s11097-015-9433-z

Hougaard, R., Carter, J., & Hobson, N., (2020). *Compassion leadership is necessary but not sufficient*. Retrieved on June 11, 2021 from www.harvardbusiness.org/leading-through-a-pandemic/

Jaworski, J., & Flowers, B. S. (1996). *Synchronicity: The inner path of leadership*. Berrett-Koehler.

Jihye, Oh., & Wang, J. (2020). Spiritual leadership: Current status and Agenda for future research and practice. *Journal of Management, Spirituality & Religion*. https://doi.org/10.1080/14766086.2020.1728568

Khan, A. Z., Nawaz, A., & Khan, I. (2016). Leadership theories and styles: A literature review. *Journal of Resource Development and Management, 10*, 1–7.

Kouzes, J. M., & Posner, B. Z. (2007). *The leadership challenge* (4th ed.). Jossey-Bass.

Kovács, G. (2020). Business spirituality. In the value orientations of Buddhist and Christian entrepreneurs. In *Studies in Buddhist economics, management, and policy*. Palgrave Macmillan. https://doi.org/10.1007/978-3-030-46703-6_3

Kriger, M., & Seng, Y. (2005). Leadership with inner meaning: A contingency theory of leadership based on the worldviews of five religions. *The Leadership Quarterly, 16*(6), 771–806.

Kvale, S. (1996). *InterViews: An introduction to qualitative research interviewing*. Sage Publications.

Laloux, F., & Wilber, K. (2016). *Reinventing organizations: A guide to creating organizations by next stage in human consciousness*. Parker Nelson Publishing.

Lee, C., & Zemke, R. (1993). The search for spirit in the workplace. *Training, 30*(6), 21–27.

Lindholm, J. (2014). *The quest for meaning and wholeness: Spiritual and religious connections in the lives of college faculty*. Jossey-Bass.
Lloyd-Smith, M. (2020). The COVID-19 pandemic: Resilient organizational response to a low-chance, high-impact event. *BMJ Leader, 0*, 1–4.
Luthans, F., & Avolio, B. (2003). Authentic leadership development. In K. S. Cameron, J. E. Dutton, & R. E. Quinn (Eds.), *Positive organizational scholarship* (pp. 241–261). Barrett-Koehler.
Mackey, J., & Sisodia, R. (2014). *Conscious capitalism: Liberating the heroic spirit of business*. Harward Business Review Press.
Maddock, R. C., & Fulton, R. L. (1998). *Motivation, emotions, and leadership the silent side of management*. Quorum.
Marques, J., Dhiman, S., & King, R. (2007). *Spirituality in the workplace: What it is and why it matters, how to make it work for you*. Personhood Press.
Maslow, A. (2005). *Motivation and personality*. Retrieved on June 10, 2021 from http://www.zaadz.com/quots/Abraham/Maslowhtml
Miller, D. W. (2022, August). *Faith and work initiative*. https://faithandwork.princeton.edu/what-we-do/research/workplace-chaplaincy/sky-pilots
Miller, D. W., Ewest, T., & Neubert, M. J. (2019). Development of The Integration Profile (TIP) faith and work integration scale. *Journal of Business Ethics, 159*(2), 455–471.
Mitroff, I., & Denton, E. A. (1999). *A spiritual audit of corporate America: A hard look at spirituality, religion, and values in the workplace*. Jossey-Bass.
Moustakas, C. (1994). *Phenomenological research methods*. Sage Publications.
Neal, J. (2018). Overview of workplace spirituality research. In S. Dhiman, G. Roberts, & J. Crossman (Eds.), *The palgrave handbook of workplace spirituality and fulfillment*. Palgrave Macmillan. https://doi.org/10.1007/978-3-319-62163-0_45
Noghiu, A. (2021). Spiritual capital: A fresh conceptual framework for business spirituality. In D. P. Sakas, D. K. Nasiopoulos, & Y. Taratuhina (Eds.), *Business intelligence and modelling*. IC-BIM 2019. Springer proceedings in business and economics. Springer. https://doi.org/10.1007/978-3-030-57065-1_53
Northouse, P. (2019). *Leadership theory and practice* (9th ed.). Sage Publications.
Obregon, S. L., Lopes, L. F. D., Kaczam, F., da Veiga, C. P., & da Silva, W. V. (2022). Religiosity, spirituality and work: A systematic literature review and research directions. *Journal of Business Ethics, 179*, 573–595. https://doi.org/10.1007/s10551-021-04856-7
Palmer, P. (2009a). *A hidden wholeness: The journey towards an undivided life*. Josey-Bass Publishing.
Palmer, P. (2009b). *An undivided life: Seeking wholeness in ourselves, our work, and our world*. Retrieved on June 17, 2022 from https://www.soundstrue.com/products/an-undivided-life
Palmer, P. J. (2004). *The journey towards undivided life*. Jossey-Bass.

Peltz, D., & Wilson, J. (Eds.). (2020). *True leadership: Leadership styles and kenotic relationship*. Palgrave Macmillan.

Pendleton, D., Furnham, A. F., & Cowell, J. (2021). Five enablers of leading. In *Leadership*. Palgrave Macmillan. https://doi.org/10.1007/978-3-030-60437-0_5

Puchalski, C. (2021). Spiritual care in health care: Guideline, models, spiritual assessment and the use of the ©FICA spiritual history tool. In A. Büssing (Eds.), *Spiritual needs in research and practice*. Palgrave Macmillan. https://doi.org/10.1007/978-3-030-70139-0_3

Ravishankar, R. R. (2006, October). *Corporate culture and spirituality conference: Corporate social responsibility press release*. http://www.socialfunds.com/news/release.cgi?sfArticleId=6570

Reb, J., Allen, T., & Vogus, T. J. (2020). Mindfulness arrives at work: Deepening our understanding of mindfulness in organizations. *Organizational Behavior and Human Decision Processes, 159*, 1–7. https://doi.org/10.1016/j.obhdp.2020.04.001

Reese, H. W. (1997). Spirituality, belief and action. *Journal of Mind and Behavior, 18*(1), 29–51.

Rigoglioso, M. (1999, October). Spirit at work: The search for deeper meaning in the workplace. *Harvard Business School Newsletter*. Retrieved October 10, 2007, from http://hbswk.hbs.edu/item/0644.html

Roberts, G., & Crossman, J. (Eds.). (2018). *The Palgrave handbook of workplace spirituality and fulfilment*. Palgrave Macmillan.

Robinson, H. (2016). *Dualism and the modal argument*. Standford Encyclopedia of Philosophy.

Rocha, R. G., & Pinheiro, P. G. (2021). Organizational spirituality: Concept and perspectives. *Journal of Business Ethics, 171*, 241–252. https://doi.org/10.1007/s10551-020-04463-y

Scharmer, O. (2021). Ten lessons from Covid for stepping into the decade of transformation. Field of the future blog | *Medium*. Retrieved on July 23, 2021.

Schein, E. H. (2017). *Organizational culture and leadership* (5th ed.). Wiley Publishers.

Seidman, D. (2004). The case for ethical leadership. *Academy of Management Executive, 18*(4), 134–138.

Self, D. R. (2021). Armenakis, Achilles: A journey of discovery—Seeing change through new eyes. In D. B. Szabla (Eds.), *The Palgrave handbook of organizational change thinkers*. Palgrave Macmillan. https://doi.org/10.1007/978-3-030-38324-4_66

Silveira, K. (2021). *Wholeness in business: Rethink business*. Retrieved on January 15, 2021.

Singh, R. K., & Singh, S. (2022). Spirituality in the workplace: A systematic review. *Management Decision, 60*(5), 1296–1325. https://doi.org/10.1108/MD-11-2020-1466

Smith, N. (2006). *Workplace spirituality: A complete guide for business leaders.* Axial Age Publishing.

Stephen, M. (2002). *Spirituality in business: The Hidden success factor.* Inspired Productions Press.

Stevens, P. R. (2006). *Doing God's business: Meaning and motivation for the marketplace.* Wm. B. Eerdmans Publishing Co.

Tafoya, D. W. (2020). *Crisis, catastrophize and disaster in organizations.* Palgrave Macmillan. https://doi.org/10.1007/978-3-030-37074-9_4

Teasdale, W. (2003). *Bede Griffiths: An introduction to his interspiritual thought.* Skylight Paths Publishing.

Teehankee, M. (2020). *Trade and environment governance at the world trade organization committee on trade and environment.* Wolters Kluwer Legal & Regulatory U.S.

Thakkar, B. (Ed.). (2018). *The future of leadership: Addressing complex global issues.* Palgrave Macmillan.

Thompson, C. J., Locander, W. B., & Pollio, H. R. (1989). Putting consumer experience back into consumer research: The philosophy and method of existential phenomenology. *Journal of Consumer Research, 16*, 133–146.

Tinder, G. (1989). *The political meaning of Christianity: An interpretation.* Louisiana State University Press.

Vaill, P. (2000). Introduction to spirituality for business leadership. *Journal of Management Inquiry, 9*(2), 115–116.

van Manen, J. (1983). Reclaiming qualitative methods for organizational research. In J. van Manen (Ed.), *Q. Methodology* (pp. 9–10). Sage.

van Manen, M. (1997). *Researching lived experience: Human science for an action sensitive pedagogy.* The Althouse Press.

van Manen, M. (2006). *Researching lived experience: Human science for an action sensitive pedagogy.* The Althouse Press.

Warnke, S. (2022, August). *Faith force at Salesforce.* https://religiousfreedomandbusiness.org/salesforce-has-a-faithforce

Williams, O. F. (Ed.). (2003). *Business, religion and spirituality: A new synthesis.* University of Notre Dame.

Young, J. E. (2002). A spectrum of consciousness for CEOs: A business application of Ken Wilber's spectrum of consciousness. *International Journal of Organizational Analysis, 10*(1), 30–54.

Yukl, G., & Gardner, W. (2020). *Leadership in organizations* (9th ed.). Pearson Publishing.

Zsolnai, L. (Ed.). (2004). *Spirituality and ethics in management (Issues in business ethics).* Kluwer Academic Publishers.

CHAPTER 2

Wholeness: A Model of Spiritual Intelligence

An in-depth inquiry into the lived experience of the phenomena of wholeness manifested in top leaders from both profit and non-profit sectors, resulted in the discovery of critical insights that helped to construct a model of spiritual intelligence. Spiritual intelligence is defined as the higher consciousness and innate ability to respond with wisdom, compassion, and courage while maintaining a sense of equanimity (*sthithaprajna*, Gita 2:54; 2:55). This book explores the perspective of spiritual intelligence that plays a crucial role in leadership and management today. As a result of the growing body of research in psychology, neuroscience, and spirituality, many conceptualizations of spiritual intelligence (SQ) have emerged in the past two decades (Atroszko et al., 2021; Griffiths, 2017; Wigglesworth, 2012; Zohar & Marshall, 2000). Neurological studies have established that the brain has three distinct processing modes: serial, parallel, and synchronous (Werk et al., 2021; Zohar, 2010). Serial processing is associated with IQ functions in the left brain, parallel processing is associated with EQ functions in the right brain, and synchronous processing is associated with SQ functions in the whole brain. Holistic development, whether motor, language, social, or spiritual, is the functional expression of the complex brain process throughout one's life span. Spiritual intelligence (SQ) manifests as deeper awareness,

T. Thakadipuram, *Leadership Wholeness, Volume 1*,
Palgrave Studies in Workplace Spirituality and Fulfillment,
https://doi.org/10.1007/978-3-031-08053-1_2

meaning, and purpose where rational intelligence (IQ) and emotional intelligence (EQ) function optimally in light of higher consciousness.

Emmons and Sisk (Emmons, 2000; Sisk, 2019) identified spiritual intelligence as an instrument of mature personality that enables the fulfillment of spiritual goals with self-awareness, wisdom, and tenacity. This definition of spiritual intelligence assumes an adaptive, perceptive, and meta-cognitive capacity with several abilities and skills that may be part of one's leadership competency relevant to problem-solving situations. Wilber (2006) developed the integral psychology and spirituality model of four quadrants: subjective, objective, collective, and universal. Similarly, Wigglesworth (2011: 446) developed a spiritual intelligence model based on four quadrants of self-awareness, universal awareness, self-mastery, and social mastery comprised of 21 skills of spiritual intelligence that can be learned and developed in leaders. Accordingly, Wigglesworth (2011: 447) states, "Spiritual intelligence is the ability to act with wisdom and compassion while maintaining inner and outer peace, regardless of the situation."

Based on original research of leaders' lived experience of wholeness, I created a new spiritual intelligence model. I interviewed twenty-three leaders from different cultural, spiritual, and organizational contexts across the globe inquiring into their lived experience of journey towards wholeness. The participants were top leaders who were known for their high integrity, compassion, resilience, and deeper awareness. The group of leaders in this study had reputations across cultures and traditions even though they were each rooted in a certain spiritual tradition. Analysis of the four themes that emerged from the in-depth interviews forms the basis for the current model. The four essential themes that emerged from this research are: ***sensing crisis, embracing crisis, awakening hidden wholeness, and serving the greater good.*** Analysis of the four themes that emerged from the interviews forms the basis for this model of spiritual intelligence.

First, this model describes the inner dynamics of leaders' journeys towards wholeness (see Fig. 2.1). The four quadrants of sensing, embracing, awakening, and serving indicate an intense path of progressive self-realization and awakening of higher consciousness leading to greater wholeness of life. The wholeness model of spiritual intelligence conceptualized focuses on both the inner and the outer dynamics of the quest for wholeness for leaders.

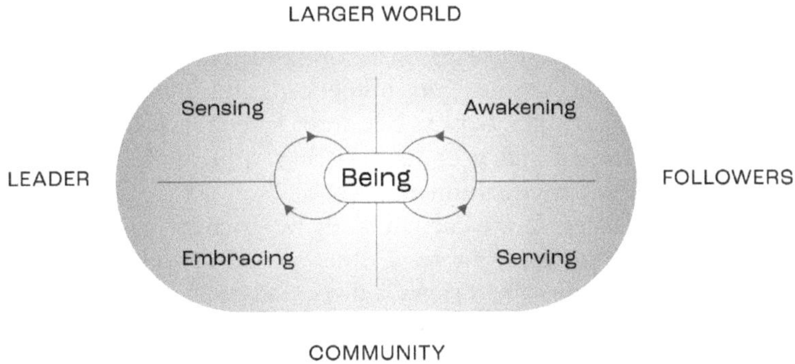

Fig. 2.1 Wholeness/spiritual intelligence model: Inner Dimension

Wholeness/Spiritual Intelligence Model-Inner Dimension

The leaders in the study demonstrated the ability to sense the existential crises in themselves and the crises happening around the world. Having sensed the crises, they gradually began to accept the crises after encountering the initial trauma of shock and awe. Embracing the crises as a challenge helps the person not to see the issue as a problem producing negativity in the mind but rather activate creative inner faculties to look at the crises with a positive and audacious outlook to find solutions. This state of embracing crisis as a challenge urges the soul to search for deeper dimensions of consciousness that leads to an awakening of hidden wholeness. This spiritual awakening enables one to see the bigger picture of the current reality and experience deeper meaning progressively through the journey. The awakened leader with a higher consciousness experiences oneness and the reality of the interconnectedness of the world as one family. This realization of world as one family enables the leader to dedicate his or her life serving the greater good in the world. In the following section, the outer dimension of the spiritual intelligence quadrant is explained.

The leaders who engaged in a genuine quest for wholeness experienced four key factors in their journey: sensing crisis, embracing crisis, awakening wholeness, and serving the greater good. These top leaders apparently used four types of intelligence in their journey towards wholeness: logical intelligence (IQ) in sensing crisis, emotional intelligence

(EQ) in embracing crisis, spiritual intelligence (SQ) in awakening wholeness, and holistic intelligence (HQ) in serving the greater good (Fig. 2.1). As a result, the leaders are inspired, influenced, and impacted followers, community, and the larger world. The interdependencies among these four key factors rooted and grounded in the *being* of the leader highlighted the pattern of spiritual intelligence.

Firstly, all the leaders in the current study experienced existential crises in themselves or were deeply aware of other's crucial crises that led them to question the previously held views, values, and perspectives of life. The experience of the crucibles of crises urged them to look at life with a new lens as the old meaning and patterns faded. The crises provoked both danger and opportunity, and thus, those leaders who used spiritual intelligence to navigate the crises inevitably lead to positive change. Secondly, when the experience of crises led the leaders to embrace them as a challenge rather problems, it led to a process of deep exploration and self-acceptance through reflective learning. The attitude of embracing crisis generated positive and resilience feelings to face the crises and explore creative solutions. This learning happens by looking at the past failures and weaknesses with honesty in spite of the drive to resist and deny. These leaders dared to deal with their crises constructively to break through the darkness of negativity and helplessness to a deeper awakening of the soul igniting the hidden fire of wholeness.

Thirdly, awakening to wholeness resulted in a new vision that helped the leaders to see the whole picture of the current reality in the context of the crises and take responsibility for their lives and the lives of others. This spiritual awakening was made possible by their steadfast spiritual practice, inner silence, interior transformation, and discovery of the hidden wholeness and the power of higher consciousness. As a result, the leaders began to experience their sense of whole self with higher consciousness and discovered their interrelationship with the community and the larger world. "Man, lives in the spirit, says the Jewish existentialist philosopher Martin Buber, if he enters into relationship with his whole being" (Quoted in Heintzman, 2011: 27). On the other hand, if one does not enter in relationship with the whole being, one hardly lives in the spirit. Fourthly, a sense of responsibility and co-responsibility demonstrated in a robust relationship between not only the leaders and followers but also between their community *and the larger world* as depicted in Fig. 2.1 resulted in a greater transformation.

The key aspect of spiritual followership is in the dynamics of learning and teaching one another in the process of leading and following the mission and vision of the organization (Crossman & Crossman, 2018). "Spiritual followership functions as a process, most notably operating in its teaching and learning relationship with leadership. The spiritual follower is emancipated, empowered, and courageous" (Crossman & Crossman, 2018: 2) in the process of developing this bonding and relationship with the leadership who seeks the greater good of the organization and the employees. Followership has been taken for granted as it seems to be subsumed in the very nature of leadership. Leaders have to learn to gain the support and the consent of the followers by inspiring and challenging them to work together as a team based on the shared mission and vision. "Indeed, without followers, the concept of leadership would have no meaning at all" (Billot et al., 2013: 91). This close relationship between the leader and the followers will eventually pave the way for developing competent leaders for the future of the organization. By engaging in an authentic search marked by integrity, honesty, and compassion, the top leaders made great spiritual progress in their journey towards wholeness and inspired the followers to join hands to accomplish the mission of the organization. Detailed discussion on the spiritual followership and its intrinsic relationship with leadership will be explored in the second volume of this book. Fueled by the spirit and passion for the common home, the earth and compassion for the world inspired leaders to commit to serving the greater good of the organization, society, and environment beyond partisan politics and polarization. The impact of this intentional journey led them to experience greater harmony and wholeness in their own life.

The key four dynamics of spiritual intelligence: sensing, embracing, awakening, and serving displayed in the four quadrants' interplay with one another from a deeper consciousness at the center of the leader's being (see Fig. 2.1). The path through four quadrants becomes an infinity loop resulting in ongoing spiritual progress and greater self-awareness, universal awareness, and self-mastery. This process and pattern of spiritual intelligence is an ongoing natural and supernatural process in a non-linear fashion discovering new meaning and harmonious relationship with the community and larger world in and through crises and spiritual awakening process with inner renewal and evolution of the spirit. Having explained the inner dynamics of the spiritual intelligence, I discuss the outer dynamics and dimensions of the spiritual intelligence in the following section.

Wholeness: A Spiritual Intelligence Model: Outer Dimension

The outer dimension and dynamics of the quest for wholeness are depicted in Fig. 2.2. From the awakening of the hidden wholeness deeper explorations collective intelligence emerges making them feel greater responsibility for their own life and the life of others. A spirit of service with a sense of co-responsibility manifested at five levels of being: personal trust, organizational responsibility, social justice, global compassion, and environmental stewardship as indicated in the model above. The trajectory of the journey is non-linear, after the pattern of an infinity loop and transformational process of learning and growth that results in adaptive intelligence enable leaders to become resilient to survive and thrive in times of uncertainly (Sternberg, 2021). Further, this model supports empirical and normative research on self-knowledge and wholeness formation (Draper, 2010; Kraus, 2020; Zohar & Marshall, 2000) augment existing research theories and findings by describing the outer dynamics of the quest for wholeness (Taylor, 2017).

Leaders' spiritual intelligence demonstrated both interior and exterior dynamics as an integrated whole, which is depicted in leadership wholeness model (Fig. 2.2). The interior dynamics contained four factors of sensing, embracing, awakening, and serving centered on the *being*, and the exterior dynamics contained five ethical dimensions of co-responsibility as it pertained to the leader, followers, community, and the larger world. The flow of spiritual intelligence moves through the processes of sensing crisis, embracing crisis, and awakening hidden wholeness, that is, igniting deeper dimension of being manifesting an ethic of co-responsibility towards community and the larger world. The five dimensions of co-responsibility are: *personal trust, organizational responsibility, social justice, global compassion, and environmental stewardship.* These five dimensions of engagement with the community and larger world depend on the level of self-awareness and universal awareness cultivated and sustained by the leaders.

The spirit of personal trust was operative at the intimate and personal level between the leader and the inner circle of his or her team, where each one had the courage, willingness, and mutually assured confidentiality to be who they are without any mask or pretensions (Palmer, 2004). The spirit of trust based on consistency, empathy, communication, and credibility enabled them to connect authentically with their team and followers

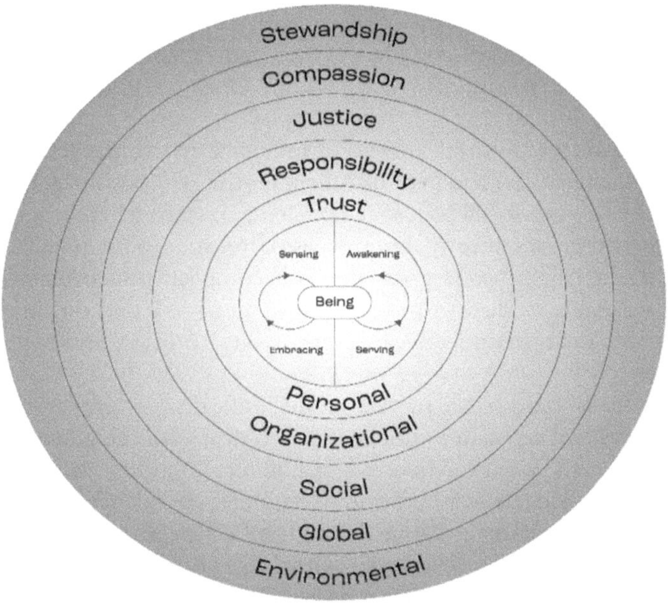

Fig. 2.2 Wholeness/spiritual intelligence model: Outer Dimension

laying the foundation for their greater journey to wholeness. Sri Sri noted, "Trust is the breath of business, ethics its limps; and uplift the spirit is its goal."

The spirit of responsibility was exercised by the top leaders so that the whole organization was helped move to a higher level of responsibility as a whole. The realization that to be human is to be responsible for the other without counting the cost was the bedrock of sustainable organizational culture. A robust sense of values and ethics guided the leaders to discover their authentic voice from a deeper level to take collective responsibility not only for the success but also for the failures in moving the organization to a new sustainable future.

The spirit of social justice demonstrates the enlightened perspective with which the leaders were able to champion the cause of justice, human rights, and peace in the society by their deeper sense of solidarity with the people in margins and advocacy for the less privileged, and disadvantaged. Gandhi asserted, "There is a higher court than courts of justice, and that is the court of conscience. It supersedes all other courts" (Quoted in

Joseph, 2019: 71). This spirit of social justice emerged from their higher consciousness and deeper conscience. The leaders' ability to pay attention to the small voice of the conscience within amidst complexity gave them power, poise, and persistence to be voice of the voiceless. Covey (2004: 83) made a distinction: "the circle of influence where the leader is able to make an impact on the lives of others by the witness of their own life and intervention in social issues, and circle of concern where leaders show sympathy and great concern about issues of injustice, poverty, and health, even without having done great things accomplish justice for all." The leaders were able to discern to response to an issue based on this understanding of situation and ethical responsibility to bring about justice in the society.

The spirit of compassion in this model indicates the leaders concern, involvement, and activism of nonviolence to deal with the global issues of humanitarian crises, natural disasters, pandemic, political polarization, and racial division, especially for the most vulnerable and deprived sentient beings including humans, animals, and other creatures. The spirit of compassion is the essence of the culture of non-violence which is an antidote to the culture of violence today. Gandhi (1920: 3) asserted:

> Nonviolence in its dynamic condition means conscious suffering. It does not mean meek submission to the will of the evil-doer, but it means the pitting of one's whole soul against the will of the tyrant. Working under this law of our being, it is possible for a single individual to defy the whole might of an unjust empire to save his honor, his religion, his soul and lay the foundation for that empire's fall or its regeneration.

Non-violence is not a weapon of the weak. It is a weapon of the strongest and the bravest demonstrating moral strength and spiritual intelligence rooted in the spirit of compassion. These leaders expanded their circle of compassion globally, having charitable, service, and non-violent activism to uplift the downtrodden and made substantial efforts to put an end to the culture of violence across the world as a new beginning to inspire the world with empathetic intelligence. Their leadership demonstrated that there is a gentle and compassionate way to shake the world for the better.

The spirit of stewardship points out the interest and involvement of the leaders in environmental protection and sustainability issues for the sake of the future planet. The leaders expressed solidarity, mostly for issues of peace and justice, establishing organizations and networks for wider cooperation. The spirit of stewardship led leaders to be proactive in the face of challenges and engage in responsible actions to address climate crisis and catastrophic effect across the world to assure the sustainability of the future planet. As we live in an interdependent and interconnected world, these leaders understood the need for global cooperation in a spirit of solidarity, addressing the unbridled greed and unhealthy competition to tackle global issues, and advance world happiness reducing world misery (Maak, 2007). The leaders believed that the care of the soul today cannot exclude the care of the planet's soul.

The quest for wholeness was expressed in these practical ways of co-responsibility and global initiatives from many of the top leaders. They nurtured the notion of earth as a family, and the planet common roof under which everyone belongs, and everything is connected to everything else. Leader's ethic of co-responsibility flowed from their sense of values and obligation to the whole universe as they became aware of the deep connection between the individual self and the universal or cosmic self. This enlightened spiritual awareness was the platform from which their sense of universal responsibility and solidarity emerged. Leaders' quests for wholeness revealed the interior dynamics of wholeness and spiritual intelligence that emphasize the importance of learning from crises, embracing crisis, connecting with the deeper dimensions of being while recognizing the interconnectedness among personal, organizational, social, and environmental dimensions of life. This model offered a unique opportunity to discover the essence of the leaders' spiritual intelligence. Emerson rightly noted, "Great are they who see that the spiritual is stronger than any material force, that thoughts rule the world" (Quoted in Nazareth, 2006: 1). The highly perceived value of experiencing deeper journey towards wholeness that manifest spiritual intelligence was clearly identified in the findings. None of the experiences shared in this study were part of an intentional career plan of the leaders—they occurred naturally in various contexts. All the leaders in this study highlighted the fact that their quest for wholeness is a non-linear journey with iterative patterns of trial and error, ups and downs, with life-long aspiration, continuity, and dynamic transformation.

Embracing the challenges with positive attitude helped them not to see life as a problem producing undue negativity but as a challenge to overcome. Facing the crises constructively with profound courage and willingness to deal with the most difficult problems, these top leaders broke through the negative patterns of the past and reinvented themselves with enlightened vision of life. In contrast to the previous literature, the current study gives an in-depth view of the quest for wholeness, not only from an intra-individual perspective, but also from extra-individual framework (Campbell, 2007). This model focuses on the existential, learning, spiritual, moral, and ethical dimensions of leaders' wholeness that manifested spiritual intelligence. Moreover, the previous literature looked at spirituality as an extrinsic component for organizational leadership, whereas this model looks at spirituality as an integral aspect of leadership and whole system transformation (Fry et al., 2017; Vaill, 2000).

The essential themes depicted in this book are present across gender, cultures, organizations, and spiritual traditions. The components of these essential themes can be used for holistic leadership development and can help educate potential leaders and others who wish to lead and guide others towards wholeness of life. The themes define the essential components of spiritual leadership and wholeness and, as such, they help to provide insight into applying spiritual leadership in current organizational contexts. Top leaders who aspire to lead holistically can benefit from leadership development focused on the whole self that can put a leader in touch with the true inner self, personal values, interconnectedness, social responsibility, and dynamics for creating a productive spiritual workplace.

In business, leaders and managers have to face an environment that is highly volatile and uncertain, with constant crises and unprecedented changes in the marketplace (Dasgupta, 2019). This wholeness model provides insights for leaders to engage in genuine self-reflection and help them engage in a meaningful journey towards wholeness in the business environment through coaching and guidance. The essential themes of this model can provide broader and deeper perspective to leaders to engage in executive coaching to enhance the whole self. The model provides holistic framework for leaders to cultivate positive organizational environment based on hope and resiliency in the wake of crisis and uncertainty in the business environment (Youssef & Luthans, 2007).

This book adds insights to the concepts of workplace spirituality and spiritual leadership literature (Altman et al., 2022; Fry, 2008; Gull & Doh, 2004; Obregon et al., 2022; Mayer & Wilke, 2022; Singh & Singh, 2022; Smith, 2006). As organizations become global and the workplace becomes more multicultural, the findings in this study provide insights for developing and training global leaders focusing on key factors of spiritual intelligence. In addition, this model provides support to develop and train organizational development consultants and change. In addition, connecting both leadership wholeness and spiritual intelligence with ethical leadership from a broader perspective of corporate social and environmental responsibility could strengthen the emerging picture about leadership and organizational wholeness in the context of rising global ethical challenges, and escalating environmental crisis (Weiming, 2001). As the ethical values and approaches are based mostly on their spiritual worldview, it should be beneficial to explore the relationship between ethical leadership and spiritual leadership in light of leaders' journey towards wholeness.

As a spiritual leader who is engaged in organizational transformation, I was deeply moved by the gracious presence, warm hospitality, and the rich descriptions shared by these top leaders about their quest for wholeness. Although getting access to these prominent leaders who have high visibility and watertight schedules was quite a herculean process, I was amazed to witness their genuine interest, openness, and eagerness to share their stories with me. I marveled at their grit and grace as they were cheered and honored by thousands of followers, disciples, and well-wishers across the globe and within their organizations, demonstrating their profound influence in the world. This research project made me travel to the four continents of Africa, Asia, Europe, and the Americas in search of the top leaders, making it a heroic adventure with a short span of time. I admired not only the generous willingness of these leaders to share their unique stories with me but also gained opportunity to stay with most of them for a few days, experiencing how they lived their values in their organization with utmost integrity, authenticity, and transparency. I was deeply touched by their sparkling intelligence, powerful vision, and deep empathy shining through their magnificent presence, voices, and descriptions. This outreach was not possible in the case of meeting the top leaders from business and non-profit sectors due the advent of the unprecedented pandemic. Still, I am fortunate to have interviewed some of them using the virtual technology and gained access to them across the world.

I gained considerable personal insight and inspiration by being with them and listening to their stories and witnessing the impact of their leadership on the organization and larger society. The personal encounter with these top leaders stimulated my own exploration and quest for wholeness and spiritual intelligence. I began to develop deeper sensitivity to feel my own personal crises of meaning and burnout due to over work and lack of focus on deeper spiritual dimension of being. It led me to take a break from ministry and work and do sabbatical to spent time in nature and do inner exploration of the purpose and meaning of my own life. I embraced the challenge of emotional vulnerability and inner emptiness and loneliness felt in the midst of busy work life of merging and transforming organizations. Exploring deeper dimensions of being led me to feel the awakening of the hidden wholeness of joy and turnaround from break down to a new breakthrough of happiness, freedom, and peace in my ministry and organizational work. The daily spiritual practices of meditation, divine liturgy, daily walk, biking in nature and monthly spiritual support group sessions and over all spiritual focus in life helped to be deeply rooted in wholeness and grounded in spiritual intelligence as a leader serving the greater good in and through my own organization. I was deeply moved by the testimonies of these leaders in uplifting the vulnerable, challenging the process, and making concerted efforts in protecting the vulnerable planet. This encounter has challenged the way I used to take top leaders for granted due to my own indifference and pride, and how I interact with people and learn from them as a spiritual leader, consultant, educator, and counselor. It is my ardent hope that others who read their stories and insights will have a similarly profound inspiration and impetus to engage in deeper journey towards wholeness of their life.

I was surprised by the findings of the study; my elevated notions of these leaders crumbled as I began hearing their down to earth, honest, and excruciating stories of crises with twists and turns in their quest for wholeness. It hit home for me that these leaders did not reach lofty reputation and a sense of wholeness without encountering adverse experiences and breaking through the illusions of life with courage, tenacity, and undying hope. I was delighted to hear their eagerness to share their experiences in the hopes that it would assist others engage in their own journey towards wholeness in and through their brokenness, crises, trials, and tribulations. For leaders, managers, and consultants who are engaged in leading, guiding, and managing others, I hope this exploration will enhance their awareness of the existential, ethical, spiritual, and learning dimensions of wholeness. Moreover, it is my hope that leaders at all levels of organizations recognize the importance of cultivating spiritual intelligence by developing daily reflective practices, mindfulness, centering prayer, forming circles of support, and engaging in the quest for wholeness consciously and intentionally to strengthen their capabilities as holistic leaders and make profound impact in the life of others and the planet. The leaders interviewed for this study have all stated that this topic of wholeness and spiritual intelligence is of paramount importance because the entire humanity at this juncture is experiencing various crises across the globe as a sign of the loss of wholeness (Weiming, 2001). The statements regarding their keen interest for this topic of the quest for wholeness made me feel that the research effort was indeed worthwhile, although I felt deeply passionate about this adventure early on. The enthusiastic interest of my colleagues, consultants, and leaders regarding this idea of wholeness and spiritual intelligence invigorated my own exploration and research journey. This experience indeed was an incredible adventure of research, learning, and advancement of one's own quest for wholeness without losing sight of the fact that humanity is part of the whole. Indeed, leadership is a spiritual journey; it is a matter of spirit, heart, and mind and the whole spectrum of life that revolves around. I was glad to see that other scholars were interested in this model and took steps to apply them in their research and practice. The next four chapters will focus in-depth on the four aspects of the leader's journey towards wholeness that led to the creation of the model of spiritual intelligence: *sensing crisis, embracing crisis, awakening hidden wholeness, and serving the greater good* by practicing the ethic of co-responsibility.

References

Aishah, S., Elias, S., Hosseini, M., & Krauss, S. (2010). A review study on spiritual intelligence, adolescence, and spiritual intelligence, factors that may contribute to individual differences in spiritual intelligence, and the related theories. *International Journal of Psychological Studies, 2*(2), 179–188. https://doi.org/10.5539/ijps.v2n2p17

Altman, Y., Neal, J., & Mayrhofer, W. (2022). *Workplace spirituality*. This book is published by open access at http://www.degruyter.com

Amram, J. Y. (2009). *The contribution of emotional and spiritual intelligences to effective business leadership* (Unpublished dissertation). Institute of Transpersonal Psychology.

Amram, Y. (2007, August). *The seven dimensions of spiritual intelligence: An ecumenical grounded theory*. Paper presented at the 115th annual Conference of the American Psychological Association, San Francisco, CA. Retrieved September, 2021, from http://www.yosiamram.net/papers

Amram, Y., & Dryer, D. C. (2008, August 14–17). *The Integrated Spiritual Intelligence Scale (ISIS): Development and preliminary validation*. Paper presented at the 116th annual conference of the American Psychological Association.

Atroszko, P. A., Skrzypińska, K., & Balcerowska, J. M. (2021). Is there a general factor of spiritual intelligence? Factorial validity of the Polish adaptation of spiritual intelligence self-report inventory. *Journal of Religion and Health, 60*(5), 3591–3605. https://doi.org/10.1007/s10943-021-01350-2

Benefiel, M. (2005). The second half of the journey: Spiritual leadership for organizational transformation. *The Leadership Quarterly, 16*(5), 723–747.

Billot, J., West, D., Khong, L., Skorobohacz, C., Roxa, T., Murray, S., & Gayle, B. (2013). Followership in higher education: Academic teachers and their formal leaders. *Teaching & Learn Inquiry, 1*(2), 91–103.

Block, P. (November, 2021). *Leadership is a spiritual journey*. http://www.peterblock.uploads.

Campbell, J. L. (2007). Why should corporations behave in socially responsible ways? An institutional theory of corporate social responsibility. *Academy of Management Review, 32*(3), 946–967.

Charnley, F., Lemon, M., & Evans, S. (2011). Exploring the process of whole system design. *Design Studies, 32*(2), 156–179.

Chin, S. T. S., Raman., K., & Eze, U. C. (2012). Relationship between emotional intelligence and spiritual intelligence in nurturing creativity and innovation among successful entrepreneurs: A conceptual framework. *Procedia: Social and Behavioral Sciences, 57*, 261–267.

Covey, S. (2004). *The 8th habit: From effectiveness to greatness*. New York Free Press.

Crossman, J. E., & Crossman, B. (2018). Spiritual followership: Emerging conceptualizations. In G. Roberts & J. Crossman (Eds.), *The Palgrave handbook of workplace spirituality and fulfillment*. Palgrave Macmillan. https://doi.org/10.1007/978-3-319-62163-0_30

Dasgupta, M. (2019). Business model innovation: Responding to volatile business environment in the Indian Banking industry. *Journal of Asia-Pacific Business, 20*(4), 260–280. https://doi.org/10.1080/10599231.2019.1684168

Dhiman, S. (2017). *Holistic leadership: A new paradigm for today's leaders*. Palgrave Macmillan.

Draper, B. (2010). *Spiritual intelligence: A new way of being*. Lion Hudson.

Emmons, R. A. (2000). Is spirituality an intelligence? Motivation, cognition, and the psychology of ultimate concern. *The International Journal for the Psychology of Religion, 10*(1), 3–26.

Fry, L., Egel, E., & Neal, J. (2017). *The Handbook of personal and organizational transformation*. Springer International Publishing.

Fry, L. W., & Slocum, J. (2008). Maximizing the triple bottom line through a strategic scorecard business model of spiritual leadership. *Organizational Dynamics, 37*(1), 86–96.

Fry, L. W. J., & Wigglesworth, C. G. (2013). Toward a theory of spiritual intelligence and spiritual leader development. *International Journal on Spirituality and Organization Leadership, 47*, 1–41.

Gandhi, M. (1920). *Non-violence.* Retrieved June, 2022 from https://www.saada.org/item/20121225-1207

Griffiths, R. (2017, September). *Spiritual intelligence paradigm.* The Spiritual Intelligence Paradigm. http://www.RichardGriffiths-Academia.edu

Hagen, S. (2011). *Buddhism plain and simple: The practice of being aware right now, every day.* Tuttle Publishing.

Heintzman, R. (2011). *Rediscovering reverence: The meaning of faith in a secular world.* McGill-Queens University Press.

Joseph, T. (2019). The state and the individual: Mahatma Gandhi on dissent. *Parliamentary Studies, 65.*

Kouzes, J. M., & Posner, B. Z. (2007). *The leadership challenge* (4th ed.). Jossey-Bass Publishers.

Kraus, T. K. (2020). *Kant on self-knowledge and self-formation.* Cambridge University Press.

Mayer, C. H., & Wilke, K. (2022). Leading through VUCA times for a successful future of work: Expert views on the global automotive industry. In K. Dhiman, S., & F. Marques, J., (Eds.), *Leadership after COVID 19. Future of Business and Finance.* Springer.

Maak, T. (2007). Responsible leadership, stakeholder engagement, and the emergence of social capital. *Journal of Business Ethics, 74*, 329–343. https://doi.org/10.1007/s10551-007-9510-5

Nazareth, P. A. (2006). *Gandhi's outstanding leadership.* Sarvodaya International Trust.

Obregon, S. L., Lopes, L. F. D., & Kaczam, F. (2022). Religiosity, spirituality and work: A systematic literature review and research directions. *Journal of Business Ethics, 179*, 573–595. https://doi.org/10.1007/s10551-021-04856-7

Palmer, P. J. (2004). *A hidden wholeness: The journey toward an undivided life, welcoming the soul and weaving community in a wounded world.* Jossey-Bass.

Senge, P., Scharmer, O., Jaworski, J., & Flowers, S., (2004). *Presence: Human purpose and the field of the future.* Society for Organizational Learning.

Singh, R. K., & Singh, S. (2022). Spirituality in the workplace: A systematic review. *Management Decision, 60*(5), 1296–1325. https://doi.org/10.1108/MD-11-2020-1466

Sisk, D. A. (2019). Spiritual intelligence: Developing higher consciousness. In B. Wallace, D. A. Sisk, & J. Senior (Eds.), *The Sage handbook of gifted and talented education*. Sage.

Skrzypińska, K. (2014). The threefold nature of spirituality in the inclusive cognitive framework. *Archive for Psychology of Religion, 36*, 277–302.

Skrzypińska, K. (2021). Does spiritual intelligence (SI) exist? A theoretical investigation of a tool useful for finding the meaning of life. *Journal of Religion and Health, 60*, 500–516.

Smith, N. (2006). *Workplace spirituality: A complete guide for business leaders*. Axial Age Publishing.

Sternberg, R. J. (2021). Transformational vs. transactional deployment of intelligence. *Journal of Intelligence, 9*(15), 1–15.

Sternberg, R. J., Chowkase, A., Desmet, O., Karami, S., Landy, J., & Lu, J. (2021). Beyond transformational giftedness. *Education Sciences, 11*(5), 192.

Subramaniam, M., & Panchanatham, N. (2015). Impact of spiritual intelligence and mindfulness on organizational citizenship behavior. *International Journal of Scientific Research, 4*(1), 228–230.

Tacey, D. (2003). *The spiritual revolution*. Harper Collins.

Taylor, S. (2017). The return of perennial perspectives? Why transpersonal psychology should remain open to essentialism. *International Journal of Transpersonal Studies, 36*(2). https://doi.org/10.24972/ijts.2017.36.2.75.

Vaill, P. (2000). Introduction to spirituality for business leadership. *Journal of Management Inquiry, 9*(2), 115–116.

Weiming, T. (2012). A spiritual turn in philosophy: Rethinking the global significance of Confucian humanism. *Journal of Philosophical Research, 37*, 389–401.

Werk, R. S., Steinhorn, D. M., & Newberg, A. (2021). The relationship between spirituality and the developing brain: A framework for pediatric oncology. *Journal of Religion & Health, 60*, 389–405. https://doi.org/10.1007/s10943-020-01014-7

Wigglesworth, C. (2011). *Integral theory and its relationship to spiritual intelligence and the SPI assessment*. Selected Books.

Wigglesworth, C. (2012). *SQ21: The 21 skills of spiritual intelligence*. Selected Book.

Wilber, K. (2006). *Integral spirituality*. Shambhala Publication.

Workplace spirituality. (2008). https://doi.org/10.1007/978-3-030-84867-5_15.

Youssef, C. M., & Luthans, F. (2007). Positive organizational behavior in the workplace: The impact of hope, optimism, and resilience. *Journal of Management, 33*(5), 774–800. https://doi.org/10.1177/0149206307305562

Zohar, D., & Marshall, I. (2000). *SQ: Connecting with our spiritual intelligence*. Bloomsbury.

Zohar, D. (2010). Exploring the spiritual capital: An interview with Danah Zohar. *Spirituality in Higher Education, 5*(5), 1–8.

CHAPTER 3

Sensing Crisis

This chapter presents a crucial part of leaders' journey towards wholeness: their deep awareness of the various levels of crises happening in their life, in their social contexts, and in the life of the world (Wilson, 2019). The word "crisis" does not connote here impending catastrophe; instead, it is accepted as a necessary turning point, a crucial moment when the development moves one way or another, marshaling the resources for growth, recovery, and more profound transformation. Thus, the crisis becomes a crucible for change. But, first, the leaders in the study experienced a period of crisis where they felt traumatized broken. They experienced the deep pain of looking for a breakthrough for themselves or others. The experience of spiritual crisis ranged from personal, social, and collective trauma such as the absence of self-worth, setbacks in careers, emotional brokenness, addictions, business losses, spiritual emptiness, and depression, to catastrophic external events of social conflicts, war, and natural disasters that triggered new direction for growth and development.

The experience of existential spiritual crises can be categorized into two major types: internal crisis and external crisis. The various aspects of internal crisis can be described as identity crisis, value crisis, and meaning crisis, and the various aspects of external crisis can be categorized

T. Thakadipuram, *Leadership Wholeness, Volume 1*, Palgrave Studies in Workplace Spirituality and Fulfillment, https://doi.org/10.1007/978-3-031-08053-1_3

into social crisis and ecological crisis. These crises provoked questions of meaning, trust, and purpose at the internal level and questions of justice, freedom, and responsibility at the external level. The internal crises manifested as identity crisis, value crisis, and meaning crisis are intrinsically connected. Some leaders experienced the internal crisis in all these three dimensions, while others experienced certain aspects of it in their leadership experience. The leaders also identified the experience of spiritual crisis manifested externally as social crisis and ecological crisis. These external crises also reinforce the internal crisis as well.

The leaders were deeply aware of the massive injustice and disruptions in society (social crisis), alienation of the self from nature (ecological crisis), inner brokenness, alienation from the higher self (existential crisis), and those experiences informed their spirituality and leadership perspective (Scharmer, 2015). The experience of spiritual crisis in their life journey led these top leaders to be empathetic to the people who suffered injustice and opened new doors to their souls and spiritual selves.

There is an intrinsic connection between the various aspects of the spiritual crisis, which manifests itself as internal crisis and external crisis. The various aspects of the internal crisis, identity crisis, value crisis, and meaning crisis can lead to social crisis and ecological crisis, which are the external aspects of the internal crisis. Experiences of some crises can lead to other crises but not necessarily happen in a logical order. Crisis, by its very nature, is chaotic and turbulent, and thus, it can provoke danger and create opportunities for growth and evolutionary progress.

The theme of *Sensing Crisis* illustrates one of the core themes of wholeness that manifest spiritual intelligence. The subthemes provide an increased understanding of this core theme of *Sensing Crisis*, as shown in Fig. 3.1. The experience of the existential spiritual crises and the various dimensions of the crisis are presented graphically, as shown in Fig. 3.1: Spiritual Crisis

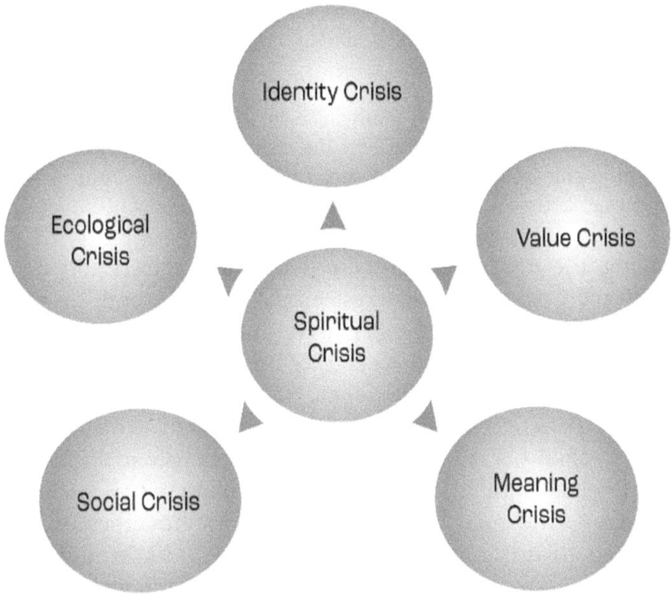

Fig. 3.1 Spiritual Crisis

Existential Spiritual Crisis

Leaders experienced existential spiritual crisis in different ways depending upon the context of their lives and business environment. A spiritual crisis is an existential crisis with crucial episodes of brokenness in which fundamental questions regarding the meaning and purpose of life are raised (American Dictionary of Psychology 2021). Scharmer (2022) categorized the experience of existential spiritual crisis into three divides: between self and nature resulting in ecological crisis; between self and other self-resulting in sociological crisis; and between self and the higher self resulting in existential crisis. Some of the leaders experienced spiritual crisis manifesting personal trauma and inner emptiness. Palmer noted, "I have not encountered anyone who is on a journey towards wholeness without having an existential crisis." Learning about other people's crisis helped leaders like Palmer to understand the meaning and purpose of experiences of crisis and traumas in life. Ingrid Vanderveldt, CEO of

Empowering Billion Women Global Network, described her moment of crisis:

> It was a very dark moment in my life in 2017; the most challenging moment in my business; I was very depressed, I was angry and hurtful, a scary moment, and I wanted to give up not seeing the light at the end of the tunnel and still waiting for a breakthrough.

Experiencing the emotional stress and mental anguish and depression made the leaders to undergo darkest moments in life and business situations and discover unexplored inner strength and vitality to rebound from the situation of break down to a stage of breakthrough.

Nick Nissley, President of Michigan Community College, shared very candidly his experience of the messy period of family brokenness and the turbulence of child hood trauma as excruciating existential spiritual crisis. The unhealthy and severed relationship in a family can have serious impact on the psyche of the child and it's amazing to see how these excruciating situations lead to existential crisis and eventual breakthrough for good. Hard times make people stronger and stronger times make people seek better life and lead a clear path towards wholeness. Nissley describes his childhood trauma and crisis:

> Forty years later, when I look at my childhood which was incredibly messy with family brokenness and existential crises, I experience the impact of alcoholism, domestic abuse, and mental illness that made me end up as the ward of the state. And as hard as that moment was, it created an opening. And the door was that led me to a place called the Milton Hershey School and an indeed breakthrough in my life.

The heart wrenching moments of family crisis with abuse, addiction, and psychological traumas created deeper life crisis and eventually paved the way for a new opening and new opportunity in the life of leaders like Nissley who learned to cope with crisis in his life. He explored the brighter side of life with good support system and caring mentors who showed the path towards greater success and meaning in life. This shows the indispensable vital role of family environment and supporting and nurturing environment for the holistic development of the person. Abbess Pema from the Plum Village, founded by the legendary Buddhist Monk Thich Nah Hanh, noted her experience and awareness of her spiritual crisis in the form of spiritual aridity, restlessness, and inner emptiness. It is appeared like an experience of dark night of the soul characterized by a combination of distress and subjective incompetence: the loss of meaning and purpose in life; lack of caring social support; a sense of being trapped in the vicious cycle of personal failure and hopelessness and pessimism. These crucibles of crisis propel a more profound journey and spiritual realization seeking advice and inspirations from the spiritual masters over time.

> The critical challenge for me is that I feel I am in a dry place at a certain point, in that dry place where the routine of life becomes a sort of meaningless. The challenge is inside me, a sort of spiritual aridity. And I am looking for something more profound. But it is excruciating to remain in that state of dryness and night. Some emptiness of self-restlessness and distress grappled me, and a feeling of fragmentation and inner brokenness; a quiet sense of despair propelling breakthrough to a profound sense of being in the world.

Williams (2021: 2) noted, "A dark night of the soul is defined as a spiritual journey that forces you to shed previous beliefs, habits, and relationships so that you can make a more mindful, fulfilling life." It shakes every aspect of your life; it makes you question everything about life and make you experience a deep transformation from within. Drawing insights from the classical text of John of the Cross, Dark Night of the Soul, a brilliant teaching on love, emptiness, and wholeness, Williams (2021: 1) identified seven signs of the dark night of the soul that many leaders in the study have experienced and manifested in their life: 1) "Feeling completely lost, powerless and hopeless, 2) No longer interested in things you once loved, 3) Your definition of success is not the same any more, 4) Distressing physical symptoms such as anxiety attacks, insomnia etc., 5) Having really intense dreams, 6) Connecting with the inner child and inner voice, 7) Despite everything, you somehow feel more free and authentic." The leaders experienced the trajectory of the dark night of the soul triggered by both internal crises and the external crises. The disharmony and fragmentation that occurred outside due to conflicts, social unrest, and war caused them great inner anguish and a deeper sense of the various crises happening in the world around them. Sri Sri Ravishankar, the founder of the global movement, Art of Living, was concerned about various wars and conflicts in his childhood days that provoked critical thinking about the meaning and purpose of life. This perspective of the spiritual crisis facing humanity led him to establish the global spiritual movement of the Art of Living which focuses on spiritual regeneration and holistic development across the world:

> Why are people in disharmony? I could not conceive all these wars around me: How can we unite and create better understanding? Why all these fights and conflicts? Why do people fight and destroy life in the name of the land and territory? My childhood days were a time of wars: India Pakistan war, India Bangladesh bar, India China war. These were deeply disturbing me in the sense that I would wonder why people live in disharmony, fear, and conflicts. Is there another way of living life?

Despite the agonizing experiences of inner crisis and distress, deeper soul-searching questions emerge in the hearts and minds of the leaders opening up uncharted journey towards wholeness. For Immaculee Ilibagiza, a Rwandan American Spiritual Leader, a powerful modern voice for the victims of war and genocide, the experience of psychological trauma, fragmentation, and agony that occurred during the Rwandan genocide caused severe crisis during her youthful days in Africa. The near-death experience in the wake of the tribal war made Ilibagiza go through the most excoriating crisis in her life while a group of ladies were kept hidden in the bathroom by a pastor for the fear of persecution and genocide towards the Tutsi tribe. These are harrowing and distressing events that go beyond the scope of the normal human experience, and they are life-threatening moments which make one susceptible to post-traumatic stress disorder. She describes the turmoil, trauma, and tempest in those crucial moments of existential crisis in 1994:

> I recall being put under fire, undergoing deep suffering for 91 days hiding in a bathroom in Rwanda during the genocide. It was a horrible and shattering experience beyond description. When I stood up, I was stretching, and I looked through the small window, and I saw about 400 people, the killers from the other tribe with weapons in their hands, coming after us. I remember my whole body went almost shut down, almost like my body thin air flying around floating in a vacuum. I remember my saliva dried instantly, and something swiftly swept out of my body; I couldn't feel my arms, my legs. It was like numb. Even though I was born in a beautiful country called Rwanda, people try to destroy it through conflict, war, and ethnic genocide.

For some leaders, the experience of brokenness resulted from their superficial living without a sense of deep purpose and meaning in their life but fleeting through the life of immediate gratification devoid of fulfillment. As a result, they underwent a deep emotional crisis and sought external means of drugs, alcohol, sex, and accumulation of material possessions to soothe their pain, confusion, and distress. An impressive body of research (Kasser et al., 2014) supports those addictions to materialistic aspiration, a trait that can affect both rich and poor, a system that can eat us from the inside out and which the researchers define as "a value system that is preoccupied with possessions and the social image they project, is both socially destructive and self-destructive" (Monbiot, 2022: 4). Increase in materialistic aspirations leads to decrease in inner well-being and increase in inner well-being leads to decrease in materialistic aspirations. It erodes the happiness and peace of mind of those who succumb to consuming the so-called low hanging fruits. It's associated with anxiety, loneliness, depression, and broken relationships. Abbot Phap Son, a Spanish Buddhist monk, shared his moments of crisis from the excessive pursuit of materialistic aspirations during his years of search and experimentation with life:

> Because I lived on a tourist island, there were a lot of drugs, sex, and parties. It was very alienating and distressing, even though those things offer instant gratification. Life looked like a party but very superficial and empty inside. I was living in isolation and brokenness within while appearing to be alright. You feel broken and emotionally shattered, feeling deep loneliness and crisis within.

Thurston, a modern mystic and South African artist, experienced spiritual emptiness at an early age, and a feeling of inner crisis led her to seek wisdom as an adolescent girl and reach the height of spiritual wholeness and fulfillment. She says, "The next significant moment in my journey towards wholeness came when I chose to seek wisdom at the age of about 16 because nothing else seemed very meaningful at all." However, Thurston also felt deep confusion, isolation, brokenness, and helplessness when her spouse and family misunderstood her, leading to separation and divorce. Standing up for what one believes is a very important part of the self-discovery and this can lead to turmoil and turbulence at the family level and tensions in old ways of relationship and traditions. Thurston describes how she experienced the crisis:

> I could tell nobody, not a single person; I didn't even have the words to express my deep spiritual experience. One day my husband opened the drawer and found my journals and inner revelations: he asked, what is this? I started reading the aphorisms or spiritual insights from my deep meditation experience; they are very profound to the one who is spiritually receptive, but they sound like nonsense for the uninitiated. He turned and looked at me with this fear, and I could see the fear on his face. He was doing an elective in a mental asylum where he finished his internship. I said I didn't know. I hear them (the aphorisms) in my head. He told me the only people I ever heard of who listen to voices in their head are in this place, an insane asylum, where I am working. I freaked out, and I thought he would have me committed (to the mental asylum), so I shut down. No, I did not shut down the inner channel. I shut down my communication with him, and eventually, we separated and divorced.

Greg Mc Brayer, Chief Flight Controller, one of the Major Airlines, described his moment of deep trouble encountering business turbulence, recessions, living a life of religiosity without spirituality that led him to the door of alcoholism and addiction hitting the rock bottom yearning for an authentic breakthrough and inner freedom from the bondages of anxiety, depression, and spiritual emptiness. The work stress and organizational stress added to the individual stress and threw life out of balance. In order to escape from the reality of work stress and personal crisis, he began to take recourse to alcohol and succumbed to addictions.

> In my profession in the airline industry, I began seeing a real journey of crises after crises; we saw mergers, pay, cuts, layoffs, and all those things continued to bring complexity and high stress into my life, and then I would lose my beloved Father and had not found my full spiritual bearings. Even though I was also serving the church in leadership roles, I had not felt the inner satisfaction and fulfillment. And I began to drink and drink to escape the pain hitting the rock-bottom, which pointed me to the doors of Alcoholics Anonymous for a deeper search and eventual breakthrough.

One of the ways the leaders were able to gain insight that they were going through crisis moments was by getting feedback from inside. It is important to maintain a close circle of trusted friendship to process the internal struggles and receive sincere feedback to make sense of what is going on inside oneself when encountering a deep crisis. Creating a psychologically safe place to process, the internal crisis will pave the way for healing, recovery, and wholeness. As Parker Palmer, a leading educationist and spiritual guide, says, “When you wake up in the early morning at three quite regularly worried and anxious, you know you have a crisis.“ In the similar vein, Carolyn Washburn, the Editor of Des Moines Register, noted, “There is no security; neither in public sector nor in the corporate world; you learn to live with ambiguity to figure the next storyline in your life.“ Learning to deal with the regular occurrence of ambiguity makes one feel vulnerable and insecure. The experience of the absence of security outside makes one to search for inner security and well-being through the pursuit of spiritual path. William Jarema, the Director of the Psychotherapy Center, noted, “Borrowing the phrase from Albert Schweitzer, I would like to say, “All pain is a messenger,” and it’s vital to sense the crisis when you experience burnout or personal turmoil to move in the direction of healing and wholeness.“ Losing the ability to sense the pain within and without can lead to perpetuation of the emotional pain and trauma causing irreparable damage. Swami Veda Bharati, one of the current World Spiritual Leader and meditation genius, described how he experienced emotional distress and brokenness in his spiritual transformational journey:

> I was about nineteen or twenty years old; I used to get very angry. I was living in the house of a well-known politician in Africa. This gentleman whose guest I was said something very unkind and untoward to me for some reason. I got furious. Mrs…, I will not give the name, she used to come to my room like a mother, every morning to see that everything was alright. She saw that my pillow had a nose bleed. I used to get such a mixture of love and respect as a teacher of Veda across the globe. In the other place, I was a son and a teacher at another location. She came to me with such a loving tone, “*Brahmachariji*, you are such a great teacher, but how come you have such a great anger"; ah! It hit me; no, I can’t do that. So, within a month or two, I discovered Gandhi’s autobiography, “The Experiment with Truth,” and I read it. And I worked on myself to grow from this moment of distress and anger and profoundly transform my inner self.

Observing and experiencing the presence of brokenness in society through the issues including structural and cultural violence of racism and xenophobia, Archbishop Harry Flynn noted, “Racism is a form of xenophobia, a fear or dislike of those who are different from us. Each of us has some element of this fear within our hearts. It dehumanizes the very humanity in us." These leaders have expressed their experience of being part of the big traumas of their life time including natural disasters, cultural genocide, colonial oppressions, racism protests, and other distressing moments of encountering the evil of social injustice. Credo Mutua, Zulu Shaman, and prominent African spiritual leader and Ambassador Susan Johnson described how they experienced deep pain and brokenness in connection with life-long struggles:

> My life journey is interwoven with the existential struggles of the African people for freedom, dignity, and self-respect. My life was threatened by colonial oppression, Apartheid, and religious fundamentalism. My life has been a back entrance of a lunatic asylum both by the tragedies of African cultural annihilation, tribal rivalry, colonial domination, and oppression (Mutua).
>
> And so, for me, when I see and feel brokenness, I find the places where I can be helpful. For example, I was on the frontlines of 911, a shattering moment in the nation's history. This year we mark the 20th anniversary. The situation in New Orleans happened with the natural disaster when the levees burst. Right now, many police officers are going through distress over the tragic Floyd incident. People from New York, so we're going to go to the frontlines, and we're going to help them. I knew I couldn't emotionally handle another pandemic (Ambassador Susan Johnson).

Ingrid Vanderveldt, the founder president of the movement, "Empowering Billion Women," narrated her first significant moment of crisis early on when the school authorities misjudged her health situation and labeled her as a mentally disabled person: "I was failing out of school. And nobody knew what was going on. I was in the third grade, supposed to go into the fourth grade. And the principal called my parents in and, you know, said, we cannot help your child, she's a distraction. The word they used is we think "she's retarded", something you would never hear today." Sensing this personal crisis and the unhealthy environment of the school system, her parents took bold steps to move her to a particular school that helped them identify the issue and help her blossom in excellence.

Sister Rosalind Gefre, an American Catholic nun and a leading pioneer massage therapist in the United States, experienced a health crisis and encountered pain in her own body and in the minds of people who visited her clinic regularly. It was by experiencing the crisis of health situation of ongoing pain and eventual breakthrough with massage therapy that opened a new door to a turning point in her life and embarked on exploring the mission of massage therapy which led to a great success and a new healing ministry that became a new holistic phenomenon against all odds of cultural bias at that time. While doing massage therapy, she made people psychologically safe to open up their lives and recognized their spiritual emptiness and make efforts to transform their life with meaning and purpose. Speaking of this turning point in her life, Sister Gefre noted:

> Before I knew it, I was on the table and had a massage. And up to that time, I kept having this chest pain that I always knew I'd die of because every night I went to bed, I had to get up and walk around or sit up in bed because that chest pain was just there continually. The days were not bad, but the nights were horrible. And then she gave me that massage, and I didn't say anything to her about that, and I didn't think about it; all I had was a massage. But that was the end of my pain, which I had for 20 years. And that just disappeared, and that's how I started searching into massage as therapy and its healing power. I encountered many people who led empty lives amid plenty" and helped them to rediscover the meaning and purpose in their lives.

These leaders consider the time of sensing their own existential crisis and brokenness as significant milestones in their journey towards wholeness. They recognized various kinds of existential crises including personal crisis, business crisis, value crisis, meaning crisis, family crisis, and career crisis. Demonstrating the first signs of deeper spiritual awareness and intelligence the leaders have diagnosed the existence of a deeper crisis in their life and this ability to be clearly aware of the crisis and its impact on their lives and their organizations is critical for their authentic journey towards wholeness.

The Psychological Impact of the Crisis

Leaders recognized that they experienced emotional turbulence and distress in their journey towards wholeness. They encountered fear, anxiety, despair, and helplessness in their life journey. Whether facing a painful business decision or confronting inner turmoil like depression, the leaders across the board shared their experience of emotional pain. They struggled at crucial moments of life that led to more soul searching and meaning. For them, emotional distress was a springboard for deeper searching and understanding of the purpose in life.

For example, Parker Palmer experienced deep emotional distress and inner devastation when he endured situational depression for an extended period in his life. He very candidly described the excruciating emotional rollercoaster experienced during his clinical depression:

> When you are in deep clinical depression, there are days when it is impossible to go outdoors. I live in a charming neighborhood, as you can see. There are days when I saw the world so full of knives. I just had to pull the shades, hunker down and stay inside. So, there is this anxiety, this fear; I believe that is an emotion of some sort. It shuts you down, and you know you are being shut down. You are not just living a half-life or just a quarter-life; one-eighth of the life. And that keeps me much deeper in the pit, deeper in the hole, deeper in the pit. It is a mystery how some people can come out of it. Well, depression is a stage of no feeling; your emotions are dead. The point of depression is that you are in the middle of it; you are no longer playing games with life. I came to a point where I thought of ending my life. It is no mystery to me why people commit suicide. Depression is just devastating.

Many CEOs of both profit and non-profit sector experienced high stress at the top managing the chaos and complexities of the rollercoaster business turbulence due to world recession, economic decline, and socio-political upheaval. They were well aware that stress can be a silent killer at the top. Larry Zimpleman, the CEO of Principal Finance Company, describes the excruciating moments of massive stress he underwent when he had to face the economic recession and the emotional turmoil of letting thousands of employees go from the company to save the company out of the crisis. Facing the challenges and complexities of business at the top creates high stress and psychological strain. The global crisis led to the organizational crisis and that led to a moment of crisis as a leader:

> "When the 2008 recession happened, it was certainly the worst time in my business career. Many mornings, my wife saw tears on my shoes while leaving my house to the office." We were 15,000 employees at that time, and I had to let go of 10 percent of the workforce. Although it was the most difficult decision, it was the right thing to do to save the company and support people.

Carolyn Washburn, a top editor of Cincinnati and Des Moines Register, expressed her moment of spiritual crisis with psychological impact when she faced the challenge of managing the declining print business: "It brought deep emotional turmoil, especially when I had to let go 100 s of employees from the company to salvage it". Corrina Linn, Executive Director of Singapore's National Association of Women for Action Research "AWARE," described her excitement of the leadership initiative in starting a technology business, Busy Body Technology, in the 1990s and the trauma of the eventual crash of the new industry during the global "dotcom" crisis: "I was burned out and probably depressed at that time, facing the challenge of crashing business venture and struggling to pivot into a successful technology business for the legal industry in Singapore." When Ilibagiza found herself amidst genocide and tribal conflict in Rwanda, she underwent emotional trauma of mortal fear, desperation, and utter hopelessness. During the 1994 Rwandan genocide, also known as the genocide against the Tutsi tribe, members of the Hutu ethnic majority in the east-central African nation of Rwanda engaged in the mass killing of as many as 800,000 people, mostly of the Tutsi minority. Started by Hutu nationalists in the capital of Kigali, the genocide spread throughout the country with shocking speed and brutality. Ilibagiza who belonged to the minority tribe of Tutsi described her experience of this collective trauma of national crisis where the entire country had become a killing field due to tribal war when she was hiding in a Hutu pastor's bathroom for 91 days along with seven other women to escape death:

> Then the herd of Hutus had stormed the house. I heard somebody calling my name. He said, "I "have killed 399 cockroaches," He wanted me to be the 400th. I'm like, Oh my God! I was so scared that he knew where I was. He's so sure. It was like dying alive, and really when I remember the pain of that place, it was like every day you are—like something is dying, slowly dying thousands of times, yeah, A deep cloud of despair and fear began to run deep into my soul. I have never been so scared in my life. I remember it was like, life swept out of your body in a second. I became dry instantly. I couldn't even find saliva to swallow.

Sister Gefre disclosed her awareness about encountering the fear of death when she had a heart attack. "Another big moment of crisis was when I had a heart attack. And it was the moment I came face-to-face with the reality of death. It was a moment of deep distress and helplessness. Somehow, I survived.“ She also described how she was in deep inner pain and suffering when she was subject to rejection and ridicule from within and outside her community. While working with the clients, Sister Rosalind encountered people with emotional struggles and turmoil. She described how she led them towards emotional healing and wholeness:

> What happened was that I was venturing into massage therapy service and business, and my community did not like it. And I lost my happy home in the community. I used to massage the older sisters. When I went to the dining room, other sisters would ask me about what I did, and I said, massage and sisters would take the plate and walk away from me, for they thought I was doing immoral, dirty work. I know I cried and cried a lot those days, especially when my massage clinic was shut down due to bad media publicity and prejudice. Facing ridicule, criticism, opposition, and resistance both from inside and outside the country was tricky.

Abbot Phap Son reflected on his emotional crises with periodic depression and alienation: "I was caught up in crisis back and forth. I underwent depression and intense emotional turmoil living a superficial life of materialistic pursuits without deeper sensibilities. It was unsettling and alienating since I had no support system to lean on. I was afraid of the unknown. It was a big struggle of inner emptiness and psychological turmoil." Similarly, Abbess Pema learned that her emotional struggles and crisis were the projections of her ego, which needed to be recognized:

> I become aware that there is something in me that is very painful; whatever I am aware of and whatever I am not aware of is part of me; my emotional struggles are part of me; that which creates pain is part of me, and I need to recognize that they are not permanent realities. I learned that my emotional reactions were the projections of my ego and not from the true nature.

Thurston, the founder of Core Light, noted how she underwent emotional trauma when she faced the moral dilemma with the idea of her unwanted pregnancy and her longing for spiritual pursuits: "Later, a couple of weeks later I learned that I was pregnant. I wasn't sure I wanted to be pregnant and so it was a trauma." Mutua, an African Civil Rights leader and Shaman, described the traumatic periods of his childhood and youth as he was succumbed to sexual abuse, violence, and rejection by his own family and community:

> One day, I was savagely attacked by a group of boys; I did not know what they were doing to me. What they were doing to me was sodomy. It was a shock; it was horror; my father came to know about it and chased me out of my house. I used to stay with my half-brother and sisters. I had to stay outside of my home. My Father said, 'I smelled of the sins of Sodom and Gomorrah.'
>
> My stepmother was even worse but kind to me. The church kicked me out, my father threw me out, my stepmother rejected me, and I was an orphan living on the street of Transvaal.

Archbishop Flynn described how he was emotionally overwhelmed when he had to deal with the clergy sexual abuse crisis at the national and local level. Holding space for the victims to pour out their hearts in disclosing the story and offering empathetic listening for long hours was an excruciating process feeling the pains and tragedies although one cannot adequately embrace the suffering, it was a very moving experience to bring healing and wholeness to the whole process. He explained how the stark sight of the discrimination the blacks encountered in the American criminal justice system tormented him and moved him to take proactive steps to fight the systemic injustice:

> Since I first began working with the victims of clergy sexual abuse and their families, I have witnessed immense pain and anger. I have seen psychological torment and sometimes loss of faith and essential trust. When these persons shared the account of their suffering, I was sometimes overwhelmed by its gravity and intensity even though I was holding space for them. Even as I tried to accompany them on their spiritual healing journey, I knew I could never fully grasp their pain and that I could never take away that horrible experience. Another experience that disturbed me deeply occurred when I first visited the prison in Angola, Louisiana. I entered the *death house*, which houses death row inmates, only African Americans. This stark experience convinced me that racism is not only a matter of individual bigotry; it is also an institutional and structural reality in society.

From the candid descriptions of these leaders about how they experienced various existential spiritual crises, including their own and others, it was evident that the deep psychological turmoil and emotional turbulence impacted their lives. The spiritual crisis manifested as internal crisis three main ways: identity crisis, value crisis, and meaning crisis and as an external crisis in two main ways: social crisis and ecological crisis. The crisis is perceived as a crucible of learning experience and not as impending catastrophes where there is no point of return from the trauma or tragedy. Their ability to sense the patterns of crises early on helped them to take stock of the situation and rally their teams together to face the crises positively to discover new opportunities hidden in these challenges The awareness of their inner suffering and the pains of others helped them to empathize and embrace the challenge of spiritual crisis. The profound suffering shaped their deeper self in the womb of fierce love. The various aspects of the spiritual crisis will be analyzed in the following section from the point of view of the leader's journey towards wholeness manifesting the emerging spiritual intelligence that transforms the crisis into a crucible of learning, discovery, and transformation.

Identity Crisis

Identity crisis is defined in the dictionary of the American Psychological Association (APA, 2022: 1) as a "the phase of life marked by experimentation; changing, conflicting, or newly emerging values; and a disenchantment with the usual roles in society" (especially in work and family relationships). Erik Erikson claimed that it is natural and desirable for adolescents to go through a period of identity crisis and that greater maturity results from experience. It is a state of inner conflict related to serious soul searching to understand who one is. At the core of the individual and communal nature, various dimensions of identity emerge in one's lifetime. The concept has been expanded to refer to adult midlife crises and other periods marked by change or uncertainty about the self and individuation process.

Similarly, Merriam-Webster dictionary (2022) defines identity crisis as a psychosocial state or condition of disorientation and role confusion occurring mainly in various stages as a result of conflicting internal and external experiences, pressures, and expectations and often producing acute anxiety due to family structural change, business context, or social turbulence. Identity crisis is a crucial moment in which our discernment process takes place to find out who we are, embracing both the strengths and shadows of life towards the emergence of the wholeness of life.

The leaders' journey towards wholeness was marked by identity crises at different stages of their lives. Many of them had to part ways with the initial group of people they worked and collaborated with or to whom they had bonded since they became disillusioned with the original mission. Invariably, they all felt that they had to part ways either because their calling was different or they had different values or perspectives on life. For most of them, experiencing failure was an eye-opener that broadened their vision and deepened their understanding that they could break free from roles constraining their lives and work. Discerning through the experiences of disenchantment and disorientation, the leaders recognized their identity crisis resulting in the transformation of their previously held beliefs and pre-suppositions. Parker Palmer described how he underwent a unique identity crisis early on due to his false sense of identity:

> I grew up in a Chicago suburb as a sort of golden boy. But in New York City, in Spanish Harlem, I saw the significant first-time signs of failures showing up in my life. I knew very little about real life. One weekend I cried in public for the first time in my life in front of the kids in Spanish Harlem. I was pretty broken down by my failures with them even though I might have been a big man due to my privileged status in Wilmette, Illinois, or New Trier High School. A moment to penetrate the illusions and touch the reality.

Palmer also identified such a crisis at a later stage in life as he recalled, "When you marry and start becoming a parent, you start learning more about failures and change of previously held idea of who you are." Similarly, Swami Veda experienced the conflict between his role as a spouse and his calling to be a monk and spiritual leader. The conflict of a life of a house holder and the spiritual calling to be a celibate spiritual leader who wants to serve the world led to an identity crisis in his life:

> I had a great conflict about my role as husband and father and a call to be a father to all. Experiences of great conflict came over me after I got married: What will you be, a monk? Are you going to be a swami? You have slipped away from your soul's ambition. And now you have to live in the world. You have to learn and find jobs to feed your family. So, it was a period of period of great depressing conflict.

Vanderveldt, the CEO of Empowering Billion Women, experienced identity crisis as a child misunderstood by the teachers and judged to be mentally retarded due to her hearing problems. Although I suffered being misunderstood and judged, I learned the power of possibility from almost impossibility. This experience resulted in my identity crisis feeling low self-esteem and total misery of being misunderstood and seeming doomed in the first school. She did not really know her potential and who she was as mistaken notions about who she is presented by her teachers and school authorities. With a change of school, good support system, the power of endurance, and positive mind, she was able to go beyond the limits of the judgment that others had put on her life:

> When I was in the fourth grade, the principal called my parents and said, your daughter, we believe is retarded for nothing is going right for her, we don't know what to do with your daughter. Being frustrated and disheartened yet loving and caring for me my parents send me to a special school with one class room. Principal and school board said that you are living very far way and so we cannot do bussing for her alone. Parents found that there is a loop hole in the law and the school had to provide the ride for an hour long. Shortie, the driver for the long yellow bus and drove me from home to the school and I was the sole traveler on the bus. They assigned a tutor to find out about my learning disability. Parents believed in my possibility and so they send me to this special school. In the six grades, they found out that I had hearing problems with good help and assistance. Thank God for the blessing of powerful parenting and belief in the power of new possibilities that I had a new breakthrough from learning disability.

Archbishop Flynn encountered deep pain and crisis as a spiritual leader when meeting the clergy's ethical scandals. The clergy sex abuse cases which were rampant in the later part of the last century were rocking the social ethics and church etiquette across the world. It was not only a spiritual identity crisis but also resulted in the agony and distress of the victims of sexual abuse crisis. In reality, some clergy are capable of heroic acts of selflessness even at the cost of their lives and shockingly capable of deeply evil acts that seem unfathomable. Archbishop Flynn noted:

> When I faced the moral crisis of clergy across the nation, it was a moment of deep personal pain and a national emergency. Cases of clergy misconduct are especially damaging because we all know that ordained persons are called to emulate Christ the Good Shepherd's charity, purity, and care. The abuse of anyone, incredibly a minor by a Cardinal, Bishop, priest, or deacon is shocking and most depraved of moral aberrations.

Mutua expressed the severe crisis he underwent in his childhood when he was ill-treated and rejected during the time of colonization of Africa and the Apartheid regime in South Africa. During a period lasting from 1881 to 1914, several European nations took control over the areas of African Continent. The main reasons that led to the colonization of Africa was economic, military, and politics. The exploitation of the local resources by divide and rule tactics and enslavement of Africa led to the extreme practices of Apartheid and racial hegemony. Mutua spoke about how he was abused, neglected, and lived through abject degradation as a Zulu boy facing crises after crises:

> I was on the street for long years facing hunger, poverty, rejection, and racial prejudice. I was a victim of cultural and religious bigotry. Missionaries and white colonialists told us that we were savage, lazy, and primitive, who knew Nothing about God. Due to the harsh and inhuman working climate in the gold mines of South Africa, where the Colonialists subjugated the Africans, I became blind. I lived in darkness for ten years until a white doctor healed me.

Thurston described her struggle with ego projections and identity crisis as she engaged in inner exploration, shadow work, and spiritual seeking. Shadow is the unconscious dark side of oneself with repressed thoughts, feelings, and emotions that block the exercise of the authentic identity of the person. Shadow work involves being honest about the unpliant part of one's own personality and processing through the inner shadow work is the way to recognize the identity crisis and rediscover the deeper spiritual identity beyond the shadows. Samadhi is the highest state of consciousness one is gifted with following intense and consistent practice of meditation which is characterized by union with the higher self. She felt that supernatural forces guided her, but not without being subject to excruciating sufferings to break free from her egocentric habit patterns and mistaken identity:

> The Shadow would come up, and the light will go up, and I have a few days of *Samadhi,* and then I plunge into shadows; into the next layer; into the next deeper layer of Shadow. This went on for months. Finally, after the ego death on the floor of the Del Mar Inn the following day, I thought I felt very different with a new identity, but I still didn't know what to do. And they didn't speak to me; it was dead silence.

Sri Sri spoke about his identity crisis mainly associated with his difficulty to connect with his peer group and friends. His experience level was far ahead of his companions as he focused on the deeper meaning of life and spiritual exploration, unlike his peer group engaged in sports and entertainment. He was far ahead of his time and naturally drawn to spiritual pursuit of yoga and meditation and devotional practices. Some of the family members did not quite understand what he is after and why he is different in his approach to life resulting in family tension and misunderstandings. This kept him alienated from his peers and led to discerning his own true identity as a spiritual master in course of time.

> I was a kid who was out of place. When you are young, you feel really out of place. I was not drawn to the world of cricket, sports, or movies like my peers. I had to force myself to engage the peer group. Otherwise, I would feel out of place and have conversations with them. I wanted to be among them, but I could not be at their level. It would never interest me, the peer group small talk. On the other hand, I was happy identifying with elders asking serious questions about life, spirituality and higher purpose of life.

Abbess Pema described her crisis of identity as a crisis of faith. She encountered a religious system which was more rubric oriented and judgmental in its approach and so did not find good sources of support to process her inquiry into the meaning and purpose of religious practices. Along with the growing pains of culture and family, the struggles with beliefs and faith continued to challenge her world of religiosity and upbringing. Without having an opportunity to go into the deeper meaning of ones' own religious traditions, she abandoned her Christian roots and began to engage in the spiritual pursuit of Buddhist meditation and monastic living. This led to a period of deep crisis and transformation. She was dissatisfied with the religious teachings she received during her younger days and so began to seek truth beyond the religious system of her upbringing:

> One of my crises is the crisis of faith. Even though every week we went to a priest for Catechism, we did not understand anything. Maybe that is not very unusual. I did not know what Mass was as I was an English-speaking person living in the Netherlands. Even though I was prepared in a non-denominational school in Catechism, I attended a Catholic school. A nun asked me, could you describe God? I said no. At that time, she told me that I was not a good Catholic. This incident challenged my identity as a Catholic person, and I was searching for something else to identify with.

This spiritual search led me to practice of Buddhist meditation and way of life.

Abbot Phap Son expressed the fact that due to his unique circumstances of family and culture, he underwent confusion about his identity experiencing a personal crisis due to upbringing in different ethnic culture identity and expectations and value system. Being caught up in the middle of the cultural conflict can make one feel deep insecurity without knowing whom to identify with or how to transcend the pressure of dealing with difference sense of cultural identity. Without the proper support of a supporting system to work through the experiences of brokenness, it is hard to gain a deeper sense of mixed identity and self-acceptance. Feeling insecure within, he sought something meaningful to identify with to overcome the sense of loss and identity crisis:

I experienced an identity crisis. My Father was English, and my mother was Swiss. I was a foreigner living in Spain. The other problem was about who I am as a person. That was part of my journey as well. I felt broken within and emotionally insecure. Eventually, I joined different local environmental groups that gave me some sense of identity.

Sister Rosalind spoke about her identity crisis as a crisis of vocation and calling: "As I got older, I was thinking very much about sisterhood; however, men became more attractive than sisterhood did. And it was tough to decide life as I was torn between the two ways of life whether to marry or to embrace religious vocation as a nun." Discerning religious life while feeling attracted to married life is a time of intense stress and inner turmoil as if being pulled apart in two directions. The focus, the prayer, and consultations with experienced Nuns helped me to overcome the moments of confusion and chaos to come to a clarity of mind, charity of heart, and make a leap of faith and trust to be drawn to the spiritual calling of religious life. Ilibagiza described how she underwent the identity crisis as a Tutsi when she was hiding for fear of the Hutu Tribe, questioning her own identity as a particular tribe and not able to grasp the brutal onslaught of the ethnic conflict that was emerging in Rwanda in the 1990s. When the peaceful environment in which she grew up began to collapse due to tribal war and ethnic violence, she began to question the meaning of her existence and identity in the wake of the crucible of suffering and turmoil:

> The reality was that they were killing everybody from my tribe. Some churches from the opposite tribe have killed 10,000 people who ran there for refuge. They destroyed churches. And they said we want to eliminate everyone. They searched homes, Hutu homes where even the Tutsi friends were hiding. It was terrible not to be sitting without light in the bathroom, without talking, not knowing what was going on: The confusion of why am I having this misery? Why did this happen? And what is wrong? Why am I sitting here? Who knows the whole village? I remember the first three days so well; the feeling that was going through was why me? How can these things happen to me? I was born as a Tutsi, so what is wrong with that? And someone wants to kill you, why? And why are you sitting here? If I go out, I will tell my mom what is happening to me? I was sitting here beating myself as if it was only happening to me? I was blaming people. How can they do that to me?

The crucial life experiences of leaders have indicated a period of identity crisis that resulted in the more profound inner transformation towards a more excellent individuation process and unfolding of hidden dimensions of the whole self. In addition, the leaders have gained greater insight into their personalities as they have turned the negative experiences into the crucible of learning and discovery of their true nature.

*The leaders' experience of identity crisis shattered their sense of self-concept, creating excruciating agony and turmoil. They experienced identity crises of many types: vocational, career, cultural, social, religious, and racial. The experience of these crises and brokenness eventually helped them to seek their deeper and broader sense of who they are and what their true potential and roles are concerning the leadership role they exercise in organizations. However, the creative confusion of one's identity resulted in self-enhancement that promotes psychological and physical well-being, albeit at the expense of interpersonal relations, cultural associations, and probably because it serves to sustain good spirits and goal-pursuit (*Hogg, 2007*). Many other identity motives have been identified in their journey towards wholeness. These include drives for meaning, continuity, coherence, communion, and agency not without a deeper awareness of one's being and becoming in the individuation process manifesting spiritual motives and intelligence.*

Value Crisis

Many leaders encountered value conflicts and ethical crises in a variety of ways depending on the context and type of organizations. Although the context of each leader was unique, their experiences of value conflict made a deep imprint on their quest for wholeness. These leaders understood that holding the noble values of human dignity and integrity was paramount to their lives. When they found that their espoused values conflicted with the actual values of their organization and culture, either they confronted this value conflict within them, or they abandoned their position in the organization to preserve their dignity and integrity. They understood the importance of holding on to their values after undergoing the crisis and seeing the negative impact on their lives and the people around them. The leaders realized that value crises were moment of learning and opportunity to chart a new course in their journey towards wholeness. The leaders' experience of moral dilemma and crisis led them to deeper understanding and transformation in their journey towards wholeness. Palmer found himself in conflict with the people in power as they compromised the fundamental human values of honesty, integrity, and justice:

> I worked in many institutions as faculty and many other positions. I started realizing that I have a pretty high unhealthy reaction when I get inside an institution. For example, one of them spent lots of time and energy conflicted with whoever was running the show, those in power, significantly when they compromised fundamental values.

Vanderveldt, Chairman and CEO of Empowering Billion Women, narrated her excruciating moment of moral dilemma and value crisis in her business deals when she encountered that there were bad actors whom he trusted to work with during the global pandemic times. Ethical and moral issues in business encompass a wide array of areas within an organization's ethical standards. Fundamental ethical issues in business include promoting conduct based on integrity and trust. This is true of both people within the organization and the partners with which business deals are done. The uncertainty and volatility of the business environment alone with the unreliability and lack of credibility of the business partners created the inner turmoil which led to regathering strengths to trouble shoot the moment of crisis:

> Many nights I didn't think I'd survive this. There were nights I was going on 1–2 hours of sleep, fighting to make this happen, knowing timing was more critical than anything I had faced as an entrepreneur. I was negotiating PPE deals 24/7 to no end and was just so incredibly tired. Finally,

> I realized I needed more help and started to grow the team. As things seemed to be coming together, we got a hard punch in the gut. Here we were trying to do good by the world and solve a major health crisis, only to learn that many of the players we were negotiating with were actually bad actors with no true intention to help our efforts. They only wanted to turn a profit for themselves. It was a devastating blow to my heart and to humanitarian effort. People everywhere were promising they had the supply and had signed legal documents for these critical supplies only for us to learn that they didn't have them. We were swift to rectify these issues and put the right team in place to eliminate our risk. I appointed tech veteran, Rhonda Parouty as President, Roberta Lang, former global VP and General Counsel of Whole Foods to ensure we had excellence and eyes, ears, and hands on every step of the PPE process. We hired Cynthia Barnes as VP of Contracts and Development, who is a Six Sigma Black Belt in process, engineer, and an attorney to trouble shoot the situation and face the issue head on to move own with our business venture.

Swami Veda had to leave the organization where he began his career, which gave him the platform to be a world spiritual teacher. He realized that its values and ideology were very constraining and narrow. He became more exposed to the world at large and different religions. He acknowledged that he was no longer comfortable belonging to an organization that changed its focus with a fundamentalist religious ideology. Religious fundamentalism believes in the superiority of their religious teachings and in a strict division between righteous people and not righteous people. He struggled with the mindset of his religious leaders and chose to go beyond such dispositions:

> My Father was a member of the ultra-radical reform movement called *Arya Samaj*. So, I spent my earlier years within that movement, but I soon felt very confined to a doctrine and organizational structures. As my exposure to people of different countries and faith grew, I abandoned being a "fundamentalist missionary," if you know what I mean. Of course, being a frog in the well, I reached a point of crisis for my soul where I couldn't survive without abandoning such a narrow ideology.

Swami Veda was also aware of the increasing disparity between the rich and poor people. The rich become more affluent, and the poor become poorer due to policies and practices across the globe. While he was overwhelmed by the enormity of such value conflict in society, he tried to challenge these values and practices in his writings. He added, "There is massive injustice in the world between rich and poor, the powerful and powerless; I feel much helpless, but I write about them and do what I can." John Abbate, the owner and operator of 37 McDonald franchise locations throughout Central Valley of California, described his value crisis as a wake-up call and warning to think about his priorities and the gap between what he believed and what he practiced as a spiritually focused business leader. He disclosed his moments of crisis:

> My wake-up call didn't come until his wife Karen called me out for being a hypocrite. It was painful and shocking to hear first but that helped me to keep to do soul searching doing inner work to be authentic and thrive in my life and business. I would profess to believe in faithfulness and commitment at Holy Mass on Sunday, but then my actions didn't back it up. She helped me to look deeper at his business talent and to understand the greater purpose of those talents from a spiritual point of view of service and dedication. It was at this point that I reexamined my life and his priorities. I came to realize that wealth, power, pleasure and honor are all substitutes for my higher purpose and focus on God and what will bring ultimate happiness. This led him to ask the big question. God what do you want out of me and my life? While on a pilgrimage I reflected on this question. I also thought about how those of us in business often react out of fear, the fear of failure and the fear of not succeeding. This led me to adopt the mantra, "Be not afraid. Be not afraid to live your faith and values in every aspect of your life, in my community, in my business and in my family. This turn around helped me to be wholesome in my leadership practice and avert further moral crisis in my life. This new perspective fueled the change in me to get my priorities in the right order.

Archbishop Flynn was confronted with the evil forces of covert and overt racism in his church organization and society, which violated the values of fundamental human dignity and equality of all before the eyes of God. Facing the issues of racial discrimination which undermined the basic fabric of human dignity and worth which was hidden and overt in the culture for centuries, it was not easy to confront the hidden demon of racism head on and explore ways help people to change the mindset of depravity to a mind of truth and reconciliation. The hidden demon of racism come into national and international attention in the same city where Archbishop Flynn served with the death of George Floyd and the aftermath of national and international protest that emerged to address the challenges of racial injustice:

> More than 20 years ago, the Catholic bishops of the United States issued a significant pastoral letter on racism, called *Brothers, and Sisters to Us*. In that letter, we declared that Racism is a grievous sin: a sin that divides the human family, blots out the image of God among specific members of that family and violates the fundamental human dignity of those called to be children of the same Father. Now, more than two decades later, I am saddened to observe that Racism remains a genuine and powerful evil force among us that destroys the very fabric of co-existence as civilized people. It undermines the moral basis of equality, justice, and freedom of humanity. Despite our efforts to combat it, Racism continues to mar our humanity as a deep wound in our midst. It is a destructive force in our personal lives, Church, and society.

Archbishop Flynn recalled how his mother helped him identify and overcome the hidden Racism and prejudice in his own heart. Tackling racism is a complex matter since it is very subtle to spot it in the workplace. It's hard for the dominant community to recognize its own flows and so the issue of racism gets perpetuated in spite of the public remedial steps taken so far. The lessons from this incident of confronting the attitude of exclusion and creating an environment of inclusion helped him to dissolve his hidden attitude of xenophobia and reshape his life based on universal love, acceptance, and solidarity:

> I remember an incident on my sixth birthday. My mother said I could invite the members of my grade school class, and I replied that I would like to, but one of the girls in my class was African American, and I said that I didn't think I wanted to invite her. Fine, said my mother, you don't have to ask her, but if you don't, then you won't have a birthday party. I still vividly remember that birthday party and my mother warmly greeting the young African American girl as she came up the sidewalk to attend the party. That single act made a profound impression on me. In an instant, my mother dissolved some of the xenophobia that had been in my heart. Racism is a form of xenophobia, a fear or dislike of those different from us. Each of us has some fear within our hearts.

Witnessing blatant racism while he was leading churches in his dioceses provoked his conscience and decided to fight against racism and be a champion for all humans who are treated without dignity. He recalled how these cultural practices deeply disturbed him. Encountering deplorable instances of racial inequality that treated human beings as less than animals helped Archbishop Flynn to champion the cause of human solidarity and social justice as a spiritual leader:

> Years later, when I became Bishop of Lafayette, Louisiana, I repeatedly heard blatant racism — both within the society and the Catholic Church. For example, during Mass in a predominantly white parish, a young African American Catholic extended his hand to give a greeting of peace and was told by the white gentleman next to him, "I don't shake hands with your type." An additional factor that must be recognized is that the tragedy of September 11, 2001, has created a growing awareness of discrimination against ethnic populations from the Middle East.

Recognizing the deep value crisis in the human heart that nurtures hidden racism and discrimination subtly, Archbishop Flynn launched his struggle against racism in all forms promoting understanding and goodwill among different races. Employees who are affected by racism are less productive and it creates negative work environment which does not allow creativity to flourish and fulfill their potential. Racism does not manifest blatantly many a times but in a very subtle form and perhaps shockingly distressing when it happens publicly. Archbishop noted his personal experience:

> I have observed that racism in Minnesota is no less real and no less severe than what I experienced in Louisiana. However, racism here is sometimes more subtle, less blatant. It might take the form of ignoring or turning a cold shoulder to people of color, rather than saying overtly, "I don't shake hands with people of your type. "Racism here is often more indirect and less open.

The recent incident of the killing of George Floyd by the police on the streets of Minneapolis, Minnesota, and the social unrest that followed rocked the entire nation during the global pandemic, sending ripple effects across the world proved the prophetic warnings of Archbishop Flynn about the reality of deep-rooted crisis of hidden and overt racism. Mutua shared his experience of an excruciating value crisis during his days of Apartheid in South Africa. He recalled how the missionaries and colonialists misled him and fellow Africans through dominant values, oppressive ideas, and suppressive practices. "We were told that we knew nothing about God; they called us heathens; that too, when the missionaries came said the same; we were told that we were savage, lazy, and primitive. That was a total undermining of our basic dignity". Mutua remembered how he experienced a profound moral value crisis as a child and adult, especially When caught between two faces of Africa. He encountered conflicts between blacks and whites and within his tribes. Moral decadence and war lead to division not only between the races but also within tribes as well:

> I was born an illegitimate child; I was not allowed to play with other children. Amongst the so-called heathens, people who wear skins, I found real friends; I realized the true face of Africa. Africa's two faces are slavish, beaten down, and savage as presented to the western world. Another front of Africa, caring, compassionate, and human, helped a man, rather a boy, who believed that he was lost forever, doomed to be bent in hell. I found that even Satan was an imaginary creature. And this is how it came, sir: That there was real Africa; an Africa, who knew many things; an Africa that was full of wisdom and civility. Africans have a light of greatness in them, but they also have a dark side of cruelty. You should see how Africans could be cruel to each other. I do not whitewash my people (Mutua).

Mutua showed great courage in helping the world recognize the actual African values and exposing the oppressive values and practices of the colonial powers. The European colonial powers dominated Africa over a century and lead to massive plunder of resources and subjugation of people's power and dignity through the business practice of slavery. Through the practices of brutal domination and exploitation leading to enslavement made the racial discrimination more acute and distressing. As an artist and sculptor, Mutua was suppressed and systematically dominated by the colonial forces. Yet, despite opposition and threat, he was able to champion the cause of ancient African wisdom:

> That Africans had its laws, which needed no policemen to enforce them. The legal system was very human and holistic. The traditional approach has rules with no need for enforcement. But I asked myself why Africa is not allowed to stand in front of the world and show the world what she is, what she is. I got shocked when I learned about an organization that systematically suppresses black art. This organization fights against black art. This organization exists in South Africa, even though we are supposed to be a democratic country. I could not sell any of my paintings, for I am not recognized as an African Artist. This is typical institutional Apartheid that continues its brutal domination.

Mutua experienced the danger and inherent contradiction of values in using violent means, including self-destructive wars, to achieve common goals. Fear and greed are the most dominant forces that debilitate the progression of the society on egalitarian principles of freedom, equality, and fraternity. But, being a victim of the unfortunate consequences of wars, conflicts, and brutal Apartheid, he became an ardent champion of non-violence and peace across the globe:

> Africa has a saying, "War is a lion that eats its own tame, so don't try it." South Africa has the future mineral; South Africa is outside Russia, which produces maximum platinum other than Russia. During the days of Apartheid, the platinum mines were on strike. It is they who brought down the Apartheid government. And so, it would happen, the next war right here. Yes, every country that is becoming very developed is looking for resources. What Gandhi said is true; "we have enough resources for our need but not for our greed." Greed is the root cause of all evils. We are on the path of juggernauts. I pray to God; let the treaty be written Let all the wars in God's name be outlawed.

Thurston experienced a crisis of values between her calling to be a spiritual mystic and, at the same time, being a mother. She almost thought that she was going insane as she began to receive messages in the form of aphorisms in her mind without knowing that she had the power of clairvoyance. Adding fuel to the fire, her husband thought she was going insane and was about to commit her to the mental asylum. She narrated her spiritual crisis:

> I was still grappling with the idea that maybe I was insane since I began to hear voices and aphorisms in my head. Then I was happy with that. And I became a closet mystic, and there was nobody to talk to. A couple of weeks later, I learned that I was pregnant. I wasn't sure I wanted to be pregnant, so it was a trauma, and then I got used to the idea that I had my first child. I had forgotten what I had written, and maybe a month had gone by. And I had morning sickness, and obviously, the consciousness level dropped significantly. After my baby was born, there was this feeling that there was something that I was supposed to do for her benefit. I had no idea what it was. I had no idea what to do and was so very vacant, like a zombie, for some time. And so here, my husband is looking at me with suspicion as though I should be committed. I was young and didn't know what to do.

The crises of family life led to the parting of ways for Thurston and her husband, and thus, she began to seek wisdom with clear focus and deep self-inquiry. Living in a strained relationship results in high anxiety, acute loneliness, and inner turmoil. She described her struggles experiencing divorce due to value conflict that is distressing and it results in ethical and spiritual crisis in relationship and marriage:

> He was a pragmatist. He just wanted a trophy wife, and I mean, I was good-looking, and that's what he wanted. He did want me to have my own life. He soon found someone else, and we were still married; then I said, okay, so be it. I was going through the end of the marriage at that time. We gradually parted ways, and my inner guides stirred me into higher consciousness.

Thurston also encountered a profound crisis of family and vocation during Apartheid in South Africa, where she was born and raised. She was torn between her white identity and her spiritual view of the oneness of humanity: "You have to understand this was South Africa in the late '60s and early '70s. There was no spiritual movement. We were in the thick of the oppression of Apartheid. It was very uncomfortable for everyone. I was sensitive enough to be miserable about it." Sister Rosalind experienced a profound conflict of values when her massage clinic was shut down, and she had to face enormous negative publicity in the media across the globe:

> And what happened was that when the authorities shut down my massage clinic, the news went worldwide, and someone brought an article from China, which said, "Nun has a touching habit" (laughing), that was in a China paper. And someone called me from Scotland to do a telephone interview and published an article about the massaging nun in Scotland. I believe God used that lousy publicity for something good and to change the very image of massage. The news went international, and I felt terrible. When I grew up, massage was something beautiful and clean. However, in Minnesota and other places, massage means prostitution. I was so upset; I said I would do something to change the image of massage.

Abbess Pema spoke about the value conflicts as she grew up during religious disputes. She recalled, "My mother said, do not fight in the name of faith for wars start at home and wars in the name of faith are the worst kind." In some contexts, the religion can be a latent source of conflict and a triggering event can lead to escalation and violence among different denominations. Abbot Phap Son shared his value crisis, especially about decision-making as a spiritual leader in the context of multicultural community living:

> The decision-making model in our community is very organic. Sometimes teachings come from Thai, our principal teacher, Thich Nhat Hanh (Thai is the Vietnamese name for teacher). Sometimes it is difficult; it is too organic; sometimes, I wish it would be blacker and whiter. When you live together, there can be cause for disharmony. We live in a multicultural environment with possibilities of value conflict among different groups.

Ilibagiza experienced a profound crisis of her human values during the Rwandan genocide, and she remembered the harrowing moments of tribal conflict between Tutsi and Hutu communities. The inter-tribal conflict destroys the basic sense of peace and harmony and co-existence in a society. A major catastrophic incident like killing the president of the country resulted in social revolt and chaos and complexity of co-existence of the different tribe in the same area. Shocking experiences cause profound shift in her psyche with major transformation and turning towards compassion and care for the universe objecting to the practice of violence and domination of the poor masses:

> Compared to what I was living before, it was shocking. That was fun, living there without being hunted. But now I am being hunted; I went through the pain, waiting for people who wanted to kill. It didn't take too long; the water in the mouth went dry so quickly, and I could not make any sense of this conflict between Hutus and Tutsis. The leaders of the people are calling people to look for each other and now calling people to kill each other. Maybe they should have taught me; I should have been told when this was bad. But I completely trusted and believed that everyone is the same as a tribe. That was the belief in my heart. It was so much entering the hell. I recall how I thought everything was so wrong; how come I ended up here, hiding in the bathroom?

These prominent leaders have a deep sense of the values they espoused and the conflicting values they encounter in society. Each leader experienced the crisis of values in their business organizations, communities, and families. The tribal conflicts in Africa, the casteism in India, classism in England, and the racism of the Americas indicate a profound moral decadence in the heart of humanity, which values in the color of the skin rather than the content of the moral character. Leaders' experience of ethical and moral value crisis resulted in personal agony and deeper soul searching. Yet, when the situations challenged them, they rose to the occasion, discerned the righteous ideals, and showed grit wisdom and courage to stand up for what they believed and felt in their hearts was right and led the people to a great future.

The experience of the value crisis or moral crisis appeared especially in leaders when their espoused values conflicted with the actual values; they are called upon to exercise t in their leadership roles. Some of the leaders left the organizations and affiliations to the societies of their upbringings due to the value conflict. The values of integrity, justice, dignity, and human rights were upheld with great courage and resilience, and vulnerability. The conflict between the superficial values and the deeper spiritual values of meaning and purpose made them leave their former state of life and even their marriage relationships when it came in dire conflict with their aspirational values of greater good and wholeness. The cultivation of spiritual intelligence enabled the leaders to face the value crisis and demonstrate greater inner strength and resilience in their journey towards greater wholeness.

Meaning Crisis

A meaning crisis involves the collapse of one's habitual ego and conventional sense of reality, meaning, and an opening to a different reality (which one could call the subconscious or the archetypal layer). It can involve a powerful sense of connection to all things, perhaps a transcending of time, space, and matter and a deep understanding of meaning and awe. Victor Frankl noted that "the greatest task for any person is to find meaning in life: life is not primarily a quest for pleasure as Freud believed, or a quest for power as Alfred taught, but a quest for meaning" (quoted in Majluf & Abarca, 2021: 35). *And* it can also be exceedingly messy, painful, terrifying, and dangerous and have psychosis-like features like mania, ego-inflation, insomnia, voices, visions, ontological uncertainty, and emotional disturbance. However, unlike a psychotic illness, it can transition to growth if handled sensitively. It is mainly a crisis of meaning. This "transpersonal" perspective was put forward by psychologists and thinkers like Frederic Myers, William James, Carl Jung, Aldous

Huxley, Ram Dass, and Stanislav Grof—who coined the term "Spiritual Emergency" to describe the spiritual crisis in modern times due to loneliness, anxiety, and depression or extreme psychic distress and experimentation.

The leaders in this research experienced the meaning crisis in their own lives in different degrees and identified with the situation of others in their lived experience. However, the problem of meaning shared by these leaders was mainly about life, passion, and purpose. For example, Parker Palmer, a leading champion of spirituality in leadership, management, and education, candidly described his experience of a meaning crisis as a spiritual crisis and reflects on his episodes of clinical depression three times in his adult life:

> My life has been deeply challenged by experiences of failures and experiences of clinical depression, times of deep darkness when I wasn't sure it was worth living anymore. The experience of depression is an experience of the destruction of self. When you are lost in the dark, you still have a self that you can use to navigate, negotiate, and grope your way towards some light. But when you become dark, you don't have anything to work with. And all semblance of religious faith or a feeling of God's presence just disappears. So, I don't understand how some people can come through depression *and find themselves more alive and more whole on the other side.* That's the real mystery to me. And I genuinely don't know, "Grace" is the only word I can fall back on.

Sister Gefre recognized the shortness of life and its preciousness simultaneously with having her heart attack. She noted, "I was quite healthy until I had my heart attack, and it became a reality for me, the death and the preciousness of life." She also found this crisis of meaning in the lives of her clients. She observed: "Who knows, maybe the children come from families with alcoholic parents; perhaps they are cruel parents, go to school, and remain clueless in their lives. I believe that much of our crime and destructive habits come from a loveless, materialistic society." For many other participants, the crisis of meaning was about their struggle with career choices and discovering their true calling. The experience of frustration in their hearts led to a more profound quest for meaning beyond the ordinary moments of life.

As Abbot Phap Son described his experience of the inner crisis after going through a life of fleeing adventures and experiments with life. The trajectory of his journey shows the deep inquisitiveness of the soul to search for what brings true joy and happiness to the soul. The materialistic comfort and pleasure did not bring deep sense of peace and tranquility to his spirit; rather, it created more restlessness and despondency in the early part of life. Due to lack of deeper inner search or spiritual practices, his youthful days were spent on pursuit of happiness in instant gratification of pleasure, power, and fame, but it led to a deeper emptiness and crisis of meaning in his life. His soul was searching for something much deeper and greater but did not know what it was until he began to engage in spiritual practice of meditation. He noted how being caught between various conflicts of worldly pursuits and inner peace and the meaninglessness of seeking happiness outside. Recalling the intensity of inner conflict and crisis of meaning, the struggle of battling depression and the inner darkness, and the challenge of making sense of the ups and downs of life, Abbot Phap Son noted how is spiritual support group and community to process his inner crisis and find meaning and purpose:

> I experienced deep confusion in my childhood days. There was no clear way. There was no clear information; there was a general one growing up, making money, enjoying sex, and achieving power and prestige. I experimented with them, but they did not satisfy me. I was not interested in any pleasure, car or money or material comforts, for I got disenchanted with them. Traveling to India opened up many possibilities, but I was afraid of the unknown. At that time, my girlfriend had a committed relationship with me. But I was not sure. I had much inspiration, but I had a crisis of discernment about the future. It created a lot of conflict in me. I was caught up in crisis back and forth. It was a very unsettling period in my life. I experienced deep shadows, depression and inner crisis. Even though I was ordained as a monk, I had that conflict. I had many ups and downs, but this community would be safe to contain those struggles. The society outside was very undermining. I was caught up in crisis back and forth. There was a big struggle; I thought there was an enemy in me, the darkness in me. I was very puzzled and confused, struggling to make sense of my internal trauma. This led to a feeling of depression and deep longing for a breakthrough.

McBrayer, the Chief Flight Controller of one of the major Airlines, noted a similar spiritual crisis in his life when he encountered significant losses due to business decline and personal tragedies: Confronted with the stress and stains of life and business turbulence in the Airline Industry, Mc Brayer began to seek instant comfort and relief to addictions but in vain. Persistent changes in mood, including anxiety and restlessness. Stress management became harder and harder as he continued to engage in alcohol consumption on a regular basis. It led him to deeper darkness and psychological trauma of depression and emptiness of life. He went through the excruciating moments of uncertainty and turmoil to figure out who he is and hat his mission would be in his life. These are moments of meaning crisis:

> But in my profession, we began seeing a real journey of difficulty; we saw mergers, pay cuts, layoffs, and all those things continued to bring complexity and high stress into my life, and then I would lose my father. We had not found my full spiritual bearings. So even though I was serving the church, I had not seen that yet. And began to drink excessively to hide my inner pain and find instant relief through the addiction of alcoholism which pointed me to the doors of Alcoholics Anonymous.

Stephen M. Lacy is a former American magazine and media company CEO. He served as Executive Chairman of Meredith Corporation, a publicly-traded publishing, broadcasting, and interactive media firm based in Des Moines, Iowa, from 2009 to 2019. He narrated his experience of spiritual struggle and the entire corporation going through a crisis during the 2008 economic downturn. Individual who experienced economic down turn had experienced the adverse effect of anxiety and high stress that come in the way leading and guiding the company out of the economic recession. Lacey's experience of economic decline resulted in distress and anxiety. Due to his faith and spiritual practice, he began to cope with it effectively and the life lessons learned helped him to more empathetic to other employees who go through difficult moments and reach out to them with care and support. The initial crisis of meaning and purpose led to a discovery of high purpose and bring greater meaning and fulfillment into his own life and the life of others.

> When we went into that horrible economic downturn in 2008, there was a real crisis. I felt very lonely at the top and spent many days on my knees praying for a turnaround for my company and me. The experience of my pain helped me realize my deeper purpose of being sensitive to others' pain and sufferings, especially in the lives of the employees. As the CEO, when employees died, I made it a point to go and meet their families and be part of their pain and suffering even though the employees come from 23 locations across the country.

The crisis of meaning for Abbess Pema led to a deeper search for the other dimension of life. She described, "I was always looking for something else, not interested in possessions or clothes." She was also conflicted over her career choice as she narrated, "Then I thought I would like to be a teacher. I did not become a teacher because I did not like the school system in the Netherlands. Some teachers were very authoritarian." She added that inner crisis paved the way to discover alternative living methods with simplicity and high purpose:

> What impressed me was that every year before the summer holiday, the nuns packed everything in one suitcase. And they left there and went home. When they come back, they will find an envelope where they are going. They would faithfully obey the transfer order. I was attracted by the suitcase possession and the simplicity of life. When I moved, I had only one suitcase and the rest I gave away. I have some difficulty now, for I have been here as the Abbess for 17 years. Having an [religious] aunt revealed early on that there is another way of living.

Sri Sri recalled how he experienced a crisis of meaning when he was a kid who felt out of place, especially among his peers: "I would rather spend time with elderly people asking philosophical questions than spend my time with peers, for I was a kid feeling out of place." He noted, "What would interest me was the stories of Mahabharata, bible stories, Buddha's stories; anything spiritual interested me and not the peer groups. My parents were scared that I would go mentally ill for I was spending long hours in meditation". He was mindful of the cry of humanity for deeper meaning, "We should not forget that whether people are in the industry or corporate or professional world, they are all human being hungry and thirsty for something beyond. They all need spirituality to gain the ultimate meaning of life" (Sri Sri). He added, "Nothing in this material world can give you contentment. An outer-looking mind seeking contentment gets more tired and unfulfilled, and the discontentment grows into inner emptiness and distress. Negativity hardens the brain, clouds the awareness, and forms a cloud of negative energy". When the crisis of meaning engulfs the human mind, it searches for purpose and direction. Sri Sri was convinced that "when the negativity reaches its peak, like an over-inflated balloon, it bursts and comes back to deeper realization and divinity".

Experiencing personal crisis through family loss, especially the loss of both of his parents at an early age, Archbishop Flynn shared how he sought spiritual consolation and strength at the time of his desperation and hopelessness:

> My dad died when I was six and my mother when I was 12. I experienced her death more poignantly because there was more loneness when both my parents were gone. After the end of my Father, he was such an incredibly kind person; my mother died so suddenly. There didn't seem to be anything to cling to. So, I think I was inclined to consolation from God in prayer for survivability.

Thurston was engaged in her deep search for meaning in life early on, and she described how she experienced a crisis of meaning: "The next significant moment came I chose to seek wisdom at the age of about 16 because nothing else seemed very meaningful at all." Later in life, she continued her search for the meaning and purpose of life: "It was like an aboriginal walkabout for me, driving through the United States in the middle of the night. This is what I seemingly was doing all the time seeking direction and purpose in my life." Surviving the Rwandan tribal genocide, Ilibagiza described her crisis of faith and meaning:

> It was a clear-cut separation between the past and the future. The radio said that all kinds of work had been shut down, no market was open, the schools were closed; everything stopped functioning. The only job which was working was killing innocent people. We were facing death every moment, hiding in the bathroom. All went quiet. And suddenly, we realized we were all going to die. It was very much like entering hell. I wondered why everything was so wrong at the same time; a while ago, everything was so lovely. Sitting in the bathroom without light, without talking for 91 days, quiet not knowing what was going on wasn't good. The confusion of why me [*sic*] crippled me. Why is this genocide happening? And what is wrong with humanity? At that moment, I felt maybe God didn't exist.

Experiencing an emotional rollercoaster, Ilibagiza described her ordeal of being hunted by enemy tribes. All her notions of faith and belief in God became shattered during her trial. Facing the unimaginable horror of encountering her own killers who marched with armed militias brought earth-shaking experience of debilitating trauma experience in her life. The scale of brutality of the genocide caused shock waves worldwide, but no country intervened to forcefully stop the killings. Most of the victims were killed in their towns or villages adding agony and terror country wide. Hutu gangs searched out victims hiding in churches and school buildings. Ilibagiza was hiding in the bathroom of the Pastor for three months watching the horror of killing marches on the outside of her windows fearing that her life could be finished at any moment losing all purpose and meaning of existence:

> The killers came dressed in banana leaves, really looking like devils. I could see them through the window openings. Some of them had horns of a goat on their heads to scare people. They had all kinds of arms, long spears, and grenades around their waists. My whole body was almost shut down, shuddering with dread. I felt a thousand needles piercing my entire body. My saliva dried instantly. I could not feel my arms, my legs; it was just numb. At that moment, I felt God did not exist. How can this evil go on? God doesn't exist; otherwise, he would have prevented such a heinous crime. I wish I were dead before the killers came and finished us. I wish I could shoot everybody, maybe put a bomb underground to explode the whole place. After that angry emotion, I came out sweating, my heart was sort of bleeding, and I was so exhausted and felt utter helplessness.

Abbess Pema described her dissatisfaction with the secular life and her ardent desire for the spiritual dimension of life. The experience of the existential distress due to the shallow pursuit of worldly ambitions began to create spiritual emptiness and deeper longing to discover meaning in spiritual journey. Search for meaning in life indicates that individual is strongly motivated to find meaning in their lives, especially finding answers to the big questions in life such as who am I, why am I here, what is truly important to me and what bring joy and satisfaction to my soul, etc. Except exploring the spiritual dimension of life which she calls the "other dimension" has led her to deeper meaning, joy, and fulfillment. The worldly and material life did not give meaning and a sense of purpose to her life until she embarked on a spiritual journey:

> I have always been yearning for something else from as far as I remember. The peripheral dimension of life, just worldly life, did not satisfy me. As a child, I had a strong feeling of the different extent, but I cannot name it. I felt I was missing something in my life. It was an unnamed ache in my heart. I know that, until I began exploring the other dimension, nothing made me happy; Nothing else. So now we call the different dimension the spiritual dimension of life.

The recurring patterns transformation in the experience of the existential spiritual crisis manifested in the lives of the leaders in such a way that there was a change in the awareness of their self-concept, self-image, and identification with the former identities of affliction and cultural conditioning. The spiritual crisis manifested as a crisis of meaning, crisis of faith, the crisis of values, and sometimes as an identity crisis. In all these experiences, the phenomenon of the alienation of the self from the higher self was evident. The positive understanding and the acceptance of the inner crisis led to greater breakthrough in their inner self. They resulted in the discovery of greater gifts and grace, and stamina in their exercise of transformative leadership roles. The awareness of the internal crisis with a greater sense of spiritual intelligence helped the leaders be mindful of the external crisis present in their lives.

Social Crisis

The social crisis is defined as a social disorder and decline due to social injustice and prolonged disparities in income, poverty level, wages, and standard of living conditions in society (American Psychological Association Dictionary, 2022). Social crisis is the result of the alienation of the self from other selves. It is a reflection of the spiritual emptiness and ethical crisis going on within the self. Thus, the root of social crisis is the external manifestation of spiritual crisis of humanity. The understanding of the meaning and context of social crisis change periodically. For example, the knowledge of the social issue of poverty had changed since the early twentieth century when pioneers in poverty research such as Charles Booth, Seebohm Rowntree, and Robert Hunter (Fried & Elman, 2017) defined uni-dimensionally as lack of income sufficient to purchase a minimum of goods and services needed to survive. Departing from this narrow definition and following the works of Amartya Sen (Boldizonni, 2011; Chimhowu, 2009) and others, contemporary thinking draws us to look at poverty more broadly as a lack of capability to live in dignity. "Poverty is not just a lack of money; it is not having the capability to realize one's full potential as a human being" (Sen, 2009: 253). Whereas concerns for justice are universal, views of just and unjust are not universally shared. Divergent opinions of justice often cause social conflicts and social crises. The parties involved in disputes are often convinced that their own opinion is solely valid. As we have no access to an objective truth about justice, conflicts may be reconciled by the judgment of an authority accepted by all parties or by a negotiated agreement between the parties. Agreements are made when the parties are equally accessible in their decision and equally informed about all relevant facts and possible outcomes.

At the core, all social crises are justice issues, whether a refugee crisis, health crisis, racism or poverty, or wage disparity. Justice is the prerequisite for freedom and equality (Rawls, 1971). It involves respect for all regardless of race, ethnicity, ability, economic status, sexual orientation, gender identity, religious beliefs or non-beliefs, or citizenship. People expect that others respect the normative standards, entitlements, fair treatment, and claims that they believe to be just. Rawls's theory of "justice as fairness" recommends equal fundamental liberties, equality of opportunity, and facilitating the maximum benefit to the least advantaged members of society (Rawls, 2001). Conflicts and crises result from violated normative expectations on how other people, agencies, etc., have to behave, from violated or disregarded claims, whatever their normative basis may be: human rights, a legal code, the codex of a religion, a formal or an implicit contract, or good manners that are valid in a culture. Fair competition is not a social conflict. If all actors in competitive markets and sports behave legitimately, frustrations and losses are possible, but they do not evoke resentment. There are winners and losers but not victimizers and victims.

Amartya Sen, an Indian Nobel Laureate in Economics, portrays the practical and comparative idea of justice while critiquing the transcendental theory of justice advocated by John Rawls (2001) emerging from enlightenment economics. While Rawls theory of transcendental justice is concerned with identifying perfectly just social arrangements defining the nature of the perfectly just society, the approach Sen (2009) favors, on the other hand, focuses on the comparative judgments of what is "more" or "less" just and the comparative merits of the different societies that emerge from the actual issues of injustice present in the current world to create a better world of social justice. "If a theory of justice is to guide the reasoned choice of policies, strategies or institutions, then the identification of fully just social arrangements is neither necessary nor sufficient."

The leaders have identified sociological crises regarding human rights, poverty, homelessness, health crisis, racism, disparity of wages for women in the workplace, exploitation of women and children, religious fundamentalism, the culture of violence and oppression, ethnic conflicts, and gender disparity. Many children, unfortunately, face many barriers to education though no fault of their own. Groups and organizations that help fight these barriers, and even specific companies who donate their profits for the exact causes, are helping change the world for a better tomorrow for the children. Mandela (2022: 2) famously said, "Education is the most powerful weapon you can use to change the world."

Through fundraising, local funding, and voluntary work, leaders and their organizations promoted social justice efforts to address many social crises of the day with bold impacts for more people than they realize, creating a future that is both bright and sustainable for today's young generations. Archbishop Flynn noted: During the past 40 years, our nation has made significant progress in the struggle for racial justice. There is a greater appreciation for the value of racial and ethnic diversity and a greater willingness to condemn blatant and overt forms of racist behavior. Significant legislation has been passed that officially protects civil rights and promotes greater racial equality. For people of color, this has meant an opportunity to make substantial advances in terms of economic and social well-being. Flynn championed the fight against racism and wrote a pastoral letter on racism (Flynn, 2003) to his church community to be aware of the various dimensions of hidden attitudes of racism and how it seriously affects the basic ethic of human dignity and social justice. He urged his leaders of various racial groups to take proactive steps to re-establish racial justice and social harmony through the practice of truth and reconciliation. The faces of racism are many and varied (Flynn, 2003), but the evidence is all around us:

- Over a third of African American children under age three in the United States live in poverty. This is more than three times the rate among white children in the same age group.
- Although Minnesota ranks first among states concerning the overall health of its residents, people of color in Minnesota are much less likely to have health insurance, have protective childhood vaccinations, and receive early prenatal care than whites. As a result, infant mortality rates are four times greater for American Indian infants than white infants.
- The disparity in the nation's ownership of wealth is a dramatic sign of the inequality that continues to exist. For example, the typical Hispanic household in the United States owns only about 4 percent of the wealth of the usual white household.

- Racial disparities in the nation's criminal justice system are well documented. For example, research on the death penalty found that murder defendants charged with killing whites were four times more likely to receive the death penalty than those charged with killing blacks.

When we see these extreme disparities in social and economic outcomes for people of color compared to whites, we need not agree on the precise cause of these inequities. However, the very existence of these disparities based on race is an offense against the basic norms of social justice, for these extreme inequalities are clear signs that the principles of human dignity and human equality are not being fully realized. These disparities are a clear call for us to respond and undo these injustices, even if we have not personally and directly caused them. Experiences and facts such as these convince me that racism is a continuing problem for all. It is a social evil we all share and from which we all suffer. Suppose we are to grow spiritually as individuals and society as a community. In that case, we all need to do more to come to grips with the sin of racism in our hearts and within the institutions that make up our church and our society. For our spiritual development, each of us must understand that loving only people who are just like ourselves, loving only those who share our own ethnic or cultural background, does not adequately fulfill the challenge of the Gospel. All of us are called to develop a sense of solidarity with our racially and culturally distinct neighbors. In doing so, we begin to live out the unity in diversity.

There is a tendency on the part of some people to say, "I am not prejudiced. I am not a racist. I did not cause or contribute to the racial injustices of the past. Therefore, I am not responsible for racism today. There is nothing I can do." This is indifference to the public affairs results in continued disclination and injustice for which people pay the price. This view is unfortunate and morally inadequate because it fails to consider the social nature of the sin of racism. It fails to see that racism is not merely a personal sin but also a structural sin. It is a social reality for which all members of society are responsible. As the US Catholic bishops have written, "The absence of personal fault for an evil does not absolve one of all responsibility. We must seek to resist and undo injustices we have not caused, lest we become bystanders who tacitly endorse evil and so share in the guilt for it" (USCCB, 1979).

To begin to fill the enormous gap of women's leadership in business, there are promising initiatives taken by other women leaders. "We are so proud to bring to light the world's top 1,000 women leaders, entrepreneurs, and intrapreneurs from the EBW Top 100 Global Women's Organizations. Our greatest desire is that these women will gain access to new opportunities, know-how, and connections. Together, these benefits are structured to help them fast track a new future, enabling them to have the tools and support to succeed as leaders, entrepreneurs, and intrapreneurs," says Ingrid Vanderveldt, Founder and CEO of EBW Worldwide. Empowering a Billion Women 2020 d/b/a EBW Worldwide is a mission-driven for-profit company focused on the Social, Health, and Economic empowerment of women and our partners and clients worldwide (the SHEconomy Project). EBW has two primary investment divisions: EBW 2020, focused on investing in leading women worldwide, and our enterprise division, EBW Worldwide, focused on investing in industry ventures that are social, health, and economically focused and is home to a fast-growing medical supply chain portfolio. EBW is WBENC and WOSB Certified, women-founded, women-run, American Sourced, and American Made. Through our She-economy Project, and in line with the United Nations Sustainable Development goals, the EBW portfolio has been created by and for women with a plan to create, with their partners, $100B of global market impact by 2030.

Steve Lacey, CEO of Meredith Corporation, articulated his concern for the less privileged children on the streets losing life opportunities due to lack of critical support for their education, growth, and development as leaders find ways to support the marginalized children on the streets to avert the social crisis of children without educational opportunities resulting in bad neighborhoods:

> One of the most recent examples, which is, maybe now I lose track with a pandemic, but I guess it opened a year ago in the fall. So, let's say fall of 2019. We built here in Des Moines on the Drake University campus, one of the country's three boys and girls clubs that are actually on a college campus. That was about a $15 million fundraising project. And as it gets fully operational, because we're not at total capacity, there'll be 250 kids from kindergarten through grade 12 who will come to campus every day, after school, where they will interact with people who look like them. And it's a terrible neighborhood. And a lot of these kids live right across the street from a great university. But a great university may as well be Mars

> because it's charming. They don't talk about college. So, this is mainly for less privileged kids giving up educational opportunities.

Washburn described the high stress the Media is going through, especially the print media, in competition with digital and social media. Information divide is a major social crisis as media outlet broadcast their perspective of news, even bending facts based on their own ideological bias to serve their own market segment bias. There is a pronounced shift from the print to digital media in the first two decades of this century. The way people consume news has dramatically changed. The easy access of the internet and digital media has resulted in the fast decline of the print media bringing social crisis for journalists and print media employees and business owners. The declining print media in the wake of digital publishing makes the information divide worse than ever.

> The media industry was highly stressful. And I had spent the last almost ten years managing decline, you know, laying people off, I laid off 100 people over ten years. And I was just cutting instead of growing and managing the social crisis of the information divide. So major corporation for all of that time, in different places, but and for most of that time, I admired the leaders I was working for. They and I were a good fit. And I would sometimes say no longer a good fit. And just it was time to go. It was time to choose the next thing (Washburn).

Corrina Lim from Singapore, a passionate leading women's rights activist, lawyer, and entrepreneur, spoke of the social issues of gender equality and women's rights, especially her efforts to champion a family violence bill in the Singapore Legislature. The women's right issues include gender equality, gender-based domination and violence, sexual exploitation and harassment, workplace discrimination, discrimination based on sexual orientation, and gender identity. Singapore is one of the pioneering countries that has implemented the family violence bill into law to protect the women's rights and Lim was the key person who championed the cause of women in Singapore for many decades:

> I did not think that women were disadvantaged until I did pro-bono legal counseling for women's issues. I often helped women who had abusive husbands and problems with family violence. This led to the movement of advocating the family violence bill and passing it to protect the dignity

and rights of women. This was my major piece of advocating for women's rights straightforwardly. Until then, the police had limited powers. They could not investigate a case of violence against women until there was a broken bone or damaged limb.

*The leaders identified many social crisis issues, including racism, tribal war, women's rights, mental illness, income disparity, poverty and hunger, and political suppression. The awareness of these crises helped to evoke a greater sense of justice and fairness while engaging in the transformation of society and organizations. Leaders' capacity for higher consciousness helped them to sense the social crisis and create awareness of the challenge in their organizations and take collective steps to co-create relevant solutions with courage, confidence, and spiritual intelligence. Research in spirituality and crisis leadership is ever-growing, and the leaders who empathize with social issues have greater success in engaging in crisis management and greater social impact to address issues of justice and fairness (*Firestone, 2020*). Another crucial area of spiritual crisis is the ever-growing ecological crisis resulting from the alienation of the self from nature is presented in the next chapter.*

Ecological Crisis

The deepening crisis of climate change is defined as escalating changes over time in the averages and variability of surface temperature, precipitation, and wind as well as associated changes in earth's atmosphere, oceans and natural water supplies, snow an ice, land surface, ecosystems, and living organisms (IPCC, 2007). Humanity, with its hyperactivity and unsustainable consumption, has created a significant deficit of resources and an excess of biowaste in the biosphere's limited volume, resulting in environmental pollution and ecological crisis (Wienhues, 2020). The impact of the current environmental crisis would lead to global instability and the extinction of species. Figueres and Rivett-Carnac (2020: xiv) ask the poignant question of recognizing the current state of the global climate crisis, "We have seen the world on fire, from the Amazon rain forest to California to Australia to Artic. Do we watch the world burn, or do we choose to do what is necessary to achieve a different future?" The answer to the questions is as follows: climate change is the single-greatest threat posed to humankind and failure to stop its progression will result in the extinction of humankind and other species from the earth. They present three mindsets of stubborn optimism, endless abundance, and radical regeneration to address the issue of ecological crisis and create a sustainable future.

Extinction-level climate destabilization will cost the nations of the world hundreds of trillions of dollars and billions of lives along with environmental disasters, maybe the survival of the human species itself. Moreover, there is a possibility that extinction-level climate destabilization may never correct or re-balance itself to some new equilibrium level. A sense of new ecological justice can pave the ways for managing the biggest crisis of our times. The Cop 26 global climate conference involving 200 nations proposed the four paths for restoring climate sustainability: mitigation, finance, renewable energy, and collaboration. The root cause of the ecological crisis is the alienation of the self from nature, and the following facts are to be recognized across the globe to deal with the impending crisis. The Economist (2022: 2) reported the following vital contributing factors to the current climate crisis:

- Today's global warming emergency is not a natural disaster. Instead, it is a human-made disaster, which can be curtailed with human intervention.
- A slight increase in average global temperature will eventually create catastrophic changes in the world and lead to significant damage and loss.
- As global warming and climate destabilization continue, our local and national weather and our global climate will become much more unpredictable. Storms, droughts, floods, seasonal disruptions, sea-level rise, and wildfires will become more severe, frequent, and occur at larger scales resulting in unrecoverable destruction of life and habitat.
- As the global climate continues to destabilize, most people will not realize their lives are destabilizing after it is too late. Hence addressing climate change with global leadership is an urgent matter.
- We may have already reached irreversible climate destabilization. It will go on much longer than our human life spans. It can last for centuries or thousands of years, not knowing the gamut of damage and destabilization of the environment.
- A continually destabilizing climate due to escalating global warming will be the most significant disruptor of normal life that we have ever known—exceedingly even our greatest world wars. However, the awareness of this disruption can lead to a great sense of innovation to save the planet with renewable energy.

Our house is on fire is the story of how the climate crisis clashes into families and communities and nations through the eyes of the world-renowned teen climate activist, Greta Thunberg (Pirani, 2021). She challenged the government inaction, hypocrisy, and inspired millions to champion the cause of protecting the blue planet from its status of an endangered entity. Greta hit rock bottom when her class watched a film about plastic rubbish in the world's oceans. She could not reconcile with the consumerist excess that surrounded across the world. Since then, she is an unrelenting champion fighting to end the climate crisis and restore the pristine nature of our planet from the threat of human consumption.

The leaders in this study articulated their solidarity with people and communities based on their expanded spiritual awareness, interests in global issues, and universal perspectives. They believe that individuals are part of the larger whole and need to be interested in common affairs with broader views beyond their interests. They demonstrated that they could contribute to the welfare of the total and make a significant difference on the planet. Their circle of solidarity was based on an expanded awareness of the unity of humanity and the interconnectedness of the whole creation. For them, life is being whole, considering the body, mind, and spirit being intertwined at the personal level and human life not apart from the creation. These leaders advocated the need to go beyond the immediate concerns of charity to the deeper issues of social justice and the global issues of environmental crisis and governance issues in today's world of politics and market forces. Considering the world as one family, the leaders engaged in asking questions of ecological justice, expanding their sense of solidarity with the human and the earth family.

Larry Zimplemen envisaged a future of environmental sustainability to deal with the ecological crisis in threefold ways:

> While some might still want to debate whether we see climate change, the evidence continues to mount around us daily. I recently saw a report that 2021 was among the hottest years on record. While climate change may have different impacts on different businesses, ALL businesses can reduce the effects of climate change. That means using more renewable energy sources, looking for ways to use recyclable materials whenever possible, etc. Rather than focus on just climate change (even though it's a very, very big issue), many today are starting to talk about "ESG"—environmental, social, and governance—as a broader way to think about climate change and other related issues. Climate change is put under the "environmental" label. Social refers to general social issues like diversity, income

> distribution, and even voting rights. Governance usually refers to public companies having clear statements on diversity, discrimination, etc. I think you will see more focus on "ESG" and what companies and individuals can do to impact all three areas. As an investment business, The Principal Company is well aware of the impacts of climate crisis and its global impact on the planet's future. Larry identifies the insurance company's specific initiatives to deal with the ecological crisis, especially in investing in renewable energy and sustainable businesses. This is also done in collaboration with other businesses across the world since the climate crisis is a global issue.

Businesses have been gradually moving into sustainable development and renewable energy for many years, especially in the financial sector. Larry explains who companies like Principal Insurance contribute to deal with the challenge of climate change and governance. The Principal Company and other financial services companies have been focused on climate change and ESG issues for many years. The primary area where ESG comes into play for a company like Principal is its investments. Customers and investors are looking to companies like Principal to consider all elements of ESG before they make any investments. That's not always possible—but it certainly is a goal to move towards overtime. The principal is also focused on reducing energy usage, recycling whenever possible, and doing everything it can to reduce its carbon footprint.

> From my own experience, Europe is more focused on ESG than we are here in the United States (although the United States is now starting to catch up). I serve on the Board of a European financial services company, and they have already made statements about when they want to be "carbon neutral." They are also taking steps in their business model to stop providing insurance coverage to coal companies as one example. To be fair, the term ESG often means something slightly different to each person. Over time, I think there will be a convergence on what ESG means and how it should be measured and reported.

From a sense of seeking higher good and the common good, the leaders began to ask more profound questions of sustainable co-existence. Archbishop Flynn recommended, "We not only should be concerned about others' immediate needs but should ask a more profound question of existence and co-existence?".

> Why is it necessary for people in Mexico to come to the US searching for bread?
> Why racial disparity still exists even though we are all one human family?
> Why the fastest growing industry in the US is the prison industry?
> Why do we fail to invest in children across the globe?
> Why do we need to protect and preserve our common home?
> All these questions call for civil debate, and unless we ask these questions, do we stand for wellbeing and the greater good? Is there a better way to live in solidarity with the less privileged and more excellent stewardship of the environment? (Archbishop Flynn).

Making sense of these crises will lead to discovering and co-creating answers to our collective trauma in the social fields and ecosystems. These leaders emphasized the need to learn to co-exist in the world as our life on the planet is threatened with the collective trauma of global pandemic and environmental crisis. Archbishop Flynn noted that the essence of having a sense of solidarity is to keep the principles of justice and charity as twin ingredients for the transformation of the world and better environmental stewardship:

> We must not only exist in the world, but we must co-exist in the world in peace and harmony. I believe all of us are called to stand for justice and work for the transformation of the world. We must keep one foot in front of the other, charity and justice. Keep justice and charity on the front burner and we cannot but come forward with greater integrity of creation with a sense of serving the common good and preserve universal wellbeing" (Archbishop Flynn).

Climate change affects everything from geopolitics to economies to migration. It shapes cities, life expectancies, and food habits. The examples of climate events like fires, floods, and atmospheric tsunamis identify the man-made systems holding us back from progress and invite us all to join the movement of climate justice: the most significant emergent social movement in all of history. An inevitable sense of urgency on the current state of the crisis and the collective global and local efforts for lifestyle transformations will make it possible to find a way out of it gradually. As Al Gore (2022: 5) stated, "The Climate Crisis is the battle of our time," and we can win it with collective will and collaboration from all sections of society. The coronavirus brought much of the world to a standstill, dropping carbon emissions by five percent. Keeping the rates down is left to the whole of humanity. However, the steadily declining cost of wind and solar energy will transform manufacturing, transportation, and agriculture, offer a cheaper alternative to fossil fuels and nuclear power, and create millions of new jobs, paving the way for assuring a sustainable planet. Pandemic revealed the underbelly of disparities of income. Oxford economists predict the fastest growing industry in creating new jobs in renewable energy. Ingrid Vanderveldt, CEO and Founder of the Empowering Billion Women and SHE Economy, advocates the social, economic, and global transformation of the economy, focusing on women's leadership and entrepreneurship that will help address the current environmental challenges to move us to an egalitarian and sustainable future.

As an avid mountain climber and environmental scientist and the former EPA Chief of American Government, Anderson reflects on the key lessons on leadership for environmental stewardship from his mountain-climbing experience, especially the need to put full attention and intention into what you are doing and where you are going:

> One of the beautiful things about climbing to me is it demands your full attention, your entire focus, and your will and, and mine so that extraneous stuff just falls by the wayside. So that number two. Experience a wholeness moment in climbing being fully present and fully engaged with complete focus. This same focus and collective awareness as a leader will help you make the best decisions for the greater good of society and the environment. I want us to convert nearly 100% away from fossil fuel use as energy and convert. I'm talking about wind, solar, hydro, and nuclear; I want us to move out to renew; I want us to move completely. I want us to move entirely away from fossil fuel generation, especially in the energy field, and to renewable energy. That's, that would be my number one wish that I want us to eradicate. In 25 years, we could do it, we could do it, I want us to take care of global warming, but it's tied to my first two. I'd like to eradicate starvation and lack of food and clean water and a clean environment around the world that can be done for a sustainable future; it would take enormous cooperative effort and global collaboration to save the one blue planet.

Larry Zimplemen, the former CEO of Principal Insurance Company remain optimistic about the initiatives taken by the business and the government to address the climate change in spite of the political polarization and indicated how he sees the change happening with businesses:

> I think this is where you are seeing serious efforts by companies, large and small, particularly large companies, to say that our involvement extends way beyond just our business purpose. You know, yes, our business purpose has meaning. If we're a public company, yes, we have the responsibility to shareholders, but we have an even greater responsibility to society and the planet. The generation of the global GDP depends on the adaptation of renewable energy that will, in turn, avert the climate crisis.

Many companies are taking the initiative to create green spaces in the inner cities by erasing the office spaces while the work is shifting to remote and digital. The leaders are well aware of the impact of climate change and its catastrophic consequences if not dealt with courage and convictions about the situations rising above the power of big money and vested interest of the lobbies against the implementation of renewable energy for global sustainability. Caroline Washburn, the Chief Editor of Des Moines Register, confronted the presidential candidates in the public debate regarding their position on the issue of climate change, which was a hot button issue since most of them denied that climate change due to human factors:

> The presidential campaign always starts in Des Moines. And so, the Des Moines Register always hosted a presidential debate. And the editor, the Des Moines Register, always moderated the debate. One of the things that had changed over all that time, though, was, of course, our political world changed. And what used to be a debate for the people of Iowa on Iowa, public television suddenly had become a national interest, and now was on CNN and everything. And the national political parties became much more involved. So, when it was my turn to moderate the debate, the candidates were in the state of Iowa for a year before that happened, so residents see them a lot. So, we did a statewide poll and said to Iowans, in all the years of listening to all of these candidates, what do you feel like you understand very well about their positions? And what do you still feel the need to know more about? So, they thought they understood very well, so we didn't ask questions about those. And we focused on the things they wanted to know more about, right. But, of course, that made the candidates mad. Because they did not want to talk about the hot-buttons issues, climate change?

Washburn did press the political candidates to demonstrate their stance on climate issues, and she had to face adverse reactions and media attacks due to her courageous and principled disposition. Political debates in United States became very brutal at the onset of the social media for any one could voice their anger and reactions without having any filter to keep it civilized and decent engagement as citizens of the second higher democracy in the world. Maintaining civility in dialogue and discussions has become increasingly challenging as the media persons get abuse from both other media out lets and political rivals. Sensing the crisis of civil dialogue and engagement was the need of the hour to counter against the suppression of freedom of speech and search for truth in a messy political world. Standing firm on the principles of journalistic truth and transparency to serve the public during the course of the presidential debate, Washburn took bold stand on enquiring into the truth and understanding of the issue of climate change even though it was a polarizing issue on the ballot. Her experiences show that how divided the society is and how challenging it is to engage in civil discourse of the most pressing matters of today, especially the climate challenge. She noted:

> Well, climate change is one of the things people want to know more about. And they did want to know more about climate change. You know, there were 15 candidates. And so, I remember saying to the group of them, you know, we'll talk more about this in detail. But just to get a lay of the land, give me a show of hands who believes that climate change is partially caused by man. And so, some people started raising their hands, and then one candidate just stopped and said, I'm not raising my hand, and this is ridiculous. And they were, some of them misbehaved. And he just started giving me grief. And this is live television. So, after those debates from social media, I took the abuse. So that was the first-year social media was a big deal during debates. I was just brutalized. I mean, it was awful. Well, fortunately, my friends and my family were very supportive.

Despite the severe consequences that Carolyn has to face, she gathered strength and courage with the support of the family and colleagues with a mind of wisdom, spiritual intelligence, and fortitude. She recalled how she was able to confront the presidential candidates in the media to clarify their positions on climate change and how they are going to tackle this impending catastrophe on a global scale. This was a difficult task for some of the candidates took position that climate change was a hoax and denied the scientific reports regarding the issue. The challenging questioning and inquiry had exposed the hypocrisy of such a stand and it made them more aggressive on the debate platform. Being rooted in ethics and internal values enabled Washburn as the chief editor of the newspaper to conduct the public debate with clarity, confidence, and boldness as a leader:

> My company was moderately supportive, which was part of what was hard. They had never had that kind of reaction to one of those debates before. I think, you know, I realized after the fact that that was kind of the first year that the candidates made the media, the story, you know, that diverting attention by making the media the bad guy, but you only see some of that after the fact, you know, you know, how did I deal with it? I did lots of second-guessing myself, talking to friends and other journalists, and talking to my husband, and then you just come to work every day, you know, I mean, it's just you. I just kept going. I have no regrets now. Yeah. I mean, I, I look back, and I'm proud of the questions we ask. I was taking the long view. I feel good about it; I just kept going; I mean, I, you know, it was ruthless. But I just came to work every day and just kept going.

In matters of governance, the politics and the media, the public have to align in their understanding of what is at stake due to the impending catastrophe of the ecological crisis well beyond the collective trauma of denial, non-civility, and polarization. Appreciating the universe as an emergent living phenomenon can be done only from the inside by cultivating the capacity to understand the world and ourselves as an interconnected whole (Capra, 2003). This holistic perspective can be gained only with a mind of wisdom, crisis care (Bailey et al., 2021), and a spirit of courage, and not in fear and division resulting from a myopic vision of a fragmented world.

The International Rescue Committee (IRC, 2021) has released its 2021 Emergency Watchlist, a global list of humanitarian crises expected to deteriorate the most over the coming year, creating significant psychological distress for humanity. The ongoing threat of war and conflict, climate change and global warming, COVID-19, and global health challenge are driving the crises in nearly all Emergency Watchlist countries, threatening famine in several in 2021. These global issues have impacted the lives of leaders, and their perspectives enabled them to adapt according to the changing circumstances uncovering higher consciousness and discovering new solutions with holistic intelligence.

The leaders demonstrated the ability to sense the existential spiritual crisis they underwent or pre-cognition of the emerging challenges in manifold ways. This spiritual crisis manifests into the three big crises of today: the ecological, social, and ethical crises. The spiritual crisis presented itself as alienation from self and nature, alienation from self and the other, and the alienation from self and one's higher Self. These leaders experienced this brokenness as an ethical, social, and ecological crisis. Their *lives were shaken for some time by intense psychological and emotional turmoil leading to traumatic experiences, both personal, social, and collective traumas (*Linstroth, 2022*). The traumas caused by social crisis can be divided into particular episodes of trauma, "synchronic trauma or over a long period or synchronic trauma. These necessary and critical life experiences have shaped their journey towards wholeness and outlook on leadership and spirituality. They described their experiences as crucibles of learning. The process of sensing or pre-cognition of crises manifests deeper intelligence and awareness that helps leaders take a bold stand of conceiving and embracing the challenge with a positive and constructive attitude. Lastly, these prominent leaders manifested how they learned from these crises by embracing them as a challenge rather than problems to discover critical insights in their journey towards wholeness through Lenz of spiritual intelligence. The next chapter will show how the leaders transitioned from their ability to sense crisis to embrace the challenge of crisis with tenacity, courage, and confidence in turning the crisis into an opportunity for awakening hidden wholeness.*

References

American Psychological Association Dictionary. (2022, November). *Spiritual crisis*. https://dictionary.apa.org/identity-crisis

Bailey, C., Poole, N., & James, A. (2021). Crisis care: Tackling the climate and ecological emergency. *Bjpsych Bulletin, 45*(4), 201–204. https://doi.org/10.1192/bjb.2021.3

Boldizonni, F. (2011). *The poverty of Clio*. Princeton University Press.

Capra, F. (2003). *The hidden connections*. Flamingo.

Chimhowu, A. (2009). Poverty. In R. Kitchin & N. Thrift (Eds.), *International encyclopedia of human geography* (pp. 408–415). Elsevier. ISBN 9780080449104. https://doi.org/10.1016/B978-008044910-4.00116-4

Figueres, C., &, Rivett-Carnac, T. (2020). *The future we choose: Surviving the climate crisis*. Vintage Books.

Fried, A., & Elman, R. M. (2017). *Routledge revivals: Charles Booth's London (1969): A portrait of the poor at the turn of the century, drawn from his "life and labor of the people in London."* Taylor & Francis. ISBN 978-1-351-98157-6.

Flynn, H. (2003). *In God's image: A pastoral letter on racism*. Center for Ministry.

Gore, A. (2022, January). The climate crisis is the battle of our time, and we can win. *The New York Times*. nytimes.com

Hogg, M. A. (2007). Uncertainty-identity theory. *Advances in Experimental Social Psychology, 39*, 69–126.

Firestone, S. (2020). Spiritual leadership and crisis. In Biblical principles of crisis leadership. Christian faith perspectives in *Leadership and business*. Palgrave Macmillan. https://doi.org/10.1007/978-3-030-44955-1_5

IPCC. (2007). Climate Change Report. *Synthesis Report Contribution*, 2007.

IRC's. (2021, February). Emergency watchlist: The triple threat of COVID, climate change, and conflict threatens 200 million people without urgent action | *International Rescue Committee (IRC)*. Retrieved on February, 2022 from https://www.rescue.org/press-release/ircs-2021-emergency-watchlist-triple-threat-covid-climate-change-and-conflict

Kasser, T., Rosenblum, K. L., Sameroff, A. J. Deci, E. L., Niemiec, C. P., Ryan, R. M., Árnadóttir, O., Bond, R., Dittmar, H., Dungan, N., & Hawks, S. (2014). Changes in materialism, changes in psychological well-being: Evidence from three longitudinal studies and an intervention experiment. *Motivation and Emotion, 38*, 1–22. https://doi.org/10.1007/s11031-013-9371-4

Linstroth, J. P. (2022). Racial trauma and racism. In *Politics and racism beyond nations*. Palgrave Macmillan. https://doi.org/10.1007/978-3-030-91720-3_5

Majluf, N., & Abarca, N. (2021). *Sensible leadership: Human-centered, insightful and prudent*. Routledge.

Mandela, N. (2022, February). *The quotes of Nelson Mandela*. https://www.nelsonmandela.org/content/page/researcher-resources

Merriam-Webster Dictionary. (2022, November). *Identity crisis*. https://www.merriam-webster.com/dictionary/identity%20crisis

Monbiot, G. (2022, August). https://www.theguardian.com/2013/dec/09/materialism-system-eats-us-from-inside-out

Pirani, S. (2021). Overcoming the imaginative asphyxiation of climate protest. *Capitalism Nature Socialism, 32*(1), 128–131. https://doi.org/10.1080/10455752.2020.1828561

Rawls, J. (1971). *Theory of justice*. Cambridge University Press.

Rawls, J. (2001). *Justice as fairness: A restatement* (2nd ed.). Harvard University Press. ISBN 9780674005112.

Scharmer, O. (2015, November). Rowntree (formative theorists) (p. 136). Routledge. ISBN 978-0-415-35260-4. The blind spot: Uncovering the grammar of the social field. *HUFFPOST*. https://www.huffpost.com/entry/uncovering-the-grammar-of-the-socialfield_b_7524910

Scharmer, O. (2022, February). *Ten lessons from Covid for stepping into the decade of transformation*. https://medium.com/PresentingInstitute/filedofthefutureblog.html

Sen, A. (2009). *The idea of justice*. Penguin Publishing.

The Economist. (June 2022). *The climate crisis*. https://www.economist.com/climate-change?

United States Catholic Conference of Bishops. (1979). *Brothers and sisters to us*.

Wienhues, A. (2020). Ecological justice and the extinction crisis: Giving living beings their due. *Bristol University Press*. https://doi.org/10.46692/9781529208528

Williams, P. (2021, November). *7 signs of the dark night of the soul*. https://medium.com/change-your-mind/7-signs-youre-going-through-a-dark-night-of-the-soul-691e1c058258

Wilson, P. A. (2019). *The heart of community engagement: Practitioner stories from across the globe*. Routledge.

CHAPTER 4

Embracing Crisis

The leaders in the study embraced their existential spiritual crises positively and turned them into the alchemy of inner transformation. For each, their journey towards wholeness was prompted and propelled by the force of those experiences, which helped them delve deeper into the meaning and purpose of life. Engaging in self-exploration rather than self-denial and projection, the leaders turned negative experiences into catalysts for change and growth. They developed a holistic perspective embracing strengths and the shadows for greater integration, considering the crises and failures as challenges, and learning experiences rather than a burden was a salient feature in their journeys towards wholeness. The interviewed leaders expressed the conviction that their understanding of spiritual crisis led them to embrace it as a challenge rather than an impending catastrophe. The ability to embrace the crisis as an opportunity made the leaders challenge their own assumptions and discover their capacity for spiritual intelligence to adopt creative cooperation in their journey towards wholeness.

The five aspects of the process of embracing the crisis can be described as follows: awareness of strengths and weakness, self-acceptance, failure as a learning experience, matching soul and role, and growth in authenticity, as shown graphically in Fig. 4.1. The qualities of deeper awareness, acceptance, learning, and integration helped them grow as authentic, creative,

T. Thakadipuram, *Leadership Wholeness, Volume 1*,
Palgrave Studies in Workplace Spirituality and Fulfillment,
https://doi.org/10.1007/978-3-031-08053-1_4

Fig. 4.1 Embracing Crisis

and wise leaders in the organization and the world. The supportive network of resources and the model of other leaders helped them grow in resilience and wisdom to embrace the crisis in their lives and turn them around as opportunities for growth and development, integrating a synthesis of productivity, people, quality, safety, and reliability (Hollnagel, 2022). The creativity of crisis emerges from embracing the polarities and forging new pathways for change and growth.

Awareness of the Strengths and Weaknesses

In their intentional journeys towards wholeness, the leaders became conscious of their strengths and weakness through their successes and failures. Holding the paradox of forces and shadows in their lives helped the leaders gain a deeper consciousness of their gradual change and growth towards the wholeness of life. For example, Larry Zimpleman of the Principal Company was aware of the strength of his business organization while embracing the crisis of recession in the financial industry. "There were days when I put my shoes on to go to work, my wife has seen tears falling on my shoes. I want to save 13,000 jobs, but it was painful to cut 1500 jobs to make the company survive the crisis." Archbishop

Flynn was aware of the indomitable power of the human spirit amidst the tragedy of pastoral abuse scandals across the globe. He expressed the spirit of hope and confidence amidst discouraging moments, "I also came to know, however, that no matter the brokenness, the human spirit can indeed heal and move beyond it." He also noted that deep awareness of his strengths and weakness helped him embrace the crisis with humility and exercise his Leadership with sensitivity and resilience. "I would dare say that I would probably be one of the most sensitive persons with a thin skin anyone could meet; born out of that sensitivity is the care for others, but I did not ever lose any sleep." Similarly, Saint Augustine noted, "Struggling with one part praising up and the other part falling" (Chadwick, 2008: 147). John Abbate, the CEO of over 2000 McDonald Branches in California, expressed his ability to hold the paradox of being aware of both his strength and weakness as a business leader:

> I was very proud of my strength as an authoritarian leader initially in the restaurant business in California; however, my challenge was how to be a good leader for people. A leader that can get the results that are needed for the business and at the same time be a good servant of the people. It's incredibly easy to be a tyrannical leader; it's incredibly easy to be a warm and fuzzy leader everybody likes. But it's very critical to be aware of one's strengths and weaknesses to be an effective leader who is tough and caring at the same time.

Jarema, a psychoanalyst, pointed out the fact that while acknowledging one's strength, the way of growth and development lies in looking at the least noticed area of one's life where the potential is dormant: To discover the hidden potential, one has to look at the least unexplored area and embrace the new pathways to realize area of change and development. Embracing the shadow or the dark side of the personality is critical for rediscovering the hidden wholeness of the person and unleashing the least explored dimension of the psyche and the potential of the person. When you get stuck in a rut at work, your focus becomes what you dislike and it makes one demoralized and frustrated. Whereas when one focuses on the hidden passions to find out what makes one happy, energized, and excited, you begin to discover the hidden wholeness of life. Jarema expressed his perspective of helping leaders rediscover their hidden potential and passions:

> What I found in leadership development, it's good to acknowledge your strengths. It's good to look at, let's say, your dominant function on the Myers Briggs. I want to know what is the least used function, your profile because that's where your potential lies. And I've also learned there is no growth in the familiar. Indeed, there's mastery and refinement. Growth begins with the unknown and the unfamiliar. So as a leader, I want to know what you are unfamiliar with? What is it you've never done before? That's where you discover your hidden wholeness. I worked with many leaders who rediscovered their passion by embracing the least explored dimension in their psyche.

Palmer spoke about his journey of becoming more conscious and intentional rather than moving through life in auto pilot, as he fully embraced his setbacks in life, "And I know I have got to do something about it. And so, you started journeying more consciously and intentionally because you know that your survival is at stake here if you don't embrace shadow." In the wake of the colonial domination, Mutua had to break through the cultural barriers of apartheid between whites and blacks in South Africa, embracing the goodness and fragilities. The domination of the colonial powers suppressed and oppressed the indigenous people in Africa and it took herculean efforts to rediscover the goodness lost without spreading hatred and rivalry in the nation. He was aware of the paradox of human nature for good and bad alike:

> We became aware that what our grandparents told us and what we were taught in the schools during colonial times were as different as cold tar from milk. I asked myself, why were we taught such untruths about ourselves? We were told that we knew nothing about God; that too, when the missionaries came, they said the same; we were told that we were savage, lazy, and primitive. However, when we listen to the stories of the old ones, they are different. They told us that we were human, vibrant, and noble. What breaks my heart is that human being is basically good, but human beings also can be like a hand grenade.

Thurston walked through family misunderstandings and intuitive spiritual stirrings in her soul to be aware of the shadows and the light in her own life (Chappell et al. 2019; Fosu, 2022). Moving back and forth from the deep awareness of light and deep shadow within, Thurston embraced her crisis gradually. She described the evolution of her consciousness as moving through the dark tunnel of life discovering the lighter and better side of her personality by embracing her own personal crisis and working through the shadows of her life a journey through the rollercoaster going through ups and down of life:

> In the daytime, when he wasn't there, I was walking around; we had this beautiful prominent place with lots of acreage by a river. And I would wander along the river bank. I was still grappling with the idea that maybe I was insane. Then I was happy with that. And I became a closet mystic, and there was nobody to talk to. And after my baby was born, there was this feeling that there was something that I was supposed to do for her benefit. I had no idea what it was. I had no idea what to do, and so I walked very vacantly like a zombie for some time. It was another deep dive from a high state into the deep shadow.

Working with her spiritual guide, Thurston became aware of her unconscious shadows, the hidden childhood emotional trauma that haunted her for long life, and breakthrough into the light of consciousness within (Molen, 2018). Shadow self is the site of repressed desires, emotions, and impulses hidden from the conscious awareness. Shadow work involves bringing these unconscious desires to the forefront so that we can better understand them, heal them, and integrate them in a healthy way to lead a productive and fulfilling life. By embracing the shadow, Thurston overcame the resistance to growth and began the transformation towards the wholeness of life. She described the internal process of working through her negative parental imprinting and transcending to higher consciousness through the virtuous and vicious cycles of trauma and light by embracing the shadows layer by layer as a gradual unfolding process of self:

> Since I had nowhere else to go, I went back to Los Angeles to visit Francis Sterns. I slept on her couch for about six weeks. Every morning we would process for hours, and she took me through the process of parental imprinting, my childhood, my father, mainly who is a dominator and quite violent. And I worked consciously through those unconscious shadows to bring out the light within. The shadow would come up and the light will go up and I have a few days of *Samadhi* (higher consciousness) and then I plunge down into shadows, into the next layer; into the next deeper layer of shadow. This vicious and virtuous cycle of inner drama went on for months.

Sri Sri spoke about accessing the strengths of the higher self by embracing one's boundaries and limitations and letting one go to the universal dimension through prayer and meditation. Embracing what is going on within is a significant step towards exploring the greater dimension of being embedded in peace and unlimited potential for transformation. Turning the inner turmoil into a spiritual process will be a catalyst for discoveries of inner strengths. The powerful meditation process which Sri Sri cultivated throughout his life became very handy to be aware of the limitations and work through the boundaries to the infinite dimensions of self-discovering the inner freedom, peace, and infinite spiritual potential within and the power of hidden wholeness:

> Whenever you are unhappy, you are just coming in touch with your ego boundaries! And what can you do? You can feel thankful: Oh, I came in contact with my boundary, my limitation. This was my limitation. You just turn the whole situation into a prayer or a moment of meditation. Take a deep breath. Let there be peace, not just in me but in everybody. At that moment, what can you do? You can say that you made me aware of my boundaries, my Lord, my God. You bring peace. I am giving it all to you. That very moment you will start smiling. However hopeless the situation is, you will breathe through it, walk through it, sing through it, dance through it! You experience your boundless and innocent love in the heart. Then nothing can rob you of peace.

For the leaders, upholding humanness while embracing the good aspects of science and technology was a priority to be on the path towards wholeness. Sri Sri addressed the need to embrace the power of science to make humans creative and productive. However, it has limitations, but not to neglect humanity's more profound and broader spiritual side for realizing wholeness in life. In this way, the rational intelligence and spiritual intelligence work hand in hand for the advancement of the whole life. Townes (2022: 1), the Nobel Laureate in Physics, noted, "Science and religion are often viewed as separate aspects of our beliefs and understanding. But religion is an attempt to understand the purpose of our universe and science an attempt to understand its nature and characteristics, so the two are necessarily related." The spiritual intelligence and scientific wisdom do not contradict one another but can complement each other to enhance the quality of human life and the sustainable progress of the humanity as a whole:

> In this era of science and technology, we can be creative and productive and at the same time not lose the humanness that we are all born with. Just material things or comfort alone do not make you comfortable. You may have a good bed to sleep on but cannot sleep because of insomnia or worry! You need to get a broad understanding of yourself and your priorities. In science, knowledge comes first, and then faith follows. In spirituality, faith comes first, and then knowledge follows. Thus, spiritual intelligence and scientific knowledge do not contradict each other but support and enhance life.

These leaders were excellent at practicing self-observation and identifying what was happening within them. For example, Abbess Pema expressed that she was internally aware when she reached a higher contemplation stage. She was mindful when her awareness level dropped down to mundane levels. The practice of self-observation, that is, observing the patterns of thoughts and emotions, was helpful to growing deeper levels of being and cultivating inner peace and tranquility. Self-observation is an awareness practice where you turn your attention inward, and nonjudgmentally watch what you think, feel, and desire. Imagine that a kind, neutral person has full access to your inner landscape and this awareness is the key for deeper inner transformation. Self-observing allows a person to change or correct their own thinking, behavior, and effects in the world as they emerge moment to moment, and eventually to apprehend them before they are manifest into full behavior. Pema's deep sense of self-awareness was a force of transformation in her journey towards wholeness:

> Something I tell you is significant in my life. Since I became more contemplative, I have a considerable concentration; after sitting meditation practice for a few months, I can go into a place of deep peace. However, I found my attention was weakening, I was getting a bit disturbed, and it was bothering me; I was getting distracted. When I sat in meditation, I thought about what I had to cook. I hardly knew how to cook Japanese food, for I knew only about cooking Western food. Thought my meditation practice was going down the hill being bothered by external circumstances. I had a bit of resentment in me. This practice of self-observation and awareness of what is going on within helped me to embrace my weakness and the deeper layers of shadows gradually. Recognizing and embracing what is going on within enabled me to work on myself so that the shades could become a trigger for inner transformation.

Participants' experience of the crises triggered deeper awareness of what was happening, and they learned to be proactive in those times. Learning to listen to the inner voice of wisdom and guidance helped them go beyond the immediate crisis situation of their life and embrace life with new possibilities. Ilibagiza spoke about the discovery of her spiritual strength. Facing the inevitable extreme crisis situation in which her life was at stake, Ilibagiza underwent psychological trauma but her spiritual attunement in deep prayer helped her to travel the deeper recess of the spiritual dimension that enabled her to embrace the crippling fear and terror and move into a place of peace, serenity, peace, and security within. When confronted with extreme crisis situations such as a near-death experience, some people experience breakdown and some are able to endure the inner turmoil and turn their life around by embracing the inevitable to discover the deeper source of strength and grace within. Ilibagiza attributed this inner transformation to the divine forces and spiritual awakening of the hidden wholeness:

> When I was trapped in the pastor's bathroom, where all I saw was terror in the eyes of the other women and all I heard were the howls of blood-drunk killers, praying took a new meaning. My mind was entirely focused on God for hours on end. At first, my petitions were driven by my fear. I simply wanted to stay alive. But later, as I spent long periods in communion with Him, my prayers transported me to a spiritual level I'd never imagined possible. Praying was no longer a request for Divine intervention; it became my gateway to God, and when I passed through, I felt there was no fear, there was no pain, and there were no doubts... there was only the light of the Lord and the certainty that He loved and cared for me. I felt the Holy Spirit moving within me, and I could hear God's voice assuring me that He was with me and always would be. When I wasn't praying, the light dimmed, and the hopelessness and horror of my situation returned. It was like growing spiritually during a crisis; somewhere, something was changing, and much was inside my heart. Finally, I could find the light at the end of the dark tunnel.

Leaders in the study manifested great capacity for self-awareness. They were not only aware of their inner strengths but also their weaknesses, limitations, and shadows. Their sense of self-awareness enabled them to recognize what was not working well and helped them to discover new ways to cope with crises. Leaders' profound sense of inner awareness, resilience, and awareness of their shadows and weaknesses helped them embrace a problem as a challenge and turn it into a positive force for inner growth and transformation.

Self-Acceptance

Leaders in the study demonstrated their ability for deep self-acceptance, especially when situations were not going in their favor. The natural tendency to deny the existence of problems and failures to give a positive impression was more complicated for the leaders to resolve (Prigatano & Sherer, 2020). Although they tried to hide the problems initially, they understood early on that ignoring the issues would not make them go away but reappear with double force. A profound sense of self-acceptance made a significant difference in their ability to embrace their weaknesses and draw lessons for their continued journeys (Foster, 2017). They recognized early on that non-self-acceptance would stand in the way of realizing leadership wholeness. Lim reflected on the challenge of embracing her own identity as a gay person, and the power overflowed from the moment of self-acceptance:

> In 2009, I was asked to be the executive director for the national women's advocacy group in Singapore, but I did not feel the courage to step up as I struggled with my own identity. Although I did not go to church regularly, I was not against it. One day I went for the prayer at the stations of the cross for children in the church and walked along with Jesus carrying his cross through his most excruciating path to Calvary. It was a moment that hit me deep in my heart to embrace my suffering and challenge to come out as a gay person despite the fear of the unknown future and the adverse reactions of my family and society. It was a moment of relief, acceptance, and inner freedom for me as I had been hiding in the closet for many years, although the more extensive community did not welcome it positively but denied our existence as a legitimate way of life.

Palmer felt that his journey towards wholeness was indeed a journey towards a fundamental level of self-acceptance. The ability to embrace both the polarities of light and shadows, part and the whole in the same perspective is the way to unfold the deeper dimension of being and discover the hidden wholeness. Instead of denying the existence of brokenness which leads to deeper pain and trauma, acceptance led to a greater level of healing which took place gradually and enabled the person to live life more fully and alive. To be fully human, fully alive, and completely awaken is to be thrown out of the comfort zone and go deeper into the spiritual zone of being. Positively embracing one's flows will help one to be proud of one's essence and existence and embrace others with their flaws and strengths:

> For me, the journey towards wholeness means a journey towards a fundamental level of self-acceptance, both the light and the shadows together, and both the whole and that which is broken are placed together. I no longer see them as impending or up and down or better or worse. And my experiences enable me to embrace everything I am. The shadow or brokenness does not disappear. But they somehow start to become healed. The brokenness is part of my life experience rather than what I am trying to sweep under the rug.

When the acceptance process becomes internalized, Palmer acknowledged that it could become transformative. "When you embrace your enemy, something softens. Maybe you realize you don't have to be enemies." Palmer added, "If something goes wrong with my work, I have no one to blame but myself. I wish I had someone to blame, but I don't." Palmer's sense of awareness suggests that acceptance of failures helps one take responsibility for one's life rather than blaming someone else for abdicating the responsibility. "Enemies do not need to kill each other. Embracing the enemy in you deeply is based on this principle of self-acceptance. It is transformative" (Palmer). Embracing the crises is like a mother holding a crying baby with unconditional love and acceptance until the baby stops crying. Comfort the afflicted and afflict the comfortable to be wholesome. Accept the things you cannot change and change the things you can and have the wisdom to know the difference. Embracing one's own struggles and sufferings helped Sister Gefre to hold others' pain and sufferings with compassionate care:

> People are skin hungry because they experience emotional brokenness and lack of love in their life. In the context of massage, you can bring out these emotional pains, and when they are open, they are on the way to healing and emotional wholeness. During the massage, I found many who were holding in emotional burdens, and I would help them share their inner struggles; through many sessions, people would get rid of their distress and guilt, which led to bodily and mental stress.

Palmer emphasized accepting failures as the alchemy of transformation rather than justifying one's own mistakes. Alchemists are the highest level of identified leadership in the Seven Transformations of Leadership (Rooke & Torbert, 2002). Alchemist leaders have an extraordinary capacity to deal simultaneously with multiple levels. They are skilled in reinventing themselves and their organizations in amazing ways. They build on the skills and action logics of strategists and take them to another level. They encompass a wider range of skills than other leaders, integrating material, spiritual, and societal understanding and abilities to drive change at a huge scale. This sense of self-acceptance creates an environment of vulnerability, authenticity, and creative change. Palmer identified this disposition of self-acceptance as an alchemy of transformation:

> For me, when realizing that failures are inevitable, shadows are inescapable, limitations are unavoidable, and tensions are unavoidable. Some people say, oh, then, in the harshest form, you justify your sin; I say no, that is not what I am talking about. I am talking about failures, accepting failures as the alchemy of transformation. And I think God's relationship with our imperfections, I am told, is that of forgiveness and grace. That is the alchemy that is the condition under which we transform. So, the answer almost has to be [that] you got to be intentional about the shadows to make it more whole.

Highlighting the significance of self-acceptance from the point of view of yielding or giving up resistance by turning into his experiences of setbacks, Palmer acknowledged that when we become absolutely powerless and vulnerable, we begin to discover the power of deep listening, patience, positive choice, and acceptance of our authentic selves. Surrendering the ego to a higher power of awareness and acceptance is important to unfold the deeper dimensions of being. It takes humble leadership to maintain trust and openness in times of crisis (Schein & Senge, 2018). The experience of depression can be a moment of self-abandonment and total surrender to let go of the shadow side of self and rediscover the empathetic dimensions of higher self:

> Acceptance is yielding, emptying, and laying down without giving resistance. And experiences of depression are part of my story where I turn to. But people have different versions of this. When you are down to the point where yielding is all, you can do. The terrifying thing about depression and the exciting things about it later is that all the tools like resistance

> and coping are dead and gone. You cannot think your way out of it; your Ego is defunct, shattered, and emotions are dead; all the energy sources depression deprives you of. I worked hard to train my intellect to use it as a tool or weapon or whatever, my will is strong and my emotions indeed energize me for better or worse. In depression, all of that dis-empowers. The switch is turned off. You can't energize yourself. So, I say, here I am, I will listen, and I am going to take things in, stop fighting the resistance to understanding fully what is going on.

Leaders emphasized another aspect of acceptance: how we accept others as they are. Instead of blaming or accusing the other of fault, a graceful acceptance of the people as they are and understanding their situations will bring more remarkable healing and harmony. Seeing the goodness in others is important to embrace them as they are in spite of their faults and failures. Accepting others as they help the leaders to work together for the greater good of the organization holding the complexity of the shadows and light simultaneously, Palmer expressed the view that profound change happens when there is unconditional acceptance:

> I can tell you a straightforward thing that I have learned in life: if you want to help another person, engage in the alchemy of transformation, the last thing you want to do is beat them up on their limits or failures or shadows. The best thing you want to convey to them, on the contrary, is, I love you, or I accept you no matter what. Paul Tillich, a protestant theologian, says it more elegantly. "Accept the fact that you are accepted." Profound change happens when there is unconditional acceptance and love.

Swami Veda shared how unconditional acceptance and compassion brought profound changes in his life and the life of his young friends. The grace of unconditional acceptance manifests in greater understanding and a positive outlook in life to win the hearts of both friends and foes. So, it's essential to keep the mind in a pleasant and compassionate place. Naturally, the mind becomes more joyful, and the negativities are dealt with in a positive frame of mind. Cultivating a mind of equanimity and inner calmness would enable the leaders to embrace negative or provocative situations with a proactive mind and that positive disposition will eventually transform the negative situation for good. Swami Veda understood that unconditional acceptance is another way of practicing non-violence and inner calm in the face of violence and conflicts:

> I was sharing an apartment in London with some other young people. And so, there was a hotheaded Bengali boy; by that time, I was a convinced proponent of Ahimsa. He was all for Subhash Chandra Boss, a proponent of violence against the British to win freedom. He said, you talk of all these Ahimsa; if I slapped you, what would you do? I did not say anything. Later we were sitting in the living room, and suddenly out of the blue, he got up and slapped me. God gave me wisdom; I smiled. Now you can imagine what happened to him. Well, he melted. He cried with remorse. He became a friend and almost became a devotee. You can do that. So, my experiments worked, so one does experiments in life, the virtue of unconditional acceptance and love wins. The practice of daily meditation helped me to maintain a yogic mind.

Unconditional acceptance made a significant impact on the lives of leaders. In the moments of rejection and personal crisis, total and deepest acceptance helps a person to grow in health and wholeness of life. Mutua acknowledged the profound influence on his life when his original tribal folks extended unconditional acceptance while his own family rejected him as an unwanted child. In the moment of rejection and opposition, it is important to find ways of comfort of acceptance and respect from sources which are trustworthy and credible to process the negativities of life and turn them into positive force of transformation. Mutua described how he found such source of comfort and strength in times of turmoil and personal crisis:

> But amongst the people who wore skin skirts, who were said to be savages, I found solace, security, and unconditional acceptance. My grandfather, a traditional Zulu Shaman, healed me while my family rejected me as an illegitimate child. He taught me the conventional wisdom and healing, which enabled me to be the chief Zulu Shaman.

Similarly, Sri Sri's family misunderstood his spiritual pursuits as deviant, but they later accepted and embraced him with kindness, support, and care. Discovering the unique mission in life makes one pursue a different path in life. This creates dissonance with the familiar surroundings and makes one go on the less traveled road. When you are making a deeper search and approach to life, it's naturally to be misunderstood by family, peers, and those who hold you in high esteem. Breaking through the barriers of conventional cultural expectations is needed to discover one's own identity and sense of mission in life. Therefore, removing misunderstandings eventually is essential to cultivating unconditional acceptance and support for the unique mission in life.

> I would sit in meditation for long hours. It was very natural for me. "Why do you sit in meditation," they asked me. Then, they told me to go and play. Then, my mother asked me, "Why can't you be like other people"? They were afraid whether I would go crazy. My parents were scared that I would go mentally ill, for I spent long hours in meditation. But later understood what I was doing, and they accepted and supported me (Sri Sri).

Leaders believed that self-acceptance had a lot to do with surrendering to a higher calling in their lives. Pondering over their life experiences and choices made them discover their inner voice and pursue the different paths that lead to tremendous fulfillment and serving the greater good in the world. Discovering the higher purpose in life naturally leaders to surrendering the other apparent priorities in life. Without a sense of surrender and sacrifice, it is rather impossible to realize the higher vocation in life. Despite the odds and challenges, Thurston was open to divine inspiration. She recalled how she was able to sort out her calling and marriage issues by learning to surrender to the higher motivations of life:

> We immigrated to the United States. And as soon as we got to Los Angeles, I started meeting people on a spiritual journey. And I came out of my closet. I had to tell my husband; you know, the people here understand what I am talking about. I am out of the closet. This is what I want to do. And he was not very happy about it at all. And so, we did not stay long after that. In the meantime, the aphorism, inner voice, coming into my head the voice coming became a full-time voice guiding me. And I surrendered to the authentic voice within. I did not have to go through many problems with marriage, you know. There were some tests I went through. We did not have a big fight in court or anything like that. I was just guided right out of it to a new way of life.

Thurston learned to surrender and let go of her relationships with family and children after an excruciating discernment process to be a spiritual mother for many. Self-acceptance is a process of break down to a breakthrough that opens up the more profound and higher reality of life. She realized that she was responding to a higher calling in life. Thurston did not allow her family relationships to stand in the way of her higher calling and moved forward with a new sense of spiritual mission. She was able to pursue her calling with solid determination and perseverance after accepting it as her life mission. She stated:

> After a year or so, I lived with my children; I was guided to let my children go with the father. They were pretty small; there were two of them by then. And so, first, I resisted. I am not letting my children go, and then the voice in my head said, it was so vivid, I can remember where I was standing and what I was doing: I was in the garden raking leaves or something. And a voice very loud and commanding said, it's time: stop being a mother to the few but be a mother of many. I didn't know what the hell it meant. But it got my attention. I did not see the destiny where I was drawn.

Ingrid Vanderveldt experienced the struggle of discerning and accepting the challenging and life the mission of starting the adventure of "Empowering Billion Women by 2020" through a spiritual encounter during an unusual trip through the gravel road on her farm in Texas. Self-acceptance is what allows you to be authentic and it is the primary spiritual relationship with yourself, love yourself, and a greater door of discovering one's mission would emerge from the spiritual encounter:

> In 2011, my husband and I were on a ranch in Dallas, Texas 2011. I was driving down the dirt road and praying that a breakthrough would happen in my life. I was a business TV host until then. And the day before, I had made an authentic commitment to be more spirit-focused to receive guidance. And I know exactly where I was; I've got pictures of it, you know, I've gone back many times. I asked, "God, what do you need me to do? I'm ready. I heard the voice telling me, "We need you to empower a billion women by 2020". I was inspired, challenged, and urged to embrace that mission in my life.

Abbess Pema also shared a similar experience of discerning and discarding the ego projections that keep one divided and seemingly happy with the current sense of false security and comfort. Discerning whether your reactions coming from the ego or from your soul needs self-cultivation through meditative awareness. It is like sifting through the false projections of one's ego self versus the deeper self. Ego seeks comfort and convenience whereas the soul looks at the deeper need and greater good of the situations. Ego looks at what is it for me whereas the soul looks at what is good and need in this situation for the sake of the community. With this realization and self-acceptance, the ego is ready to drop the resistance and show willingness to love and serve. The fact of resistance to let go of the old and become familiar with greater self-knowledge accepting a higher inspiration to love and serve.

> I also started to look at myself. For instance, I had a monk who had a habit of ordering me around. I would react by saying, why me? I would argue, and then I would do it later. I noticed that I had a habit of reacting; I don't like being ordered around. What would if my teacher came or Buddha came? I would fly and do it. That means there is something in me called Ego. Even the monk and I wanted the same result of being clean. The next day also, the monk asked me to clean; then again, why me? Then I stopped and looked at myself. It is my ego that puts up the resistance and not my soul. Where is my resistance to love? That's where I started to grow to remove my resistance to love by gracious surrender and acceptance (Abbess Pema).

Johannes Tauler (Quoted in Stinsissen, 2011: 31–32), the fourteen-century mystic and spiritual genius, writes about the power of accepting one's faults and failures as manure for growth. The resistance to accept one's faults will create a sense of false peace and will maintain one's own attachment to pride and other physical attachment for the sake of the ego self. In itself, the manure is dirty and repulsive but when it is mixed with the soil and seed it produces greater growth and harvest. In the beginning, it is bitter but eventually the self-acceptance will yield great positive results. Humble surrender is key to self-acceptance as a process of realizing the wholeness of life.

> In itself the manure is repulsive and pollutes the air. However, the same horse bears it with much toil to the fields, where it produces a precious harvest of fine wheat or excellent wine, a harvest that would not have been good if it had not received any fertilizer. Your own faults, which for the time being you have not mastered and which you will never succeed in overcoming, are your manure. Give yourself to carrying them diligently to the field of God's good pleasure in true surrender. Spread your fertilizer over the good earth, and without the slightest doubt, precious and sweet fruits will grow rom it with humble surrender.

Leaders in the study recognized that when they are unable to change the outside situation, they are challenged to look within and change from the inside—looking at the pattern of one's own thinking and belief and breaking through the illusionary concept of the divided self. For example, Abbess Pema testified how authentic and non-judgmental acceptance by her teacher led her to deeper self-knowledge and inner transformation. She realized that self-acceptance is the key to change and noted:

> There was something and experience in my life that came all the time that colored my interaction with my sisters. I wanted to share it with Thai (Thai is the Vietnamese word for a spiritual master or teacher); I do not want to go to Thai. I want to be completely clear as possible; every time I sit in silence, I imagine I am sitting with Thai and meditation on it. I say to myself. When I met Thai and shared it, Thai sat there looking out through the windows but with deep listening; there was no approval and disapproval and no judgment. In my meditation, it came to me that this is *beeja*, the seed of mental formation; there was full awareness, silence and solitude, acknowledgment, and complete acceptance. Thus, there is a dramatic effect, a profound inner transformation.

Self-acceptance also means learning to recognize the presence of positive and negative elements in oneself and embracing both of them with openness. Abbot Phap Son shared this aspect of unconditional acceptance. It is like holding everything in unconditional love and radical receptivity going beyond the field of right and wrong, beyond the area of division and contradiction, to a lot of most profound acceptance and oneness. Out beyond the field of right doing and wrong doing a field of wholeness and well-being where one is able to embrace both the good and bad, positive and negative with a greater sense of equanimity and open-mindedness. This process of self-acceptance itself is self-healing. Having an expanded awareness helped him to hold the paradox of strengths and weaknesses in a balance of wholeness:

> The teaching of Thich Nhat Han was very helpful. He said, "The *Buddha* and *Mara* are not enemies." What is negative in me and good in me are not enemies. They both are part of me. There was a big struggle; I thought there was an enemy in me, the darkness. I was very puzzled. I learned not to fight but to embrace what is within me. It's like holding your negative emotions like a mother holding a baby in her alms; it is like a flower that is not yet blossomed is being open when the sunlight comes and penetrates

> the petals, and thus the flower blossoms. The problems may blossom like a flower but at the end of the day or the week, its going to whither away.

Self-acceptance, in another sense, means allowing room for mistakes and handling the errors of others with care and respect. Sri Sri expressed the view that dealing with the person who committed mistakes with benevolence and kindness is very important instead of making the person feel guiltier by picking on their mistakes. It is a naturally tendency of the mind to focus on the fault of others and project it further. The person with a quality of self-acceptance has a different approach of life; instead of pointing at the fault of others, learn to look at the goodness first and eventually with love and compassion one can offer guidance and correction for the greater good of the person. A deeper sense of compassionate self will enable one to accept people as they are focusing on their goodness and eventually bring transformation into their lives with love and care:

> You can be both authoritative and sweet when you allow room for mistakes. That is how the Divine is, the right balance of both. *Krishna* and Jesus had both. Don't make a mistake by pointing out mistakes! Once a lady came to me and said her husband had lied to her. She was distraught. I asked, why does your husband lie to you? Because he loves you and he is afraid to lose your love or hurt you. If he did not love you, he wouldn't lie to you! Do not tell a person a mistake he knows he has committed without accepting their goodness first. By doing this, you will only make him feel more guilty. A generous person will not pick on the mistakes of others and make them feel guilty; he will correct them with compassion and care but fully accepting and embracing the person as they are.

The leaders spoke about a fundamental level of self-acceptance with deep awareness in their journey toward wholeness by acknowledging all parts of being, including their life's best and worst aspects. The phenomenon of self-acceptance resulting from self-inquiry resulted in the more profound transformation of discovering who they are. Being non-judgmental and allowing room for mistakes gave them a broader understanding of people and the power of unconditional acceptance. They accepted themselves wholly with their light and shadows and found it easier to accept others with their fault and frailties and win them by love. These leaders learned to surrender to their higher calling despite ordeals in their journey towards wholeness. When the outside situations were hard to change, these spiritual leaders learned to embrace the challenges gracefully and began to change from within, finding courage and strength in times of crisis. Self-acceptance was indeed a pathway to excellent learning and exploration.

Failure as a Learning Experience

The leaders considered failure a gift and learning experience rather than treating it as a discouraging phenomenon in their journey towards wholeness. Leaders understood the need to uncover hidden messages and meaning in every failure they encountered. The significant failures made them think about what is essential to living and what makes life worth living. They found that real learning comes not from successes but from the crises and failures that push them beyond their comfort zones and superficial level of living (Allio, 2008). In the crucibles of crisis, the five facets of character: humility, courage (moral and personal), caring, integrity, and perseverance, are tested. Leaders with great character are followed and trusted in times of crisis and change (Blunt, 2022). Failures are perceived as the birth pangs of inner transformation that helped them build a learning culture to gain wisdom and tenacity in their lives. Maintaining a healthy self esteem helps the leader to expand the boundary of leadership in times of crisis (Panteha et al., 2021). Bells (2019: 7) encourage the leaders in crisis to "hope for the best, prepare in crucible." Washburn reflected on how she helped her staff learn from failures and periodic changes to navigate the strategic growth process in her business:

> I gathered all my staff, 200 of them in the print industry, from the most senior to the recent ones. And the common theme was, we've constantly been changing over many decades, even the person who's only been there a month has experienced change, and they've done it successfully through learning. They know how to change, and change happens from learning from failures. And sometimes, change is done better with the collective wisdom. And so that helps the staff see the trajectory of change through learning and see it through their own lives. It was a great day of processing all those stories, and sort of you could almost watch people discover the confidence that they were capable of more change. And so, hold learning sacred and build a learning culture to change and grow.

Archbishop Flynn, in the similar vein, reflected on his story of how learning from failures led to a significant turning point in his life. He accepted that although he was living a responsible life, he was not giving his best as a spiritual leader. Reflective learning allows one to engage in self-examination of what is working and what is not working or missing in the path of spiritual progress and make corrective steps to move in a clear direction of spiritual commitment and priority of life. Reflective learning is a process of stepping back from action and looking at life from one's values and priorities of life and seeing how one can realign one's life with mission, vision, values, and strategies of accomplishing the goals in life. He discerned what was missing, learned lessons, and moved forward with a positive initiative and disciplined commitment of meditative practice daily to grow in spiritual intelligence and wisdom:

> And this would have been at the end of my seventh year studying theology. It was a graced moment that I felt I was giving God only left-over time. That is all I could describe. I was praying, doing everything I should have done, but I was not giving God quality time. And I think in any relationship, relationship in marriage, the relationship among friends, there needs to be the nurturing of that relationship through quality time. So, I realized that I failed to give priority time to God even though I made my commitment to God. And that grace hit me. And then I promised from that moment onwards I would give God quality time. Every day I spent an hour of quiet time before the Lord in silent prayer, meditation, and contemplation. And out of that commitment came some beautiful reflections and a deeper understanding of a holistic life.

In dealing with the clerical sexual abuse scandal at the national level in the United States, Archbishop Flynn acknowledged how he learned from these failures to be empathetic and caring: "I learned that I should never try to minister to another who is in pain until in some way I could experience some of that pain. I learned to listen before I tried to speak." The successes in life may be gratifying, but learning from the failures makes a person whole. It is the learning that helps a person grow and not just succeed. Palmer shared his insights about this life learning process, which is focused on self-inquiry, and taking lessons for life. An attitude of learning helps a person gain a holistic perspective of life, embracing its positive and negative sides. Palmer described how he undertook this learning process in his journey towards wholeness. Learning about one's limits and weakness helps one to be aware of the boundaries one places oneself not only to succeed but also to be wholesome:

> And I feel gratified, and when you feel that way, you don't think. What you think is, Oh! This I have figured out. I don't have anything to learn here, for I have these excellent reviews, awards, feedback, etc. Your failures, my failures, make you wake up at three in the morning and chew them. You have to say to yourself, what happened? What went wrong? What do I need to learn about myself, the other person, the situation, and my relationship at all? What do I have to know which will help me grow? One question is to help you succeed, but the other question is, what makes me whole? That doesn't mean getting rid of imperfections, which can never be got rid of. I've come to believe that just as each of us have God given gifts, on the flip side of our strengths, every one of us have weakness, potholes, a limit. And so, there are things that I can do very well and I worked hard to develop those skills. But right on the flip side of it, I am aware that I have limitations where I shouldn't go, or it is not my gift.

Palmer disclosed that when he initially resisted learning from his failures and lived in denial as he was driven by sheer success, life became very burdensome and inauthentic, putting up a mask not living from the true self; this turmoil pushed him into the abyss of clinical depression. Inauthentic life is a threat to physical and financial well-being and not to mention the spiritual decline comes along the road very quickly. When one is not living a balanced and authentic life, it is more draining to live busy lives and the universe brings crisis situations to look back at your life and engage in profound reflection to alter one's life. Later, these moments of failure became moments of profound learning and, thus, crucial turning points in his life.

> I was so I, and the failures began to surprise me; the failure experience with youth in Spanish Harlem, losing a research job at Berkley; I started to rub my nose in failures. The struggle to pretend that I am always light and have no shadow, limit, or weakness becomes exhausting. You wear yourself down until defenses start to crumble. During my forties and fifties, that took me to prolonged periods of clinical depression. However, the turning points in my life bring me toward profound moments of the learning experience (Palmer).

Learning to admit and embrace failures, one becomes more human and humbler. However, it is also noted that if one doesn't take steps to internalize lessons from failures, one might show pathological behavior over time. The cost of inauthentic life is beyond measure even to the point of experiencing depression. Living with false image of oneself is costly and contributes to unhappiness and lack of fulfillment. Learning from failures is quite humbling, but it is also ennobling in the sense that one can grow to greater heights of authenticity and true happiness. Therefore, building a learning culture by reflecting on the losses is vital to authentic life and growth. Palmer reflected on his approach to failures as a process of self-discovery and spiritual growth.

> For a couple of decades, I said to my folks and myself: the truth is that I have learned a lot more from my failures than I ever had learned from my successes. Successes simply make me feel self-satisfied, and I pat myself on the back and say, "what a golden boy I am." You are not saying it doesn't matter that I messed around; those things matter. But to go back and embrace that failure as a place where I learn something about my true self. This learning never comes from counting the merits of success alone. I know from junior high school students in Spanish Harlem that real people can't connect with somebody who looks perfect. Those who either willingly or unwillingly reveal one's weakness that brings in the connection. There is a crack in everything, and through the crack comes the light. It is not about failure sucks; that is not the lesson. The lesson matters how you understand and appropriate, and internalize those lessons. Quakers used to say; I am a Quaker; when I am not walking in my light, it shows in pathological behavior.

Leaders expressed that the journey towards wholeness is a journey of trial and error; it is a messy journey that is non-linear and not a straight path. The process will test your strength, reveal your weakness, and empower you to embrace the crisis with grace, grit, and determination. Dive deep into answering the questions you refused to answer and learn to engage life with greater sincerity, clarity, and wisdom. Spiritual growth is like learning to climb the ladder; when you make two steps higher, you might fall back to the lower ring and the ability to bounce back and climb again brings greater tenacity and resilience to go higher in the journey. This wholeness journey is an iterative process of trial and error all the way. The journey might involve many failures, but the aspirant to wholeness is engaged in the pursuit with undying optimism. Palmer articulated this notion through the help of a metaphor of climbing the mountain as expressed by this ancient story:

> Embracing the failure to learn and grow is like the story where a fellow was living at the foot of the hill, and at the top of the mountain was

> a monastery, and he lived there for years, and one day he became more curious. He thought they must be living an exotic lifestyle, and he went up the hill one day and knocked on the gate and asked the Abbot, "What is the trick you are doing here?" Then the Abbot said, "it is straightforward, my son, we get up, we fall, we get up, we fall ... we get up and fall; that is how the journey looks." The journey towards wholeness: is messy; it is a journey of trial and error; it is a journey of experimentation.

Mutua described how African people learned from their mistakes. In the beginning, they innocently believed the colonialists and became victims of domination. Colonialism's impacts include environmental degradation, the spread of disease, economic instability, ethnic rivalries, and human rights violations. This was a time of excruciating suffering and crisis for the natives. It took many years of struggle and sacrifice to learn from the colonial tragedies and rebound as free people. The natives learned from the past mistakes that they needed to be shrewd to understand the evil intention of the colonial masters and resist being exploited and denigrated.

> We learned from our grandparents that many of the wars fought between Africans and colonial people were often accidental due to misunderstanding. When the colonial people came to South Africa, they just asked for a place to make a home because they did not fight us first. They were polite first; then the king said, anywhere you can build a house. The king of the Zulu did not understand that the colonial mind and the Zulu mind were different as chalk is from cheese. We learned about the greed and viciousness of the colonial mind only much later. We began to understand how we were I and were victims of colonial exploitation. We were innocent, but we learned that we need to be wise enough to know others' evil intentions so that we resist being exploited.

Learning from historical mistakes is how Africans will regain confidence and lasting freedom from colonial misery and depravation. Describing the historical situation of women having high status in Africa, Mutua indicated that the bitter lessons of colonial exploitation and abuse couldn't be overcome without strong self-esteem and pride in their culture. He advocates the belief that education is the key to transformation and self-development. Learning from the aftermath of colonialism helped the natives to remerge in greater strength to claim their place in the human civilization and it took the spiritual awakening of their soul force to overcome obstacles and crisis to create new opportunities of freedom and growth from within and stop the colonial exploitation down the road:

> Women had high status in African society and enjoyed enormous power and authority. In those days, our women had the power of buying and selling, and black women-owned all the farms all over the Transvaal. Then, there came a new law by the colonialists where women lost the right over the land overnight. The colonialists took over the grounds. We were angry, and some of us thought about fighting. Great African John Dube called us and told us, "Do not be stupid. You cannot defeat the white man in a battle". They have already created a new kind of Africans, Africans without self-confidence, Africans without identity. There is no way to win your land unless you regain your self-esteem and confidence. You will rescue them and begin fighting for your lasting freedom and independence with education. Even though your body is broken, your soul is not defeated. You have an unbeaten soul. We are trying our best to learn from our historical mistakes.

These leaders consider failure and success not as opposites but as polarities because one can see the interconnection between them. Through a shift in awareness, they discovered their true worth and significance. Questioning and exploration, the spiritual search happens from the perspective of someone who made plenty of mistakes along the way showing willingness to discover new dimensions of life. Polarities are ongoing and chronic between two point of views that are co-existing like breathing in and breathing out. The genius of learning from polarities is to learn the benefits of both sides and challenges of both perspectives. With reflective understanding, one can uncover insights from failures and rebuild the life one is called to be. Thurston learned to reconcile the opposites by gaining insight into her traumatic childhood experiences and learning to integrate them. She disclosed her process of embracing the shadow by holding the paradox of life:

> I met with Francis Sterns; she was a Jungian psychologist; I said I was supposed to be learning about the reconciliation of the opposites. She said I know about that because it is a Jungian thing. So, she taught me how to process. In other words, I learned about the Ego, the shadow, my weakness, and the polarities and how to work with them; it was psychological, but she was very spiritually oriented. The law of contradiction lets us know

> that we have *failed* in our lives; we can also expect to uncover *success* in those failures also.

Abbot Phap Son spoke of how he and his community support each other to learn from one another's mistakes and grow as a community of enlightened seekers. A strong learning community sets the ambience for life-giving and uplifting experiences necessary to advance an individual and a whole community. This is done through reflective dialogue, active listening, and personal commitment. He cited a learning process, *beginning anew,* which is done in a safe and trusting environment. This process of "beginning anew" starts with a positive approach of appreciating the individuals in the community and thus creating a safe environment to discuss deeper issues of conflict or disagreement to arrive at a create solution that helps both the individual and the community at large. True learning happens in an atmosphere of compassion, deep listening, and respectful dialogue:

> The elements of the beginning anew-learning process are: The first step is watering the good seeds. That means giving feedback about the beautiful qualities of the other. Even simple things, like telling the other person that you have a beautiful smile, are essential. Secondly, express regret for the mistakes you have made. When mistakes happen, and you express regret as quickly as possible to begin anew, you take care of your interpretations but bring up your perceptions out in the open; otherwise, it can go deeper and become a more significant conflict. Such a practice will create a rich soil for good seeds to grow in the community. Usually, one person may share; we try not to interpret but speak lovingly. There is a bell master monitoring such sharing to create a safe environment. If we have any difficulty, we need not share it in the community first, but we can share it one-to-one for learning and healing. We as a community help each other learn from mistakes and grow gradually.

Similarly, Abbess Pema spoke about a Buddhist personal learning practice of beginning anew, especially from one's failures. Although it is excruciating to receive open feedback about one's failures, in a climate of trust, the growth and transformation began to occur gradually. Moreover, in the community context, when there are interpersonal difficulties or misunderstandings, the beginning of the anew-learning process is constructive to restore and renew relationships. Learning through feedback is a healthy process of recognizing the flaws and rectifying it with a healthy sense of self-esteem and affirming the positive aspects of personal learning and spiritual growth.

> For me, beginning a new-learning process is what I do all the time, or once a week; it is a continuous process. I become especially aware of it when I am stuck in an idea, feeling, or concept. It creates space within, beginning anew in specific interactions when I lose my freedom and hurt others unknowingly or knowingly. As soon as I became aware of it, I expressed my regret for my mistakes in renewing my relationship with others. Some can push your button all the time. I can say something to the sister, but that is the beginning of the learning but not the end. In the practice of relationships, beginning anew is the essential process of change. If I am aware of the nature and the effect of the interactions, I can deal with them much better. If I see my interaction has not helped me to touch the spiritual dimension or the sisters are not happy with me, I make a change. If I make a change, I can already learn about the shift happening in others. Learning to begin anew is a way to grow spiritually.

Rowling (2022: 3) noted the invaluable benefits of failure as a true gift and how she climbed out of poverty and failure to become the world's richest author. When she treated failure as a friend, she discovered the gems hidden on the other side of failure, true success. The failures in life have taught her about the right priorities in life based on her passion for literature and gift of writing to bring out the best and contribute to the humanity the best from her soul.

> Failure taught me things about myself that I could have learned no other way. I had discovered that I had a strong will, and more disciplined than I suspected. I also found out that I had friends whose value was truly above the price of rubies. The knowledge that you have emerged wiser and stronger from setbacks means that you are, ever after, secure in your ability to survive. The truth is, failure is not your enemy to be dealt with, it is your friend and ally, to be embraced and used to fuel every future effort you make. You will never truly know yourself, or the strength of your relationships, until both have been tested by adversity. Such knowledge is a true gift, for all that it is painfully won, and it has been worth more than any qualification I ever earned. And so rock bottom became the solid foundation on which rebuilt my life.

Cultivating a learning culture in the organization makes it a psychologically safe workplace (Edmondson, 2019). Considering failure as a learning experience help one to embrace life a journey of trial and error. Recognizing the limits and pains and embracing the shadows help one to integrate and heal the imperfect dimensions of life with grace and new strength. This deep sense of learning from failures turns life around from brokenness to wholeness. Hence, those who are showing the willingness to look back at setbacks with a positive frame of mind to learn lessons will experience the comeback in their life.

Considering failure as a learning experience, the leaders showed how they learned crucial lessons from personal losses and historical mistakes in their journey towards personal wholeness. Creating a psychological safe environment for employees to speak up and share their feelings and thoughts candidly paved the way for best learning experience for the organizations. Giving permission to explore and experiment with various scenarios of strategic solutions helped the employees to make calculated risks for the organization. Lessons from the critical moments indicate that they are extraordinary in their ability to sense opportunity in failures and embark on a deeper journey to begin anew. They were able to turn the negative experience of failure into a joyous blessing and a great gift by shifting perspectives. Willingness to learn from failures made the leaders humble and empathize with the suffering humanity. This learning process made them capable of discovering the deeper meaning of life, which they otherwise would not have learned from the mere experience of success.). Maintaining such a learning experience and culture helped the leaders to allow room for others' mistakes developing a spirit of magnanimity, empathetic intelligence, resilient leadership, and authentic living.

Growing in Authenticity

These leaders emphasized living and growing authentically in no uncertain terms. People can live authentically by being honest to themselves, their positive values, interests, and accomplishments, and by acknowledging their failures, weaknesses, and limitations. If people do not live authentically, they have to pay a high price in their journey with the pain of wearing a mask drifting towards pathology. Living a life of self-impersonation (Collins, 2021) has become the order of the day for many leaders today, and therefore to live authentically, people have to walk consciously and intentionally. Focusing on living authentically and stop being carbon copies in life brings out the original vitality, clarity, and creativity it oneself. Leaders demonstrated their progressive growing in the five essential dimensions of authentic leadership—purpose, values, heart, relationships, and self-discipline. Authentic leadership offers inspiring lessons to all who want to lead with heart for those they serve (Blunt, 2022; George, 2004, 2007). A spiritually intelligent leader explores the three courses essential to leading-reflective work that results in a guiding life purpose, learning from the mentors' experiences, and being part of the community of practices that knows together and holds each other accountable. Given that there is a cultural craving and expectation to appear successful all the time, there is a tendency to hide all shame and embarrassment for fear of being judged by society. Leaders in the study demonstrated that living authentically is a sine qua non in their journey towards wholeness. The need for growing in authenticity and the risk of inauthentic life are noted below:

> There is something in the human organism that is hard living falsely. And if you live falsely, you are going to drift towards pathology. May be depression, alcoholism, and may be drugs, sex addiction, false relationship, may be overwork, may be constant stimulation and distraction, some form of anesthetic you are using, and you are reminded that you are not your authentic self. Thomas Merton said this eloquently, boy! It merits reflection; he says, "Most of us live a life of self-impersonation." That is a Biggy, a Biggy; go around and act like who we think we are, rather than acting like us, trying to talk like who we think we should talk like. This self-impersonation partly comes from shame and embarrassment of who I am, and I am trying to pick up signals and what Tom wants me to say or what society expects of me or what my role requires, and how the president should act. You can appear to be suitable by pleasing people. I believe people are afraid of self-revelations. It is true of all areas, not just the academic arena (Palmer).

One of the congresswomen described her struggle to live authentically when her campaign manager wanted her to fake her true self. When society is in a dilemma, it does not wish to counterfeit leaders, but on the other hand, it does not want to hear certain things that true leaders articulate from their authentic selves. The price of authenticity is beyond measure that it brings enormous suffering and pain to the leaders who stand up for values and virtues of greater good of the society. No wonder the great leaders and heroes in the world were willing to lay down their life for the principles and did not compromise their values for the sake of personal safety or self-protection. It takes enormous spiritual stamina and strength to counter the forces of domination and culture which tend to bury the true value of freedom, truth, and authentic living. Sometimes fake leaders appear to be original and do not stand the scrutiny of authenticity in life. It takes great courage and sacrifice to be authentic, stands for the truth in one's life, and be consistent on the path towards wholeness. Palmer described the issue of authenticity in political arena:

> A congresswoman narrated the following to me: "My campaign manager told me, don't ever speak to the reporter again about your weakness that you are immersed in the grief over the loss of your husband. Of course, it is a truth about yourself, but it will make you appear weak in the eyes of the public. If it happens again, I will never be your campaign manager. And I told him, no matter what, you can quit, but I will keep telling the truth." That is a powerful story of the conflict some leaders find themselves in, including the faculty and the board, to be authentic. They are very ambivalent; on the one hand, we don't want fake leaders, but on the other hand, we don't want to hear certain things from leaders that make them human and vulnerable. Yes, the story I am telling you about my life is that there is a danger if you try to live as if you are beyond mistakes. It is a disaster; It is a train wreck. And that is the way some leaders lead their life. It takes courage to be authentic like the Congresswoman; no matter what, you can quit, but I will keep telling the truth (Palmer).

Leaders emphasized that close and trustworthy relationships are crucial for growing in authenticity and authentic life style is necessary to maintain trust and collaboration in the organizations (Yikilmaz & Surucu, 2021). When a person can speak honestly with another person about what is going on in their life, they can hear their authentic voice coming from the depth of their hearts. It is essential to listen to what you are saying, and most of the time, we don't hear what we are saying. It is possible to listen to your authentic voice in the circle of trusted people, for they act as a mirror to your soul. The significance of honest relationships and effective feedback on the road to authentic wholeness cannot be underestimated. On our road to wholeness, we need those relationships where they can speak honestly about their own lives. Of course, what is essential about speaking honestly regarding your own life is not the other person hearing you talking about yourself. Still, in talking about yourself to the other, you get a chance to listen to yourself and what you are saying. Abraham Maslow stated, "Musicians must make music, artists must paint, poets must write if they are to ultimately be at peace with themselves.

What humans can be, they must be. They must be true to their nature" (Grimes, 2022: 1). Growing in authenticity is a gradual process of discovering the inner beauty and strength in the wake of adversities (Monzani et al., 2019). In the traditional systems of Africa, Mutua observed that people valued honesty and authentic living as core values of the culture. Even if someone committed wrongdoing, it was voluntarily reported to the Chief as a way of taking responsibility for their actions.

> The traditional system in Africa has laws with no need for enforcement. For example, if an African did some wrong, let us say, in the conventional situation, have stolen, he would go to the Chief and report it himself, even if the Chief is not aware of it. I did hear stories; about a group of Zulu young men who did something seriously wrong to King Dinka's wife. After running away hiding amongst the missionaries in Durban, eight of them came back and reported themselves to the Chief; they knew that they could be ordered to be executed for their betrayal. King Dinka immediately ordered their execution. These young men had known that they would be executed. Such great honesty and taking responsibility for their wrongdoing was the culture of the Ancient Africans (Mutua).

Emphasizing the importance of manifesting one self and acting from the true core of being, Sri Sri advocated that actual fulfillment cannot be gained without living an authentic life. "Life without wisdom is incomplete; wisdom that does not give rise to feeling and action is incomplete. Action that does not give rise to fulfillment is incomplete. Fulfillment is relating to your true self" (Sri Sri). "Positive energy that is unleashed when leaders give themselves permission to connect and express themselves from the core of who they are. Creativity, engagement, confidence, and a sense of inner resourcefulness emerge when they practice authenticity" (Inam, 2015: 2). In practicing constructive community living, Abbess Pema acknowledged that there is no better way to live life than being honest with oneself. The key to happiness and wholeness is being true to oneself both personally and in community living. The monks in the monastery call it a "practice of shining light," creating an atmosphere of transparency to be vulnerable and honor the gift of growing pains.

> I noticed the more honest myself, the more I see. Sometimes I am not ready to acknowledge, the more I see, the more I can admit, and I can be happier. We have a practice of shining light; we say where our habit energies are and share it with others with excellent transparency and honesty

> to shine a light on one's growing pains. No one can be happy living falsely (Abbess Pema).

Abbot Phap Son emphasized that one couldn't hide from the true self for very long in no uncertain terms. Being authentic is a hallmark of leading a life of wholeness (Price, 2005). "You cannot hide who you are and what you do for long." "The four-paned "window" divides personal awareness into four different types, as represented by its four quadrants: open, blind, hidden, and unknown (Blunt, 2022). So, when you open your mouth or do action, your being is involved. You can see a person is whole or not." While doing healing ministry as a massage therapist, Sister Gefre witnessed the power of authenticity in healing when people broke down on the massage table and opened up their pain of leading dishonest lives:

> I learned that people are hurt; I had my private ideas and bias that people with money could buy anything. So, I had spiritually impoverished but wealthy people as my clients. One of the first people who came to me was an owner of a bus company, a woman. So many people used to break down on the massage table. Finally, she broke down on the massage table and wept; here is the woman who got what she wanted. I thought these people had everything, but they were not living truly from their hearts and thus lived with a lot of distress and sadness. And when they were honest with themselves, they broke down and disclosed their brokenness, which helped with healing both her body and soul. Living holistically means living from the heart.

The power of authenticity is experienced when both the client and the consultant are sincere and open to each other and venerable for growth in authenticity. "Pretentiousness repels, but authenticity attracts, and vulnerability is the pathway to intimacy" (Warren 2002, p. 276). "A company's purpose needs to be based on a fundamental truth – this entails looking into the company's very soul and trying to extract the essence of why you exist. It's about standing up for what you believe in, not about standing out" (Massen, 2022: 4). Sister Gefre shared her experience of helping people grow in authenticity and experience great healing in body and soul:

> You must be in tune with the heart of the client while you massage by sincerely listening to people. When they open their heart, you hear, and you love them; something is happening even in the way you touch people.

> If you are sincere in your love and honestly care for people, naturally, they open up their life, and personal trust proliferates. One day a client came, and after counseling and massage, it was like his whole life had changed; he didn't have to put on a face, put on a body language, and became soft and sincere, being true to himself. I remember there was a time when I went after this wishy-washy stuff, but you know it's empty. Only the Lord gives us that sense of fear for the real and not just for life's wishy- washy things. That is what I mean when I say people are God hungry or spirit hungry and some may not be aware.
>
> Living in ignorance of the beauty of spiritual life makes people go after worldly things.

A sense of fearlessness and courage is essential to living an authentic life when one is confronted with opposition and obstacles. Living authentically doesn't always mean a life of comfort and bliss. Often it means just the opposite. When we show our true selves to the world, when we dare to live our dreams, we might just run into many obstacles we didn't expect. We might experience ridicule. We might find that our authentic life isn't what we expected at all. It can lead to sleepless nights and tensions, but eventually it's all worth the pursuit for the sake of growing authentically which brings greater joy and sense of deep fulfillment. Sister Gefre gave testimony to her courage and confidence in doing what she felt right in her heart despite the adversities along the way of her pioneering massage ministry in the United States of America:

> I no longer care about what people think about me. When I feel right in my heart, I have no fear. That fearlessness helps you break through the prejudices about massage as a dirty business to a beautiful healing ministry. I learned that people might judge me in poor light, but God knows my heart. That is so nice, my heart is open and vulnerable, and people know who I am because I hug them openly. I embrace both men and women during conferences in universities, churches, prisons, or my clinic. I am open from my heart. With all this publicity and growth, I still live a simple, humble life, and I make sure that nothing gets into my head. I am still a farmer's daughter; I know my roots. As Saint Margaret Mary says, "we are who we are, and God loves us very much as we are."

While surviving the onslaughts of the Rwandan genocide and deprivation, Ilibagiza spoke about the importance of being honest and authentic is not deserving something she did not work for. Brown (2020) noted, "Authenticity is the daily practice of letting go of who we think we're supposed to be and embracing who we are." Choosing authenticity means cultivating the courage to acknowledge the imperfectness, to set boundaries, and to allow ourselves to be vulnerable; exercising the compassion that comes from knowing that we are all made of strength and weakness; and nurturing the connection and sense of belonging that can only happen when we believe that we are enough. In addition, authenticity demands wholehearted living and loving—even when it's hard, even when we're wrestling with the shame and fear of not being good enough, and especially when the joy is so intense that we're afraid to let ourselves feel it. Mindfully "practicing authenticity during our most soul-searching struggles is how we invite grace, joy, and gratitude into our lives" (Brown, 2020). Realizing that we are not a finished product but a work in progress unfolding the goodness and greatness of our being and the weakness and imperfections, Ilibagiza described how she found inner courage and strength to admit that she is imperfect and learn to be venerable and authentic; being true to herself even in little things:

> While we had the food that Major Ntwali had supplied us within the refugee camp, we had no money, and after months of wear and tear, our clothes were practically worn to threads. So, we went to abandoned homes looking for shoes and new things to wear. In one house, I found a pair of gold earrings. I convinced myself that I deserved something pretty to make me feel good after all I'd been through, and I put them in my pocket. But I couldn't bear my reflection when I tried them on in front of a mirror at Aloise's. All I could see was the face of the woman who had owned them. The earrings didn't belong to me and held none of my memories; someone else had worked hard for them or had received them as a loving gift. I felt like a trespasser in another person's life. I didn't want possessions I hadn't earned and didn't deserve, so I took the earrings to where I'd found them the next day.

These leaders testified to the fact of growing in authenticity and inner freedom and were deeply aware cost of authentic leadership. Living authentically means having a heart full of courage and fearlessness to stand for truth at all cost. Even when leaders happen to commit mistakes, they are honest in admitting the mistakes and taking responsibility for their actions to grow in authenticity and greatness. Authentic leaders learn to lead with a heart of wisdom and compassion, and courage. The power of authenticity is manifested in wholehearted living, loving, and engaging in a fragmented world with grace, vulnerability, and courage. A sense of fulfillment and deep life satisfaction is intrinsically connected to the practice of integrity and authenticity. Jung famously noted, "The privilege of a lifetime is to become who you truly are" (quoted in Srechinth, 2022). Growing in authenticity takes a lifetime of learning and discovery. "Because true belonging only happens when we present our authentic, imperfect selves to the world, our sense of belonging can never be greater than our level of self-acceptance" (Brene, 2015: 145). These leaders gave witness to the fact that being true to oneself is indeed a hallmark of the spiritual vibrancy in their the journey towards wholeness.

Matching Soul and Role

Leaders in the study recognized the importance of integrating the soul and role, aligning who they are with what they do. When the soul and the role are not incorporated into leadership, the parts are just external skeletons. Therefore, they do not recognize the intrinsic relationship between internal values and outer behavior. This gap leads to inner conflicts and fragmentation. A conscious and intentional way of declaring values and integrating actions helped these leaders rejoin the soul and role to experience greater joy and satisfaction. Integrating souls, systems, and society is the need of the hour to find solutions to the divide we experience between self and other self, self and nature, self and the higher self, the social crisis, ecological crisis, and ethical crisis of today. Rowson's (2017: 2) research organization, *Perspectiva,* examines how social change happens across "systems, souls, and society." "If we can get better and more nimble and more generous about how we move between those worlds, then the chance of creating a hope that makes sense for all of us is all the greater," he says. Engaging his broad spiritual lens on the great dynamics of our time, from social life to the economy to the climate, he envisages to integrate the souls, systems, and society. For leaders who are already learning to live from the actual depth of their being, integrating soul and function is a matter of grounding their current activities with greater insight, values, and wisdom. Every moment and every event of my life has an imprint on my soul. Palmer noted, "The interconnectedness of our inner life of spirit with that of the outer life of action is important for an authentic life." Palmer reflected on his work of helping people rejoin souls and roles in his retreat circles:

> The work I do with the circles of trust is to help people rejoin their souls and role. That is the language we use from the perspective of wholeness. If we look at the individual and their journey, you asked about my journey. We start without knowing who we are, and we don't know our souls very well. Tiny children understand what their soul is, but as we grow older, we get distanced from it; from that knowledge very quickly, we often go into early middle age and maybe later middle age still not with much self-knowledge. What you do during that time, I think we all do in an inchoate, a need to articulate; we need an identity, where is it come from? Let us look around and find a role that makes me examine what I want to look like. Or do I enjoy being who I am and playing my role?

The path to the realization of the purpose is never straightforward. The important thing is never to lose sight of the ultimate goal while engaging in business enterprise. You cannot wait for a universal consensus before moving forward with a complex initiative, although you aim to build consensus with authentic engagement. Moving forward is often what helps to bring everything into focus and, ultimately, the soul and the role. There is a real need to articulate one's identity and match the doing according to one's values. Palmer recalled that mere identification with his positions did not give him meaning and fulfillment. Still, he ended up in crisis and situational depression as he was leading a divided life:

> This is[what] I call extra skeleton… you are propping yourself from outside, gaining an identity from the role you adorn. So, I am a professor; I am an executive, a money-making machine, or whatever, I am a social do-gooder, I am a social reformer, or I am a man of faith or whatever, a woman of faith. There are all kinds of roles we put on when we don't know who we are. It seems to give us a sense of who we are. Then there are these whitewater crisis times; you have to find something more profound than that of roles, for the positions do not sustain you anymore. I mean, I was in deep depression when I was a successful author, a much sought-after speaker, I had a million friends, and I was making an income; all did not help; the role did not help me. It doesn't save you from the darkness. What role does not give you is survivability unless you want to anesthetize yourself. So, for me, it is again a question of survivability. When my soul and role were this far [apart] (shows his hands far apart), it was a question of survivability. Depression was the manifestation of the divided life I was leading.

Integrating the soul and role from the point of view of an individual journey is a question of survival. People explore the soul differently; some understand the soul as identity and integrity. Some others describe it in spiritual and religious terms as consciousness or divine self. Integrating the soul and role will help the leaders to gain perspective of the world from a macro-point of view and will enable them to set policies and priorities that help to align the spirit, strategy, structure, and services in organizations. This holistic perspective is not realized unless the leaders are able to match their soul with the role, internalizing the values and the inner world with that of the outer world. It takes arduous search and persistence to discover the soul amid many distractions and messy life.

> Man does not live by role alone but by the soul. And so, you come to a place where you have to start understanding your soul, identity, and integrity, who you are, your truth, in whatever term you want to name it. And then find ways to manifest that in the world as roles. Some people find patterns as they come in touch with soul or truth; they see where it is, manifest that soul more fully in the position they are already playing. I was asked to be a university president, but I felt that did not match my soul. I am called to be a peace activist and a traveling teacher. Now I can fill that role with more integrity and authenticity. Other people find what they have learned about themselves. Thinking from the soul's point of view, they can manifest it differently. And that is the individual journey for those who are conscious without anesthetizing or distracting themselves. And, of course, our society offers millions of anesthetics and distractions so that the people need not worry about themselves (Palmer).

When leaders began to align their souls and roles, a positive life force emerged with more energy, enthusiasm, and ease. This alignment of soul and role takes place gradually, and greater integration and convergence of soul-lane and role-lane will happen, resulting in feeling more confidence and harmony. The duality and the polarization of life happen when there is no alignment of the soul and the role one is playing in the society. The coherence of intentions and actions, purpose and strategies helps to address the rising sense of division and chaos in organizations and society. This work of coherence building and integration is a gradual process since there are many systems that need to converge with a greater sense of wholeness (Yang et al., 2019). There is an inherent capacity for wholeness in every being and matching the soul and role will pave the way for greater sense of integration.

> When you are aligning your soul and role, the life force begins to take charge; then you are working to bring your life to more alignment with truth. Then there is a feedback mechanism, and then you start feeling better. This is interesting; I am doing my work with more energy, I am doing my work with more confidence, and I am writing better books because I am writing from what I directly know, not to some mythical audience that somehow, they want. And so, there is slow convergence, but it is not all straight lines like that. We need to go through many detours and tours. I think the oscillation of the two lines, the soul-line and the role line comes closer moving this way. Again, I don't imagine that I will ever come to a convergence ideally. I can't imagine what they would look like. Christians believe that Jesus manifested fully human and fully divine; fully God and complete man. I think that we all have that capacity for wholeness. I think that is what it means you are created in God's image and likeness, a little lower than the angels and a little higher than the beasts. We have that duality and unity in us; it constantly oscillates (Palmer).

Swami Veda stated that by doing personal meditative practices, people could integrate their souls and roles, and they can journey towards wholeness. With such personal experience of consciousness and spiritual awakening through meditation and spiritual practices, a greater sense of harmony and peace will arise, and everything becomes integrated. This is easy said than done, for it takes personal commitment and consistent practices to gain the level of integration and wholeness to go beyond the experiences of fragmentation and restlessness in the soul.

> The core of it all is meditation. Without that personal experience of wholeness in meditation, all the different parts of the brain do not become integrated, and the 10,000 wars going on under the continent called skull declare a one-hour truce, then there are no divisions; because that experience reinforces a sense of wholeness. It has to be a personal experience, not a theory, lecture, philosophy; not a reading; that wholeness, the entire cosmos, all its galaxies, the particle of dust, all little waves and ripples in the ocean of consciousness everything becomes integrated. Paradoxically when you look into your mind, you see nothing, see everything in its fullness (Swami Veda).

As the modern society puts more emphasis on material progress without cultivating spiritual resourcefulness, Sri Sri advocated that a healthy balance between material progress and spiritual advancement would pave the way for integrating soul and role. Through a three-step process of waking up, growing up, and wising up, humanity can need to find new level of integration; learning to shape culture and design institutions with ecological sensitivity, technological insight, and spiritual sensibility" says Rowson (2017: 4). This is the new path towards integration of science and spirituality as Sri Sri noted:

> Modern society puts a lot of demand on our time and resources for material progress and affluence. But, at the same time, spirituality gives enthusiasm and a sense of confidence to face the pressures modern society poses. The two together make life pleasant, vibrant, and satisfying. That is how one can find harmony with who you are and what you do.

Sri Sri also insisted that matching soul and role is possible by living in the moment and allowing your deeper self to be free from the past hurts and attachments. Maintaining a sense of deeper self-awareness helps the leaders to integrate their soul and role consistently. Living in the moment helps us be grounded in the now, aligning what you are with what you do; the being and doing are synchronized without effort when you can match your soul and your role.

> Let go of each moment as it passes; forgive others, especially yourself. Let go of all the judgments and blame and learn to pursue and honor the Divine who dwells in you and the other. The Divine is free of all responsibility, and that is how all are at the core of our being. Living in the moment will help you align what you are with what you do (Sri Sri).

Archbishop Flynn noted that his calling as a priest and a spiritual leader has been highly satisfying; he felt that his soul-aligned very well with what he was doing. His sense of personal integrity and wholesome identity has helped him face severe challenges with poise and endurance. Daily practice of silence and solitude helps him focus his life on serving God and humanity. Doing the right thing helped him stand up for justice issues despite opposition and resistance. But discerning doing the right stuff was the way Archbishop Flynn learned to match his soul and role as a spiritual leader. "When I was taking a stand for justice issues, people misunderstood me; I learned to stand my ground, even though I have fragile skin, for I felt I was doing the right thing." "Doing the right thing is the key to matching one's soul and role. It demonstrates a high level of integrity and ethical responsibility in the wake of adversity" (Palanski, 2017). The individuation process consists of purifying, refining, and integrating our otherwise diffuse, preoccupied, and fragmented existence into a wholesome living and engagement. Having the courage to stand up for one's values and conviction is critical to matching soul and role. Sister Gefre was able to face all the adversities in her profession with stability and moral integrity when she focused on doing the right thing:

> I know I cried and cried a lot those days. Facing ridicule, opposition, and resistance was tricky, but I knew in my heart that I was doing the right thing. I knew I had to change the perception of massage from that of prostitution; from its public shame. That firm conviction helped me to overcome all the odds and move forward. And today massage therapy is a healing ministry. Adversity is the testing ground of faith, and if you do the right thing, you will never lose sleep over it.

Carolyn Washburn, the former Chief Editor of the Des Moines Register, was tested in the wildfire of public opinion in the print media, significantly moderating two presidential debates in the United States. Still, she stood firm, asking the right questions to manifest the mind of the politicians who claim to stand for public interest and serve the common good. She noted, "Ability to take bold decisions knowing intuitively what the right thing to do" helped her to match her soul and role at the right moment. Mary Chind of the Des Moines Register won a 2010 Pulitzer Prize for Breaking News Photography. She won for her photograph of the moment before a rescuer, dangling in a makeshift harness, saves a woman trapped in the foaming water beneath a dam. Carolyn had to make a bold and unusual decision to use the top half of the new paper to publish this fantastic picture knowing intuitively that it was the right thing to do without realizing that it would win the top prize. Carolyn also pointed out that there were excruciating moments of decision-making and moral dilemmas about whether to publish empathetic stories like the suicide of a student that happened in a public school, which resulted in negative public opinion even though the news was already out in public. She decided based on the journalistic principle of transparency and public accountability. American Press Institute (Silverman, 2022: 4) states, "If journalists are truth seekers, it must follow that they are honest and truthful with their audiences, too that they are truth presenters." Mutua advocated a deeper soul searching to reform our life and society, for one can quickly stop being good, and instead, self-centered desires and greed can drive one. The soul needs to be cleansed of egocentric pursuits to align it with the external roles:

> People want to care, but they are not given a chance to care. People want to be well, but they are not allowed to be well. People want to be friends, but they are not allowed to be so. What stops people from being good; is their love of gain, money, and greed. We need to realize that we are not who we think we are. We are not the owners of us. Linking who we are with what we do is crucial to reforming our lives (Mutua).

Abbess Pema noted that harmonizing the being and doing is how she brings joy and peace to the people around her. Being aware of one's thoughts, feelings, and presence, one can integrate what one is inside with what one is outside. The integration of belief, behavior, and business paves way of greater harmony and peace in daily life. When one notices disharmony between ones being and doing, it is important to engage in self-examination to repair and find new balance. The integrity of her life is the hallmark of her witness, and that is how her community reaches people who reach others:

> As a community, Plum Village has been called a village of peace. Many people visit here, and when they go home, they feel calm. Through teaching and our presence, we reach people who reach other people. Some of us would like to do some charity work. But we feel it is better to reach the people who do charitable work. Thai always says that walking the talk is how we get people interested in us. Harmonizing our being and doing brings joy and peace. While I was on a train, a woman came to me and said, "You are the most peaceful person sitting on the train." It is heartening to receive such feedback. I thought, no wonder Gandhi said, "The rose does not preach except by its fragrance." The peace and wholeness within you manifest themselves naturally.

Integrating who you are with what you do is a continuous process for these leaders. Abbot Phap Son believed that constant striving to see your true self helps you match soul and role through various moments of life journey. A firm determination allows people to integrate and align their values and actions. This is an evolutionary process of the human psyche to grow in greater authenticity and integration of who you are with what you do. Self-integration is a continuous and progressive journey all through one's life:

> When I was in Bodhgaya, India, I saw myself in light of the journey of Buddha. In Bodhgaya, each stage of Buddha's life is depicted. It mirrors my trip, there are many obstacles when you try to realize your wholeness, and these obstacles mark the journey. There is a considerable determination to see your true self. The constant striving helps you know who you are and how it matches what you do.

These leaders knew the importance of integrating the soul and role for an authentic life and continuing their quest for wholeness. This integration was made possible through trustworthy relationships, self-knowledge, and genuine dialogue. They found that meditative practices and reflection paved the way for internalizing values and integrating who they are with what they do. Discernment of truth in the wake of false claims and ideologies is very important to maintain the integrity of the soul and leadership role one is entrusted with. These leaders recognized that identifying with the external role alone, without integrating their core values, led to crisis and emptiness in life. On the other hand, living through the crisis and adversities helped them recognize the significance of nurturing and integrating their values with external behavior. Congruence between the intrinsic desire to serve and the extrinsic desire to make a profit and climb up the promotion ladder ethically (Witesman, 2021). They experienced the positive effects of harmony, high energy, and flow when they matched their soul and role. The second essential theme, *Embracing Crisis*, describes the process of leaders' inner journey towards wholeness. The subtheme and elements are presented for an enhanced understanding of leaders' lived experience of the journey that demonstrated ethical intelligence in tune with their spiritual intelligence.

The leaders in the study recognized that embracing crisis in their journey towards wholeness is of paramount importance. Leaders manifested deeper awareness and a fundamental level of self-acceptance to learn from their failures and weaknesses and turn them into the alchemy of inner transformation. They understood that wholeness is not just success or strengths alone, but weakness and failures are part and parcel of the journey towards wholeness. They demonstrated the ability to hold the paradox of power and shadow in their journey towards greater wholeness. A profound shift in consciousness happened when they embraced their shadows, which broadened the base of their life and deepened the roots of understanding. Living a life of authenticity and integrity helped leaders embrace life fully and integrate who they are with what they do. These leaders showed the remarkable resilience of spirit in embracing the whole of their life with its light and shadow, which resulted in the experience of more incredible vibrancy, harmony, and integration.

References

Allio, R. J. (2008). In the crucibles: Robert J. Thomas explains how leaders learn. *Strategy and Leadership, 36*(5), 4–8.

Bells, S. J. (2019). Learning from the crucible moments: Lessons in crisis leadership. *Library Leadership and Management, 33*(2), 1–9.

Blunt, R. (2022). *Leadership in the crucible: The paradox of character and power* (govleaders.org). Retrieved on March 18, 2022, from https://govleaders.org/crucible.htm

Brene, B. (2020). *The gifts of imperfection.* Random House.

Brene, B. (2015). Daring greatly: How the courage to be vulnerable transforms the way we live, love, parent and lead. Hudson. Penguin Random House.

Chadwick, H. (2008). *Saint Augustine, confession, a new translation.* Oxford University Press Inc.

Chappell, S., Cooper, E., & Trippe, G. (2019). Shadow work for leadership development. *Journal of Management Development, 38*(5), 326–335. https://doi.org/10.1108/JMD-08-2018-0216

Collins, P. W. (2021). *A focus on the truth: Thomas Merton's uncensored mind.* Liturgical Press.

Edmondson, A. (2019). *The fearless organization: Creating psychological safety in the workplace for learning, innovation, and growth.* HBS.

Foster, J. (2017). *The deepest acceptance: Radical awakening in ordinary life.* Sounds True Publishing.

Fosu, K. (2022, March). Shadow work: A simple guide to transcending the darker aspects of yourself. *Medium.* Retrieved on from https://medium.com/big-self-society/shadow-work-a-simple-guide-to-transcending-the-darker-aspects-of-the-self-e948ee285723.

George, B. (2004). The journey to authenticity. *Leader-to-Leader, 31*, 29–35.

George, B. (2007). *True north.* Jossey-Bass.

Grimes, S. (2022, March). *What man can be, he must be.* Retrieved from https://medium.com/the-1000-day-mfa/. Abraham Maslow.

Hollnagel E. (2022). Systemic potentials for resilient performance. In F. Matos, P. M. Selig, & E. Henriqson (Eds.), Resilience in a digital age. *Contributions to Management Science*, Springer. https://doi.org/10.1007/978-3-030-85954-1_2

Inam, H. (2015). *Wired for authenticity: Seven practices to inspire, adapt and lead.* iUniverse.

Molen, J. (2018). "I keep being drawn towards Jung": Good and evil in the work of Etty Hillesum and Carl Gustav Jung. In J. Wiersma, G. Van Oord, & K. Smelik (Eds.), *Reading Etty Hillesum in context: Writings, life, and influences*

of a visionary author (pp. 227–244). Amsterdam University Press. https://doi.org/10.1017/9789048533428.011
Monzani, L., Knoll, M., Glessner, S., Van Dick, R., & Peiro, J. (2019). Between a rock and a hard place: Combined effects of authentic Leadership, organizational identification, and team prototypicality on managerial prohibitive voice. *The Spanish Journal of Psychology, 22*, E2. https://doi.org/10.1017/SJP.2019.1
Palanski M. (2017) Leadership integrity. In D. Poff & A. Michalos (Eds.), *Encyclopedia of business and professional ethics*. Springer. https://doi.org/10.1007/978-3-319-23514-1_62-1
Price, T. (2005). The ethics of authentic transformational Leadership. In Understanding ethical failures in Leadership. *Cambridge Studies in Philosophy and Public Policy* (pp. 123–146). Cambridge University Press.
Panteha, F., Pouya, Z., Vildan, E., & Asim, V. (2021). Linking Spiritual leadership and boundary-spanning behavior: The bright side of workplace spirituality and self-esteem. *SAGE Open July-September, 2021*, 1–12. https://doi.org/10.1177/21582440211040775
Prigatano, G., & Sherer, M. (2020). Impaired self-awareness and denial during the postacute phases after moderate to severe traumatic brain injury. *Frontiers in Psychology*. https://doi.org/10.3389/fpsyg.2020.01569
Rooke, D., & Torbert, W. (2002, August). Retrieved from https://hbr.org/2005/04/seven-transformations-of-leadership
Rowling, R. K. (2022, June). *The Fringe benefits of failure and the importance of imagination*. Retrieved from https://news.harvard.edu/gazette/story/2008/06/text-of-j-k-rowling-speech/
Rowson, J. (2017, November). Retrieved from https://medium.com/perspectiva-institute/waking-up-growing-up-and-wising-up-the-hidden-curriculum-of-the-21st-century-5ec659ebf198
Schein, E., & Senge, P. (2018). *Humble leadership: The power of relationships, openness, and trust*. Berret-Koehler Publisher Inc.
Silverman, C. (June, 2022). *The best way for Publishers to build credibility is through transparency*. Retrieved from https://www.americanpressinstitute.org/publications/reports/strategy-studies/transparency-credibility/
Srechinth, C. (2022, March). Retrieved from https://www.google.com/books/edition/Musings_of_Carl_Jung/
Stinissen, W. (2011). *Into your hands, father: Abandoning ourselves to the God who loves us*. Ignatius Press.
Townes, C. (2022, August). *Science and religion*. Retrieved from https://www.ctns.org/research/journal
Witesman, E. M. (2021). Values and motivation: An introduction. In H. Sullivan, H. Dickinson, & H. Henderson (Eds.), *The Palgrave handbook of the public*

servant. Palgrave Macmillan. https://doi.org/10.1007/978-3-030-29980-4_102

Yang, F., Liu, J., Wang, Z., & Zhang, Y. (2019). Feeling energized: A multi-level model of spiritual Leadership, leader integrity, relational energy, and job performance. *Journal of Business Ethics, 158*(4), 983–997.

Yikilmaz, I., & Surucu, L. (2021). Leader-member exchange as a mediator of the relationship between authentic Leadership and employee creativity. *Journal of Management & Organization*, 1–14.https://doi.org/10.1017/jmo.2021.23

CHAPTER 5

Awakening Hidden Wholeness

Leaders in the research study experienced an unfolding of the hidden dimension of wholeness throughout their inner journey and spiritual awakening through personal spiritual practices. The awakening of inner consciousness resulted in the transformation of the mind and ego, and it helped them broaden their vision and perspectives of life. The third essential theme, ***awakening hidden wholeness***, describes these leaders' profound inner transformation and discovery journey. The sub-themes present a deeper understanding of the top spiritual leaders' inner journey, as presented in Fig. 5.1: Awakening Hidden Wholeness.

The leaders experienced deep peace, harmony, and a heightened sensitivity as a result of such spiritual re-generation and the emergence of spiritual intelligence. Cultivating quietness and solitude within, the leaders were able to access a state of pure awareness and layers of consciousness. Spiritual practices such as meditation, mindfulness, and introspection led them to a realization of a new purpose and direction in their life. They called such transformation ego-transformation, awakened consciousness, and higher self-leading to an awakening of hidden wholeness. A new awareness made them capable of discovering new power and potentiality: they became very compassionate, caring, and altruistic forgoing self-interest and egocentric patterns of life. A sense of spiritual transformation, awareness, and awakening from within helped them to realize that the

T. Thakadipuram, *Leadership Wholeness, Volume 1*,
Palgrave Studies in Workplace Spirituality and Fulfillment,
https://doi.org/10.1007/978-3-031-08053-1_5

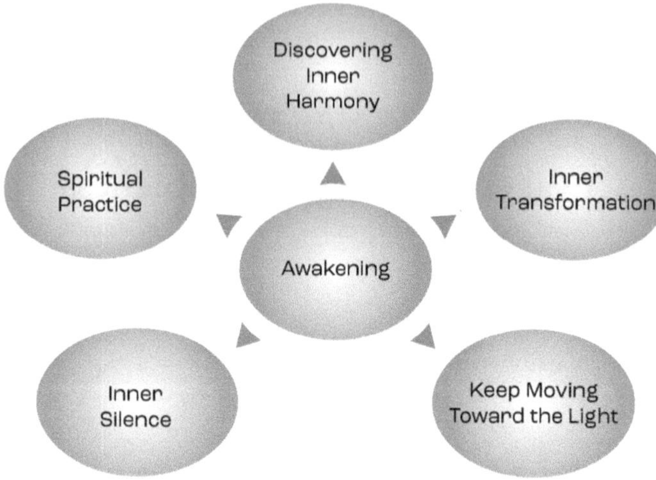

Fig. 5.1 Awakening Hidden Wholeness

journey towards wholeness as a life-long adventure. Carl Jung (quoted in Sreechinth, 2022: 18) claimed, "The person who looks outward dreams, the person who looks inward awakens." These leaders realized that the path towards wholeness is non-linear, with an iterative process of trial and error, falling and getting up, awakening and re-awakening. For several of them, the unfolding of the ultimate dimension of Being was a gradual process and not a sudden awakening. The leaders believed that this potential for spiritual wakening and wholeness is possible for every human being willing to embrace a path of introspection, reflective awareness, and mindfulness while holding the paradoxes of life. Similarly, there are four levels of awakening practiced by the Buddhism which results in the gradual purification of mind by embracing the path of mindfulness. The four levels are: entering the stream of spiritual discipline, freedom from desires of lust, greed, and delusion, path of detachment and the path of inner freedom (Anālayo, 2021a). The five dimensions of the awakening of the hidden wholeness are: cultivating spiritual practice, inner silence, inner transformation, igniting the soul, and discovering hidden harmony. These five aspects of the spiritual awakening process will be presented in this chapter.

Cultivating Spiritual Practice

The leaders cultivated spiritual practices in their journey towards wholeness. These spiritual practices ranged from mindfulness meditation, yoga practices, prayer, walking in nature, journaling and support groups. Practicing reflective awareness of their actions and interior dispositions, the leaders gained deeper insight and wisdom, freedom, and great perspective of life. The habit of meditative awareness helped them to discover the pattern of their habit energies and mental formations, which otherwise would not have been revealed to them in the busy circumstances of their lives. Awareness and attentiveness were the keys to the transformation of mind and its recurring habits. A deep sense of awareness or mindfulness helped the leaders penetrate through the illusions of life and focus their spiritual energy on more productive purposes. Gupta and Reina (2022) emphasized the cultivation of mindfulness in leadership that influences the followers' outcomes in a significant way. Snyder (as cited in Leighton, 2003) noted, "Practically speaking, a life vowed to simplicity, appropriate boldness, good humor, gratitude, unstinting work and play, and lots of walking brings us close to the existing world and its wholeness." Zenoff (2013) noted that taking care of one's soul requires a certain amount of quality time for reflection and appreciation regularly. The leaders recognized the thought loops that pulled them into adverse reactions and emotional turmoil with their reflective practice and deeper awareness. An awareness of their inner self and core values helped the leaders to maintain poise and a sense of purpose in moments of crisis and chaos. Abbot Phap Son described reflective awareness as *mindfulness*. Keeping focused on mindfulness helps to gain insight and inner freedom. Meditative awareness is a sine qua non for enhancing spiritual qualities such as compassion and loving-kindness. It also allowed the leaders to sort out inner and outer conflicts transforming destructive emotions and finding creative solutions.

> Mindfulness or reflective awareness is a tool to help yourself; it can be a refuge, and it is also a means to help you see what is going on inside and outside your thoughts, feelings, actions, or motivations. Then you recognize inner dispositions, and that recognition feeds your mind and heart. This recognition gives you understanding, peace, and stability, qualities you want to nourish, including compassion and equanimity. For example, I come back to myself when I am in conflict. When I have anger, I come back to myself and live with it. Here mindfulness gives me insights into my

> emotional states and helps me stop habitual reaction patterns. The silence, concentration, and mindfulness help me sort out the issues and develop new solutions. That is why it is said, "mindfulness sorts it out". (Abbot Phap Son)

The quality of reflective awareness depends on continuous practice. Nissley noted that he would go for regular walks in nature and that helped him relax and reflect on life and gain insights into life and work. "For my leadership practice, two key practices help me be grounded in my spirit and soul; Walking in nature and surrounding myself with my mentors and honest friends who give me genuine feedback." "Regular walking outside or hiking in nature helps Nissley relax his mind, and he can look at my past actions with greater clarity and gain a new perspective for the future." Abbot Phap Son noted that mindfulness is unique to each individual, as they develop it as an art. However, the skillful practice of mindfulness and concentration helps gain inner freedom and clarity of the mind:

> Mindfulness can be more robust for one and weaker for the other. It depends on how one cultivates it. It is like a mirror, which reflects, for example, an angry face or a peaceful face, but it is not affected by the presentations. You can be mindful of un-clarity, that your thinking is not helpful. You are not criticizing or reacting; sometimes, that is not enough; you need to develop new solutions. Each individual creates their mindfulness. Thai says, "Mindfulness is an art."

The Leaders used various methods in their spiritual practice. Some of them practiced *Yogic* meditation; others did simple daily mindfulness exercises such as breathing awareness and concentration, silent prayer and contemplation, and others seeking guidance through scriptures, teachers, and mentors who are deeply rooted in the ancient spiritual values of interconnectedness and awareness of the whole over coming to the conflicts that arise from the dualistic perceptions. Similarly, Gordon (2019) presents the reflections from Aikido pedagogy and training developed in modern Japan offer a transformative approach to relationality, one that offers contemplative education as a model to transcend the habitual conditioning of subject-subject consciousness towards peaceful dialogic interconnectedness. Abbess Pema described how she used different methods to cultivate deeper self-awareness. "My mother used to practice *Yoga*, so I got interested in it. When I was 25 years old, I began to practice *Yoga* and was hooked on it. Then, when I was 27, I began to do deeper yoga meditation practices to cultivate spiritual awareness." Abbess Pema also indicated that through mindfulness practice, she could touch the other dimension, which she calls the spiritual dimension. "I always had a yearning for something else. Now we say the other dimension." Reflective awareness leads to more profound transformation, bringing out the deeper shadows of life and transforming the negative emotional patterns. Abbess Pema described how her interior brokenness was made whole through reflective encounters and mindfulness practice:

> Some experiences in my life colored my interaction with my sisters, creating tension in the community. I wanted to share it with Thai (Teacher); when I met and shared it with Thai, he sat there looking out through the windows but deep listening. There is no approval and disapproval; there is no judgment. I came back into meditation and realized that it is my mental formation; full acknowledgment and full acceptance were there. Thus, there is a dramatic effect, and this happens in transmission ceremonies. Thai smiled at me, and I felt relieved. There is no more in me that block. Wow! This is like confession, to look deeply into your soul and bring to light the shadows of life. Being able to engage myself, I had a feeling that part of me was whole again. I felt the embrace of love.

Swami Bharati described how his sense of awakening through spiritual initiation and consistent meditative practice brought about a change in the way he perceived the world in relation to the ultimate reality. As a result, he was able to penetrate through the illusions of fleeting worldly experiences and lead an awakened life by setting his priorities in life. Many confuse attachment with love and live in possessiveness and addiction. Practicing non attachment in relationship is possible with a spiritually rooted and grounded life and gain spiritual freedom and joy:

> When you have been granted that degree of grace, *Brahman* (Divine) is not a puzzle, *Maya* (worldly experiences) becomes the puzzle; God is no longer a stranger to you; you open your eyes from that state of self-awareness and say, what is this? Where does this come from? See reality changes. No matter how devoted you are, God is a theory, and the world is the reality. After *Yoga diksa*, spiritual initiation, God becomes the absolute reality; the world becomes relative. This helps me to practice non attachment and universal love. That is what I live with.

These leaders spoke about their unique spiritual practices to cultivate spiritual intelligence and reflective awareness. Sri Sri experienced that pure consciousness, as such, is absolute while the experiences that manifest in the consciousness are subject to change:

> In the morning, I would sit starting with *Japa* (chanting Divine names), and then I will go into meditation, a time of deep silence and solitude. The experiences in meditation are not necessary; there is a danger of people identifying with those particular experiences. The consciousness is absolute; the experiences are the part of the relative; they come and go.

As a commercial artist, and a mystic, Thurston reflected on the phenomenon of supernatural intervention while she was painting. Her reflections on her transcendental experiences led her to a deeper understanding of her higher self and the deeper horizons of life. As a result of the cultivation of the yogic mind, the artistic skills are expressed with deeper spiritual meaning and purpose. An experience of the altered state of the artistic mind helped her to pain with greater imagination and disposition:

> I constantly reflected on this phenomenon without understanding it. I was in a breathless state, and when I was in a breathless state, my hands would move faster, and Everything was so beautiful. I didn't even take time to look at what I was doing. It just flew onto the canvas, and I painted the whole thing in one day. When I was tired and wanted to go home at five o'clock, I stepped back and knew it was finished. This is the best painting I had ever done. And I had to ponder the fact that a) I was not breathing; I was in a completely altered state. B) I never used both hands to paint. I felt as though somebody else was in my body. After the exhibition was over and I had to sit down and think, what the hell happened?

A sense of mystic awareness led Thurston to reflect on the inner meaning and purpose of such a strange mystical experience during her painting. She discerned the art of spiritual awakening through her experimentation with meditative painting. She came to understand that she had a spiritual calling. Thurston felt deep conviction about her experience of higher consciousness periodically. "Nobody pushes me or orders me around; many years later, when I entered into Samadhi, a state of deeper awareness and equanimity, I recognized it and remembered that when I was on the farm, it was the same state, a very expanded connected state." The spiritual practices lead to an experience of the other dimensions of life and Thurston could channel the spiritual energy finding great meaning, passion, and purpose in her life:

> Ecstatic… Ecstatic… when I was painting, there were euphoric feelings. So, Spirit used that. My medium worked for me to come and call me… it was a calling. My intuition was getting very strong, so I could sit quietly and wait for the clarity for the next move. And if the voice is not clear, I would do it for myself, whether the action is correct or not. I realized that I always had a sense of expanded mystical awareness; I was not conscious of it and couldn't put it into words. I still feel like I with a bigger border capacity and different horizons, aims, and intentions with expanded awareness.

Zimplemen noted how his practice of regular devotions, prayer, and reflection helped him gain sanity and maintain a caring attitude to make tough decisions during turbulent business environments. "My spiritual practices of prayer and devotions help me balance my work and personal life." The three dimensions of life are critical for me; the work, family, and spiritual life "to practice the best leadership that helps the organization grow." Similarly, Vanderveldt stated that she keeps a protected time in the early morning to engage in her spiritual practices:

> I get up very early every day, pray, meditate, exercise, and do most of my creative thinking during this time. It's the only quiet time of the day where I can gain clarity of mind and be productive without life and business throwing me curveballs. I value and protect this time and attribute much of my success to creating this space for myself.

Abbate acknowledged the heightened sense of awareness and cheerful disposition in times of challenging business situations due to his spiritual practices and period pilgrimages to sacred places to renew and rediscover the bigger picture of life: It is the pilgrimage to the heart of divine love and devotion. The consistent spiritual practices led him to experience centeredness to keep up with his priorities of life in a fleeting and busy world of business and family:

> My regular prayer and spiritual devotion of daily Rosary with my wife and Weekend Masses at the church helped me keep my priorities in order and deal with challenging restaurant business in California with a positive

disposition. This keeps me centered, for I need constant remaindered to be on the right track.

Several leaders noted that it is their spiritual practice that helped them to be rooted and grounded in the spiritual intelligence. Mahoney noted that he faced his odds with challenging health situations in his family and business environment with faith and confidence. "I pray every day and spend quiet time with the Lord. It keeps me spiritually grounded amidst the ebb and flow of life. My spiritual practices, faithful family, and team of great mentors help me be a better CEO who leads the company with the head and heart." Washburn noted that she learned to center herself by reading great spiritual authors to gain great perspectives on life and spent regular time with coaches and mentors to horn her inner life and skills. She stated, "Reading great spiritual authors like Richard Rohr and others helps me to reflect on what is most important in life and stay focused to lead and coach other CEOs in this time of uncertainly and complexity." Lim regained her conviction that regular spiritual practice is necessary to maintain inner peace during stress and strains in life. "I went back to the regular practice of Tai Chi and daily meditation that helps me deal with the challenges of my advocacy work and business situations with more inner poise and strength." Some leaders like Jarema spent relaxing time gardening and painting to enhance the spiritual life and the mission of healing the whole person through holistic therapy: "I engage in the spiritual practice of journaling, meditation, and gardening while guiding people to live their life to the full through whole person therapy".

As a traditional spiritual leader and healer, Mutua was convinced that self-knowledge and education are the most potent means to liberation. He asserted, "The greatest weapon to freeing people is not gun but education and self-knowledge". The wisdom of self-understanding and knowledge were the secrets of African tradition. Mutua noted, "I found with great surprise that the wisdom of the African people had great power to save humanity. I was trained in traditional wisdom and the path of *Shaman*, a *Sangamon*, a traditional healer and a wise man." The ability to see oneself in a new light is of paramount importance. Mutua reiterated, "All you need is the power of character; all you need is to see yourself in a new light."

Palmer emphasized the importance of penetrating through the illusions of life and touching reality through reflective awareness. Hearing oneself in speech is an important way of cultivating reflective awareness. Palmer noted that by sharing honestly what is going on inside oneself, especially the negative feelings and thoughts, with a trustworthy person and listening to the self-disclosure, one could gain deeper insight into one's authentic self. The unfolding of spiritual awareness happens to people in different ways: some through contemplation and others through action, devotion, and reflection.

> Not all ways look like contemplation. Some can penetrate through illusions and touch reality through action. I think I did some things by failing, but then to learn to reflect on that and internalize it; almost to reframe it to learn to hold; some people do that by walking in the woods, some through reading and meditation. You can hear yourself, and what you are saying is talking about yourself. It would be best if you listened to what you were saying, and most of the time, we don't hear what we are saying. We listen to it inside at 3 a.m., it is scary and spooky, and we think there is no way out. And if you are depressed, you are thinking that. So, this venting will help you hear yourself and keep you on track. (Palmer)

These leaders emphasized the need and importance of cultivating reflective awareness on a daily basis to lead a balanced life. Archbishop Flynn advocated that only from a deep self-reflection would a person learn to take care of the spiritual and psychological needs leading a holistic life: "And out of that solitude and reflection came an understanding of the need to fulfill the psychological and spiritual needs in one's life. The psychological needs, I think, are having a sense of accomplishment and the need for a handful of trustworthy friends, and the spiritual need to have a peaceful self." And among many leaders in the business world, these psychological and spiritual needs are not taken care of, and therefore they lead a stressful and divided life. The benefit of spiritual practice is to live a stress free and undivided life.

Cultivation of spiritual practice involves slowing down and focusing on combining attention and intention in a given situation to develop deeper perception, insight, and understanding. Scharmer (2009: 148) described the process as "opening the heart," which means accessing and activating the deeper levels of our inner perception. "The heart in any contemplative tradition is not a sentimentality or an emotionality but a deep yogic center point." Bortoft's description of the heart's intelligence embodies three principles, first, diving into the sensory experience; second, redirecting your attention; and third, activating the more profound capacities of cognition. This spiritual intelligence emerges from the brilliance of the heart. We learn to grasp reality not only from the perspective of the individual observer but also from the perspective of life and its source. The result is seeing with the heart. Goethe (as cited in Scharmer, 2009: 159) said, "Man knows himself only to the extent that he knows the world; he becomes aware of himself only within the world, and aware of the word only within himself. Every object, well contemplated, opens up a new organ within us." Therefore, the cultivation of spiritual practice is necessary to awaken inner intelligence and discover hidden wholeness.

The Leaders experienced an unfolding of the ultimate dimension of their being when they cultivated deep reflective awareness. Leaders' advanced capacity for self-awareness and self-knowledge resulted in the transformation of how they used to see the world and began to impact the world with a new vision of wholeness. Being deeply centered on Being and spiritual consciousness, these leaders were able to show wisdom, understanding, compassion, and equanimity in their journey, penetrating through the illusions of life and wakening their hidden dimensions of wholeness. The realization and presence of the spiritual intelligence enabled them to make this inner transformation through spiritual practices.

Inner Silence

The leaders developed the capacity for deep inner peace by maintaining internal and external silence and mindfulness. They cultivated regular periods of solitude and silence to enter into their inner layers of consciousness. Even though several of these leaders led very active lives traveling and teaching across the globe, they maintained a sense of deep inner peace and joy. Their lives are a testament that without cultivating inner solitude and interiority, it is highly impossible to unravel the spiritual dimension of life. Setting apart regular time for cultivation of the inner silence free from the distractions and preoccupations of life is important to gain deeper spiritual intelligence and wisdom. Mutua talked about how he experienced great solitude, peace, and heightened sensitivity in the African wilderness:

> I love the African wilderness. I feel at home in the bushes. I love the smell of vegetation. I love to walk with the animals in their silent company. There are times when I was led by supernatural forces to the African forest and remained in solitary influence for weeks. On my way back, I experienced heightened sensitivity, and Everything became very vivid, bright, and delightful, like a rainbow in the sky.

From early childhood onwards, Swami Bharati narrated how he was steeped in the ancient practice of daily meditation, with his father as one of his guides. The persistent practice of solitude and inner quietness made him discover the more profound mysteries of the mind and become a world spiritual leader of yogic meditation. The meditation practices enable the spiritual aspirant to enter into the eternal silence of the soul experiencing deep tranquility. The various forms of mediation such as yogic meditation, mantra mediation, and breath awareness meditations are practiced and taught throughout the world to help people experience deeper sense of peace, silence, inner freedom, and bliss:

> Like most Indians, I was born steeped in the ancient traditions, but it was even more profound in my case because I never went to a school and never had a tutor. My father sacrificed everything he had to put into my early years of training. And he made sure, even from the age of four and a half years old, that I sat for meditation with him for an hour every day. So, meditation was not a later discovery in life; it was part of the norm. And I cannot think of any other model for my spiritual discovery. At thirteen, some articles were published in the Hindi press about me. From February 1947 onwards, my entire life focused on traveling and teaching about the spiritual life. At the age of sixteen, I took to three days of fasting and silence, and I shut my door and began to charter my life's plan. I strayed now and then, but I stuck to the values and rules I worked out at that time. I practice yogic meditation, mantra meditation, breath awareness meditation and many other forms that helps to enjoy inner silence and bliss. When you live in the presence of God, things work out effortlessly. (Swami Bharati)

Sri Sri noted that he used to practice long hours of silence and meditation daily to explore the deepest recesses of his spiritual consciousness in his journey towards wholeness. "Meditation was quite natural to me. I would sit every morning in meditation for long hours. In meditation, you may experience light, sound, images, and vision, but the "experiencer" is the most important, and experiences will come and go." The spiritual intelligence and the absolute consciousness gained through the spiritual practice is changeless even in the mist of the reality of the changes in the external world of activities. Sri Sri affirmed, "Inner silence is the mother of all creativity, the source of intuition, and the storehouse of energy, and we all have it. "The only thing is we have locked it and forgotten the key" as we do not cultivate it daily." Sri Sri spoke of three kinds of inner silence; outer silence, stillness, and oneness:

> The first is the silence where there is no talking. This is very beneficial for people just to be aware of what they are saying and how much energy they spend talking. The second is the silence of stillness. This is the silence inside us that is detached from the noise in the world. Silence is disinterestedness in activity, an inward journey of the mind. This inner stillness is very important if we want to understand and grow spiritually. Inner silence frees us from the noise of the world. And finally, there is the silence of Oneness – Oneness with the entire universe. Oneness is the goal of silent practice. Whatever knowledge we study and understand with our intellect is limited. The knowledge that we gain by effort is immanent. The knowledge which is gained through effortlessness, through silence and intuition is transcendental.

To develop a capacity for interiority, Palmer engaged in the practice of deep listening and contemplative mindfulness in his own way. Keller (as cited in Leighton, 2003) stated, "Everything has its wonders, even darkness, and silence, and I learn whatever state I am in, therein to be content." Deep sense of interiority results from the cultivation of inner silence and solitude where the person is able to work through the confusions, anxieties, and delusions of life. According to Palmer, being contemplative would help us penetrate the illusions of life and develop the capacity for higher spiritual awareness:

> We develop a capacity for interiority and solitude from deep listening and allow the interior to do its work. There are all kinds of ways; there is a wide variety of books on spirituality and spiritual practices that you know, all about interiority and solitude and inner journey. I think each of us has to find our way of becoming contemplative; that doesn't mean chanting a mantra or joining a monastery, sitting cross-legged, or doing Yoga or whatever, those work for some people. I have this generic definition of what it means to be contemplative. To be reflective is to develop a capacity to penetrate illusions and touch reality. I think that is what all tremendous contemplatives do.

Creating a sense of deep interior quietness is vital to developing a keen awareness of self. The intentional practice of interior silence is indispensable for gaining clarity of mind and charity of heart to engage the world more meaningfully, lovingly, and productively. Seeing through the trappings of ego is vital to cultivating the spiritual nature of the wonder of reality. It is impossible to deal with today's noisy world without developing interior silence and a peaceful mind. Palmer suggested that it is hard to maintain a stable sense in modern society without regulating the distracting noises from outside, including the electronic media. Disconnecting from the external noise of the media and technology is important to cultivate the inner peace, detachment, and deeper sense of silence and awareness to deal with the world effectively:

> I think what is essential is to use a current expression: we have to turn off the radio, we have to turn off the television, we have to turn off the computer, not permanently, but I don't watch much tv, but I listen to public radio. Why should a person do that? It is to learn to reflect on life; some people do that by walking in the woods, some through reading and meditation. Because facing yourself may be the hardest thing on earth without cultivating self-reflection. You do it because you don't have a choice. It is a question of survival.

Living in a fast-paced modern society, people neglect the need to create interior silence and solitude by leading a simple life. Archbishop Flynn described how he realized the need for developing an internal capacity for silence and listening and cultivated the adventure of interior listening daily to lead a holistic life. The cultivation of the regular time of silence and prayer helped many leaders to listen to the voice of wisdom and intuition within and cut through the chase of busy life and remain efficient and effective. Leaders and busy administrators find it extremely hard to maintain interior quietness in a world full of activities. Archbishop Flynn underlines the need for such solitude to enhance the quality of their life:

> This is very difficult for active leaders in the business world and administration; there is always something more to do. And so, to sit quietly, to calm down the heart and mind is not easy because the leader, the administrator, the business leader, whatever, will tend to say, I have to do this, I have to do that, and getting it, all done. And of course, getting things all done is essential, but what would that be saying about you, about this person living in restlessness. So, that was the grace of sitting quietly every day for some time to listen to the inner self in silent prayer. And from that quiet listening came some deep reflections about holistic life. Cultivating interior silence and quietness is indeed highly transformative.

Archbishop Flynn demonstrated how his daily hour of silent prayer and relaxation helped him maintain the equilibrium and a sense of humor in handling turbulent situations as a top spiritual leader. Regular spiritual practice of prayer and meditation has enabled him to feel a sense of wholeness and well-being on a daily basis. When the world of the leader gets turbulent, he is able to maintain inner peace and clam in the midst of the storm and lead with wisdom and spiritual intelligence. Showing up with deep calm, sensitivity, and joyful presence was indeed the hall mark of his life:

> The purpose of prayer is for that divine presence to come into my company and change me according to what God wants me to be. And so, the grace of quieting my heart in prayer was great. Because as I see myself through the past 22 years as the bishop; you know, and I know that in any leadership role, there are challenges, misunderstandings, and difficulties, but I think I have been able to keep my equilibrium and a sense of humor, joy, and all the rest; a sense of presence to people, simply by opening my heart quietly in that way. I always feel delighted to be in the presence of God and rest there. I don't know, except that when I come out of that time of silent prayer, I feel strengthened. It is like having a good sleep; it is like having a good meal; you feel satisfied. My spiritual director used to say, "Have a holy hour in the morning and a happy hour in the evening, then you are all right." And he said to me, "I could always tell when you don't have a holy hour or a happy hour."

Iilbagiza experienced deep peace in her heart when she was undergoing the onslaught of the Rwandan genocide with her interior prayer and sense of solitude. She described how she found inner calmness in times of turmoil. The ability to remail in stillness in the midst of the storm all round her was a gift of grace and poise. Regular practice of prayer and inner silence and solitude enabled Ilibagiza to face the crisis and threat of her unprecedented turmoil due to the political situation in the country and rebound from the trauma and tragedies of life:

> I found a place in the bathroom to call my own: a small corner of my heart. I retreated there as soon as I awoke and stayed there until I slept. It was my sacred garden, where I spoke with God, meditated on His words, and nurtured my spiritual self. When I meditated, I touched the source of my faith and strengthened the core of my soul. While horror swirled around me, I found refuge in a world that became more welcoming and wonderful

> with each visit. Even as my body shriveled, my soul was nourished through my relationship with God. As long as I have found peace in my heart, there is no better place.

Nisley noted that he would take regular walks in nature in order to calm down the stresses of daily life and experience a greater inner space and peace. It enabled him to face the world with greater compassion, wisdom, and spiritual intelligence. "I take regular walks in nature which I deeply love and it brings peace, insights, and clarity to my life. The fresh air and the beauty of nature brings joy and peace to a stress filled life" (Nissley, 2020:2). Living in close proximity with nature helps to relive stress, anxieties, and fears of life to be productive and wholesome in engagement of business and complexities of life.

The leaders invariably developed the capacity for interiority and solitude through their spiritual practices. Silence and solitude helped them practice deep listening and attentiveness to their inner voice and penetrate through the illusions and pains of life. Cultivated solitude and inner quietness in the fast-moving, chaotic modern life, which was profoundly transformative, made the leaders wholesome in their daily living and engagement. These leaders demonstrated an extraordinary capacity for personal presence, equilibrium, and resilience in their journey towards wholeness.

Inner Transformation

The interviewed leaders saw themselves experiencing profound inner transformation in their life journey. They experienced inner transformation in different ways. For several of these leaders, the internal shift happened through an experience of spiritual crisis that triggered them to change their thinking and attitudes, especially when the outside situation was hard to change. For example, Ilibagiza underwent a tremendous inner transformation from fear and hatred to courage and forgiveness while she was trapped for 91 days during the Rwandan genocide. Thurston experienced an altered state of consciousness as an artist and a mystic being guided by supernatural powers and spiritual wisdom. Swami Bharati spoke about profound transformation as awakening his higher consciousness when his spiritual master initiated him. Palmer recognized his experience of profound inner change when he learned lessons from his major failures and struggles, including depression. Zimpleman recognized the power of prayer and inner transformation when he was facing the impact economic recession in his business organization. Vanderveldt underwent spectacular inner change and transformation at critical moments of her life and business that brought new energy, passion, and perspectives. Mutua expressed how he underwent profound interior transformation while the supernatural forces led him into the African bush for several weeks resulting in the heightening of his perceptiveness and inner awareness unfolding the ultimate dimension of his Being.

All the leaders in this study have shared their unique experiences of inner transformation, which are profound and powerful. Racionero (2018) brought out the aspect of personal and organizational change from the perspective of spiritual leadership. Invariably, the transformation experience made a significant impact on their lives and the lives of their followers. They made significant career changes and felt inner fulfillment in their personal lives and deep satisfaction in their service to humanity. Palmer recalled his experience of profound inner transformation, especially by accepting failures as the alchemy of transformation:

> When I go back and embrace failures as a place where I learn something about myself, I am being transformed. Twenty-five years ago, I came to terms with my behavior patterns where I get conflicted with people in power, significantly when they compromise fundamental values. I came to terms with it in a transparent way. I said to myself if there is some way you can work outside the institutions, if some way you can create an independent career, it is not that you abandon institutions, but you can serve them better; because you won't be spending half of your precious energy in getting conflicted with people. You keep an eye on the doughnut and not on the hole. And so, I was able to work and put together an independent career. For 20 to 25 years, I have been self-employed as a writer, a traveling teacher, and an activist. I find it very liberating. I find my creativity flowing. I no longer spend my time as I used to consume earlier in conflict. Accepting failures as the alchemy of transformation is the way to experience profound inner change.

Woiwode and Woiwode (2019) brought out that socio-cultural shifts visible in many initiatives across the world demonstrates, especially in Western countries like Germany, a new awareness and practices of spiritually informed conscious living at times. A central theme is how more profound transformations at the individual and collective societal levels take place and in which way they are brought into the public policy domain of urban community or neighborhood development. This is exemplified briefly by studying the approach of a community in the German town of Kassel and the transition town movement. The conclusion reflects on how three key areas of the discussion, Spirit, place, and people may be reconnected for a sustainable urban future. How inner transformation based on the cultivation of spiritual awareness and interconnectedness paved the way for embodying holistic Being and living in the modern society. Swami Bharati described the deep inner transformation he experienced when his *guru* gave him the spiritual initiation. Initiation into the higher states of meditation, transcendence, and spiritual energy made his being luminous. As a result, he experienced an awakening of spiritual consciousness that enabled him to overcome the projections of ego and dedicate his entire life in selfless service to humanity: He acknowledged that his heightened spiritual sensitivity and awareness with which he was able to recognize and appreciate the spiritual power present in various religious and spiritual traditions:

> The kind of things that happened to Saul on the road to Damascus, was *Yogadiksa (*spiritual initiation*),* a light touched him and blinded him for three days. It is the same tradition of Awakening. I could hardly open my eyes for three days. My guru placed his hands on my head. After a while, I began to feel the movement of the Kundalini (latent spiritual energy), all the Chakras (spiritual energy centers in the body), waves and waves of energy, and the wave of the subtle light Being; my Being was not the body. This body was not I. That was the defining moment. He gave me this finger ring. He said, I have work for you, and you will be at the service of humanity when you are granted that degree of grace. In all religions you can find such spiritual Awakening and stream of consciousness. For example, when St. John the Baptist baptized Jesus, the Holy Ghost came like a dove, symbol of peace and grace; those who are not prepared, when the Holy Ghost touches them, they dance, they sing, they go wild; they can't control movements. But for the high initiate, the Holy Ghost comes like a dove. I read the bible from that experience.

In addition, the texts of various religious scriptures are for Swami Bharati, not merely philosophical concepts, but spiritual events in which he recognizes transcendental meaning, power, and values. Meditation practices help to reducing stress, calming anxiety, increasing focus, amplifying self-esteem, expanding inner strength, and maximizing resiliency resulting in life changing transformations.

Experiencing the texts of the scriptures as spiritual events of inner transformation and awakening, Swami Bharati was able to explore the breaths and heights of spiritual intelligence and wisdom that unfold the hidden dimensions of wholeness:

> I relate to the *Upanishads*, or the *Geetha* or Bible not as *Texts* of philosophy; they are descriptions of spiritual events. So are the books like *Popul Vuh* of the ancient *Maya* traditions, or the *Sufis*, *Koran*, or *Zarathustra*. For ten years, Zarathustra sat in a cave, and the devil came to him and offered him the world's empires. But when something else becomes your reality, the empires become nothing. An experience of transcendence makes you whole. This spiritual Awakening happened to me on 26 February 1976, which I consider my actual birthday. Being born in a divine, as you call being born in Christ, sets my value.

The spiritual initiation, *Yogadiksa*, resulted in a deep inner transformation of Swami Bharati's emotional and behavioral patterns and a great transition in his career and the intimate relationship with his family. With mutual understanding and consent, he renounced his family and dedicated himself to meditation practices and spiritual teaching across the world. Consequently, he pursued a higher calling to transcend the limitation of ordinary pursuits to be a monk and prolific spiritual leader. Spiritual awakening can result in profound inner and outer transformation, including one's mindset, career, and way of life:

> This was *Yogadiska* (the right of spiritual initiation), which is a deeper transformation. I was still a married man, two more children I had after that. Finish your *karma*, duty. No, you have not loved your wife enough; love her more. Okay, I thought I would be given a renunciation, taken to the caves; here I am told to give more attention to my wife. Your guides watch over you, and then you begin to watch yourself. Change your behavior patterns, and your emotional patterns. Yes, then it affects your whole family. They may not realize it at that time, but later they begin to realize it. My children are solid Americans, but they value whatever they had with their father. They do not appreciate it at that time in their rebellious years. You know, they appreciate it now. Then, my guru told me to resign from the University of Minnesota; that was a tough one; because living in America without income, having children, and family is impossible. But he kept on it; he kept on, he kept on. He won't give up. You don't keep that relationship when you take *sanyasa* (spiritual renunciation). The marriage relationship is renounced mutually for the sake of the

> higher call. Very soon, my guru helped me establish a meditation center in Summit Avenue, Minnesota.

Mutua was transformed from an illegitimate child to a traditional healer with the help of his Zulu grandparents and elders. As a mystic and traditional Shaman, Mutua was initiated in esoteric music, oracles, and healing after undergoing strict discipline and profound inner transformation. He described how he rose from the ashes of colonial oppression to dignity and self-esteem by embracing the traditional African wisdom and spirituality. He was also instrumental, along with John Dube informing the African National Heritage Forum, a precursor to the African National Congress. His moment of awakening about his self-worth and dignity strengthened him to fight against apartheid and discrimination.

> I became a traditional healer with heightened awareness and healing powers. I saw people being healed. I ask myself, why are we told lies about ourselves by the colonial masters? In John Dube's words, 'these wars are not just killing of enemies. One of the ways to ruin the entire nation is breaking its self-esteem and its self-pride.' I saw that this is what the colonial powers knew when they came to Africa and colonized us. They knew what Africa had achieved. Records of African achievement were there, written by white men and hidden from us. I was called *Kepha Mutwas*; *Kepha* means godless heathen. I had not known that we believed in God, the mother, father, and son. I found the religion was the same as Christian tenets. I told myself even if it took many years, I was going to correct this prejudice, discrimination, and apartheid. It was a moment of Awakening to turn the page and rewrite the true history of Africa. It was a moment to reclaim our dignity and restore our lost values. (Mutua)

Archbishop Flynn shared his transformation as a celibate and a higher calling to love more with generosity and sacrifice. "Living a celibate life is another way of loving. You learn to love more through years of spiritual practices, prayer, reflection, selfless service, and learning from mistakes, transforming from within." He led the transformation of the Catholic clergy during the time of the sexual abuse crisis in the United States. He described how he envisions restoring the trust and dignity of spiritual leaders by renewing from within and through a relationship of healing and hope with its people:

> The church is facing an enormous task, a daunting task. But at the very same time, we have been given a significant opportunity at this time of crisis. Out of this time of pain, anger, and sadness, the church is being challenged to renew from within and its relationship with its people, restore trust and strengthen its commitment to the faithful. We have an excellent opportunity for healing and for the emergence of a church more robust and fuller of love and hope than we humans could ever have imagined.

Thurston spoke about her transcendental transformative experiences as a mystic and artist. A profound change happened to her while she was immersed in meditation for three weeks, and her inner Being was enlightened after an excruciating ordeal. The roller-coaster of inner transformation resulted in heightened sense of spiritual sensitivity and awareness. Thurston's cave experience helped her recognize the patterns of her ego and her unconscious emotional reactions, which resulted in a new awakening of the hidden dimensions of her soul. This approach helps participants connect with their true identity, expand their consciousness, and transform their personal and management development. It is an invitation to awaken the hero within, making a challenging journey of self-leadership and consciousness. Thurston recognized that without opening the patterns of the unconscious mind, it would be tough to break through the trappings of the ego-self: She shared that her whole Being became very compassionate, nurturing a luminous, and blissful state of awareness. She was able to live from a deeper state of awareness after the moment of spiritual awakening:

> Within a couple of weeks, in the middle of fasting and intense meditation, my back started to burn. And I was sitting there with tears rolling my cheeks, and it was agony, and the angelic Being would speak kindly but firmly: And after a few days, I do not quite remember; I suddenly broke through the *Samadhi*, awakening consciousness. And I had sat there in a radiant, blissful, and ecstatic golden light all night. And in the next night, I would be in the shadow, aching with burning back, and this area behind the heart. After three weeks, my heart was opened. I was born into a new world; I told him it was fantastic. My Spirit was open, and the *spiritual energy* went up into my heart. But I was internally focused. That is the point of the cave experience. You have to open the unconscious mind to awaken; as long as the shadow is there, it keeps you locked into ego patterns; they have to be broken. It is not everybody's cup of tea. I am not trying to fix the ego but wake up the soul. He said this is heaven's gate

> and not wishful thinking. And the reality was completely changed; I was impersonal, focused on others, not on myself. I had a whole new vision of life at a very compassionate level.

Leaders in the study expressed that inner transformation is indeed an ongoing transformation. Abbot Phap Son cited an example from his life of how his sensual feelings were transformed into spiritual attraction. He regained a sense of inner stability, peace, and joy without confusion and fearfulness. What made this inner transformation possible? The meditation practice brought inner clarity regarding the ego-centered desires and an ongoing life in a fraternal community helped him transform the self-centered desires that seek one's pleasure and are suitable to the other-centered love that will the good and welfare of the other. The practice of the three vows of chastity, detachment, and submission to the spiritual will pave the way for inner purification and spiritual capacity building. The Indian spiritual practices have still bearing on the current practices of mindfulness for inner transformation. In this way, fasting transforms into mindful eating, breath control into mindfulness of breathing process, annihilation of self centeredness into awareness of the body (Anālayo, 2021b). Paying attention to the continuous inner transformation is inevitable to the process of experiencing the wholeness of life. Abbot Phap Son recalled:

> For example, we sit opposite each other for lunch, the brothers on one side and the sisters on the other side facing each other. One day I was sitting and looking at the young sisters, conscious that I am a man and they are females. One day I thought, why I am not open to the generous love pouring out from their hearts, turning the sexual attraction into an attraction of pure love without a selfish intent? Yes, there is love there; if you are open to pure love, you can feel it in your heart. This love is without attachment but fully free to give oneself generously for the sake of the other. Now, I do not feel so confused in my life. There is more clarity, compassion, and less confusion, less fear, more focus, and direction; more joy, peace, and satisfaction with spiritual practices of meditation and fraternal community living. No doubt there are more challenges, too, as I continue the journey towards wholeness.

Ilibagiza illustrated how her deep hatred and anger were transformed into forgiveness and compassion for the perpetrators of crime against her own family and humanity during the Rwandan genocide. The spiritual awareness and intelligence enabled Ilibagiza to take stock of her harrowing situations and find sanity in the midst of terror and rise again with new vigor and compassion for humanity, especially to take care of the orphan children of the war and conflicts across the world. When Ilibagiza was confronted with inescapable violence, misery, and fear, her cry of soulful prayer, deep acceptance of the reality, and submission to the divine helped her move beyond the tragedy experiencing a powerful transformation from within, becoming a catalyst for positive change:

> I felt deep hatred and sadness that my classmate is doing such horrible atrocities. At that time, I understood what Jesus said on the cross; "Father, forgive them for they do not know what they are doing." I prayed for hours and hours, seeking peace in my heart. Somehow, I felt I could love them and pray for them. With that acceptance, I felt a piece of heavy baggage; a burden came out of my shoulder. I can see these large numbers of people lost in their minds and killing people with madness. It doesn't mean that justice will not allow them to be free of their crime, but for me, it was an experience of joy to let go of the burden from my mind, not to let my mind do planning and plotting against them in my heart, hiding in the bathroom. The whole feeling of hatred and anger is completely over with a moment of spiritual Awakening in the most excruciating time of my life.

With a sense of deep trust and confidence in the divine power and a yearning for change in her inner turmoil, Ilibagiza explained how she felt deep peace and mercy in her heart that was boiling with hatred and revenge for the killer of her tribe. She was convinced that as long as one finds peace in oneself, peace with God, despite the massive challenge within and without, the one could become a source of blessing, rediscovering the inner power to lead the way; stop being a victim of hatred and start becoming a positive force for good. She made a quantum leap in her spiritual growth and was able to transcend the limitation of hatred and revenge to a place of peace and goodwill and compassion for all. She noted:

> I began to put all things in God with deep trust. I felt I could do this; I could trust God fully. It was almost like an obstacle between them and me. My hatred is gone; my anger, my hatred of them, was nearly done. I think of it as grace. Sometimes it is so hard to explain. Before I was in hell, I

> knew that I had found myself almost in paradise. There is no better place as long as you have found peace in your heart. Forgiveness is not about holding yourself a victim, but it is also blessing those who are hurting you. Wanting them to change, wishing them good, those sentiments came from my heart. I felt a sense of deep peace, mercy, and inner security. This inner peace and courage helped me visit the people in the prison who killed my brother and offer him forgiveness from my heart.

The leaders underwent profound inner transformation marking pivotal moments in their life journey. Change of the inner self happened in different ways: from a sense of deep hatred to unconditional forgiveness; from loss of self-esteem to a profound sense of dignity and courage; from a self-seeking ego pattern to selfless service and care; from "I" consciousness to "we" consciousness; from isolation to solidarity; from a state of conflict to a state of harmony and peace; from a narrow and closed perspective to universal and open perspective. These leaders realized that without the inner transformation of the individual, no social transformation or collective transformation is possible. Ostman (2020) *explains the movement of Awakening within to evoke both inner and outer transformation. The experience of profound internal change was a crucial factor in leader experience of wholeness and well-being.*

Keep Moving Towards the Light

Everything on earth seems to be attracted to the Light. Ships for centuries used the starlight and moonlight to be their guide and compass for their navigation. All creatures, great and small, rise by the sun each day and find new energy and vitality. The sun and its light are one of life's necessities and guiding force. The light provides vital nutrients and energy. Without it, human life, plant life, and all life could not exist at all. We are bound and interconnected to physical light, as well as spiritual Light. We cannot live long without sunlight, food, or water, but we cannot live for even a second without the energy and Light of the Creator that shines anew each day. Spiritual Light sustains us to our very core of our being and re-energize our life. Leaders in this study demonstrated that their journey towards wholeness is a life-long process of moving towards the light piercing the darkness and shadows of life. In their inner journey, they went through the ups and downs, failures and successes, crises and opportunities by engaging in an iterative process of experience, learning, and reflection. The more one moves towards the light igniting the soul; the more one can recognize the deep shadows. According to Jung (quoted in Haynes, 1993: 137) "A man who is possessed by his shadow is always standing in his own light and falling into his own traps." A shadow is one's emotional blind spot. Active encounter with one's own shadow helps one to decipher the deep layers of the unconscious free the mind from the shadows of repression and projection to the light of the consciousness. "No tree, it is said, can grow to heaven unless its roots reach down to the hell" (Jung, 2014: 43). The dynamics of individuation and the cultivation of transcendence from worldly attachments to pleasure, power and fame help one to move towards the inner light and deeper awareness (Pennachio, 1992). Having descended into the crucibles of crises and embraced the crises as a challenge, the leaders began to keep moving towards the light of consciousness manifesting greater joy and generosity of heart.

These leaders compared their inner journeys with nature going through the seasonal cycles of Fall, Winter, Spring, and Summer, unfolding a deeper consciousness and creative energy. In the Summer, seeds are planted, clearing the ground; in the Fall, things shut down; during Winter, the seeds go through hibernation and dormancy to emerge in the Spring with new flowers and fruits. In the Summer, harvesting occurs in superabundance to enrich oneself and others. The seed's journey is not without challenges and threats from time to time. In similar ways, new seeds of discovery are planted in mind to go through the dormancy of reflection and introspection to emerge with the discovery of new dimensions of wholeness. The quest for wholeness is not a quest for perfection but a journey towards greater wholeness for these leaders. Some leaders in the study compared the pursuit of fullness with a trek on a spiraling path and cycles of seasons, indicating the non-linear nature of the quest. The dynamic of unfolding the deeper dimension of Being is a continuous process of conscious inquiry, learning resiliency, and profound transformation.

Arising from the darkness of crisis, the leaders were able to enlighten their minds to discover a new perspective of dealing with the world to inspire and transform the organizations. Jefferson (as cited in Leighton, 2003) noted, "Enlighten the people, generally, and tyranny and oppressions of body and mind will vanish like spirits at the dawn of day." Nessley noted how his experiences of setbacks in life became a ladder to rediscover the spark in his soul to move from brokenness to wholeness "My experiences of family brokenness, divorce, and being fired from business school helped me to look back at the life and experience deep learning to rediscover the spark of undying hope in my soul to become a wholesome and successful leader." Lim emphasized that her realization of the call to champion the cause of women's rights in Singapore and how connecting with the great stories in the life of Jesus helped ignite her soul while she was feeling the heavy burden of leadership adventure:

> I was pretty inspired by Jesus's journey from one challenging moment to the other while I was going through the burden of fighting for my organization. Jesus dared to do the right thing to stand for his core values of truth, justice, and peace, even though he had to face set back to the extent of being rejected and crucified. My parents and family were afraid that fighting for justice would expose my identity as a gay person, which was not known publicly. It would lead to substantial adverse reactions from the society but connecting with the life of Christ gave me so much courage and confidence to do the right thing in fighting for my organization and fighting for women's rights for justice and equality.

Washburn noted that coaching the CEOs like a midwife asking excellent and meaningful questions inspires and challenges her and others to discover new perspectives to solve current business issues. Providing a platform for deep listening and process is vital for the sanity and wholeness of the chief executives as they are involved in complex issues of the organization and market situations: Through the use of metaphors and reflective questions, the CEOs were able to keep moving towards their own inner light, wisdom, and intelligence. This is both an individual process and a collective process of deep listening, dialogue, and rediscovery of a higher perspective of life:

> Currently, I am working as an executive coach inviting other CEOS to form a group to challenge and support one another. The group is kept so diverse that one may inspire the other from different perspectives. I use the metaphor of being a midwife to listen to their stories and perspectives as leaders who are primarily lonely at the top and find hope in their challenging business environment and discover courage and strength to navigate the organization to more tremendous success and impact on the society. My ability to ask critical questions such as "Are you serving the greater good in this situation or the narrow interests" helps them sort out their core values and set priorities to act on."

Jarema refreshes his soul by engaging in his spiritual practice of gardening, painting, reflective journaling, and therapy sessions to find joy and strength in his life. "Gardening keeps me down to earth, and reflective journaling helps me centered on my whole being to offer my life as a healing touch for the world." Just as the fruits of growing a garden exceed the doing—the weeding and seeding and countless other tasks—so do the riches of tending a spiritual life surpass the striving. Renewing the relationship to nature and growing in deeper appreciation of the fruits and flowers of garden and life, a greater sense of being and serving is possible in the world is possible. Vanderlvedt noted that she was proud of her daily routine of prayer, scripture reading and reflection, and exercise to center herself in Spirit to inspire and transform women in their entrepreneurial journey:

> I practice daily prayer and meditation and do daily exercise early morning before the day's activities take over. I want women of all ages and stages in their entrepreneurial journey to know they have the resources to help them scale. When you activate women, you activate the economy. The underrepresentation of women in business is a missed opportunity-both socially and economically. When we invest in women, their communities, states, and countries prosper, which generates a multiplier effect.

Thurston acknowledged that the journey towards wholeness is a spiral process of learning and discovery. "Life is a spiral; we return to where we once were but at a higher vibration level." She shared her experience of moving towards her inner light and manifesting that more profound dimension of being through her organization, Core Light, which she established in Santa Fe, New Mexico, to help others in their inner journey:

> When I could still see the light in my body, in my core, actually the Spirit, I asked the inner voice what I should call the organization? The answer came immediately, "Core Light." So, I established my organization with this name in Santa Fe. I thought that was a strange name. I didn't understand it at first, but later it made sense. It took time and persistence to recognize this light within.

Sellman, an O.D. consultant and founder of business consulting through spiritual counsel, noted that he ignites his soul and the soul of other people by spending time in quiet time in the morning and journaling to listen and discern what the inner voice is telling him to do. His experience of prayer and meditation helped him experience great breakthrough from his addictions and helped people to awake from their soul to be of great service to the humanity:

> I spent hours in daily prayer and meditation to declutter my mind, gain spiritual wisdom, and focus my Spirit on touching the heart of people who go through pain, struggles, and sufferings. I have a practice of asking people this question after being friendly with them, "What is the one thing in your life that needs prayerful support?" When I ask people this question, it's fantastic to see how people open up from their hearts their deepest pain or struggle, asking for help and it brings great joy for me to offer a prayer of comfort and lift their life to the God of healing and strength.

Pope (2022) explains that classical spiritual process of enlightenment consists in a three-fold path of purification, illumination, and unification. The Illuminative way is the intermediary stage between "purification" and "union" on the path to wholeness. Also called the "Way of the Proficient," the main feature of the Illuminative Way is the enlightenment of the mind in the ways of the divine and a clear understanding of divine will in one's state of life. With intentional focus for spiritual awakening and wholeness, the aspirant needs to enter into daily practice of meditation, mindfulness, and contemplation to purify the mind from all attachment and ignite the soul with deeper serenity and love to achieve higher consciousness. The unknown author of The Cloud of Unknowing, the classical fourteenth century Western spirituality book claims, "The substance of all perfection is nothing else but a good will and how all the sensible sounds, consolations, and sweetness that affect us in this life are accidental to this perfection" (Walsh, 1981: 214). The master advices the disciples to keep a clear and consistent focus of following the inspirations in the heart towards the divine to enter spiritual awakening and enlightenment, "I pray you, then, to follow eagerly after this humble stirring of love in your heart. It will be your guide in this life, and will bring you grace in the next" (Walsh, 1981: 214–215). The master clarifies that this inspiration is from a deeper source of spiritual heart and not from the physical heart. Several leaders journey of wholeness concur with this process of spiritual wakening with purification, illumination, and union with the higher self. Palmer identified his inner journey towards wholeness through the metaphors of the seasons. The iterative process of conscious and intentional learning from life experiences helped him keep moving with undying optimism and confidence towards his inner light:

> In the Fall, things get shut down; in the Winter, it looks all are dead; in the Spring, there is new life all over, but sometimes the hail comes before even you harvest the crop. But in good years, in the Summer with its superabundance, its harvest started asking whom this is meant to feed. These are beautiful metaphors for the inner journey. There is this spiral cycle if you are in the first year. You are a farmer, hails may destroy the crop, that is pretty devastating, but if you are a farmer, you go back to the ground and try again; if you are in your 18 or 25 years of farming, I don't think it is any less painful, but you have more confidence that you can work your way through. That is spiral, double helix, or seasonal patterns I have probably seen throughout my life.

The process of awakening the deeper consciousness was gradual for these leaders. Thurston had undergone an excruciating process of uncovering her ego projections to attain deep spiritual awareness. She described the necessity of penetrating through layers of the unconscious mind, its shadows, and ego patterns by self-awareness, trial, and error to uncover the light within: "You have to open the unconscious mind to awaken, as long as the shadow there, it keeps you locked into ego patterns; the ego patterns have to be broken gradually to uncover the light within." Swami Bharati described his experience of awakening his super-conscious self, which is critical to unfolding the deeper dimensions of being open to greater wholeness. This powerful inner awakening takes one to a place of tremendous energy, focus, and vitality beyond measure. He also acknowledged that the journey towards wholeness is messy with continuous learning through mistakes and persistent practice. The practice of regular meditation reinforces the cultivation of an enlightened spiritual self which was central to his inner journey towards the inner light. Leaders testified that this spiritual intelligence is more profound than emotional intelligence and social intelligence, leading one to greater wholeness of life. In the course of time, Swami Bharati became the world-renowned meditator Master who trained people across the globe on the path of spiritual intelligence. He spoke of his awakening the hidden wholeness:

> I have experienced an awakening of my super-conscious self. But I had strayed, slept, and had temptations when I was working in service of the

> people. The meditation reinforces your spiritual self; it continually reinforces it. Meditation is the practice of keeping the independence of your mind. Meditation keep you centered on the true self and help you root out the selfishness. You learn to live experience the internal fullness and internal freedom. The four practices of interior wholeness proposed by The Yoga Sutra (1997:33) are: Maitri, friendliness, Karuna, compassion, Muditha, joy, and Upeksha, detachment. Cultivating a friendly interior and compassionate mind result in inner joy and strength to deal with the negativities in life. It is a meditation that keeps my frail and ailing body. I have many diseases in my body; I have been living with them, but meditation keeps reviving and renewing me. Meditation re-establishes your spiritual identity daily for you. You know you are something other than the mere body.

Sri Sri observed that probing into the depth is characteristic of the wise, and they keep moving towards the light of pure consciousness despite their imperfections. The wise do not remain on the surface of reality but go right deep into reality from a deeper perspective. Therefore, it is imperative to break the vicious cycle of negative thinking and mode of scarcity but become strong and courageous from within to realize wholeness. Their "vessel is always full," and "their cup overflows," manifesting their light and radiance. Movement towards the greater inner light help people remain positive and be indifferent to negativity and shine light in moments of darkness:

> The wise will not stay on the surface but probe into the depth. Things are not blurred; your vision is blurred. Infinite actions prevail in the wholeness of consciousness, and yet the consciousness remains perfect, untouched. Realize this now and be natural. In this world, everything cannot be perfect all the time. Even the best, the greatest of actions, performed with the noblest intentions, will have some imperfections. It is but natural. Unfortunately, the tendency of our minds is to grab the defect and hold on to it. And, in the process, we end up making our moods, our minds imperfect, and our souls reel with this nonsense. It is imperative to get out of these cycles and feel the inner freedom to become strong and courageous from within to awaken the higher consciousness. (Sri Sri)

Sister Gefre spoke about her mystical inner journey and spiritual encounters with the light as a Catholic Nun engaged in massage ministry. Her journey revealed her spiritual sensitivity and mystical insights. Her longing for transcendence was fulfilled in her spiritual encounters while doing the healing work of massage, and that filled her life with joy, wonder, and fulfillment. She was convinced that she was led by this mystical light:

> And one day, I was doing massage, and I felt Jesus standing there right beside me even though I did not see him. He said you know you wanted to see my father. And he just walked away, and there the *father figure* showed up. *Father* was not a person to me; what happened was: I was just wrapped in a glow of light, it was a very bright light, and I am sure it was the *father figure*. This experience of being in light continued for a week. Is it strange that nobody sees this light that I was walking in? And the *father* figure was very present, and this presence faded after a few months. But I knew I got to see the *father figure* more personally, and I felt joy and deep satisfaction in my ministry, for this light led me. I am 78 now; this spiritual encounter happened forty years back, and still, it comes. Many nights, I do spiritual reading, and I try to love him, and often he comes, and I do not fall asleep until three in the morning. I then say, why don't you go? But I say, no, I want you to be here; I will catch up with my sleep sometime during the day. Those were some of the great moments in my life where I moved closer to the divine light.

These leaders testified that their journey of coming closer to the light was a life-long adventure of transformation through the ups and downs of life. Their search and explorations helped them broaden their base and deepen their spiritual roots. Moving through the path of purification, illumination and unification, they ignited the fire in their souls. The move towards the light fuels, heals, and enlighten the soul. The non-linear process of their journey was marked by learning, reflection, and contemplation unleashing unfathomable resilience, strength, and vitality. The deep longing for transcendence kept them moving closer to the light.

Discovering Hidden Harmony

The participant leaders realized that there is a hidden wholeness beneath the broken surfaces of life. It is a sense of spiritual awakening that enables one to see the hidden wholeness amid the daily brokenness of life. This inner awakening helps one not succumb to cynicism or indifference in the wake of manifold crises that emerge from time to time. Leaders can discover this inner audacity with rigorous cultivation of Spirit and mental discipline and tap into the invisible fecundity, a fountain of wisdom. From this more profound perspective, these leaders demonstrated that there is a way for embracing Everything; the brokenness and bright spot of life. Everything becomes integrated and harmonized at this deeper level of reality. Like gentle streams beneath the mountains, innocence, virtue, and infinity meet. This spiritual disposition of hidden harmony will help one lead an authentic and audacious life, overcoming the surface's brokenness. Mix (2018) argued that the mechanistic view of the world had displaced the importance of the unifying principle of the soul. Palmer spoke about the need to cultivate the inner ability to perceive hidden harmony and wholeness in the everyday brokenness of our life:

> In his writing, Merton sees the hidden wholeness beneath the broken surfaces. It is an invisible fecundity, a fountain of wisdom. It is not hard to find; if you look at the morning paper and hear the daily news, there is brokenness everywhere. In our time, what isn't broken? Families are ruined, foreign policies are broken, the environment is broken—terminally broken; many lives are broken, and then the patriotic war machine going on; probably a third of the homeless people in this country are veterans of war. And vast numbers of people are coming from Iraq with post-traumatic disorder, depression, horrific wounds, and so forth— there is brokenness everywhere. And if that is all there, the options of how to live are pretty slim. Merton's words appealed to me; if there is a way to look at the brokenness and see the hidden wholeness; that is the path of spiritual awakening.

Several leaders in the study recognized that the core values in different religions and cultures are not entirely different, although the forms of expression differ. The practices are other, but the essential spiritual values remain the same. Although the forms of religious rituals and traditions differ, the leaders found harmonious unity in seeking the essential values reflected in each major religion. The sublime love in Christianity, the sense of deep fraternity of Islam, the non-duality consciousness of Hinduism, the kindness and compassion of Buddhism, the indomitable will and striving by the Judaism, and the cosmic consciousness of the indigenous religions. The interconnectedness of these universal values shows the deeper harmony and strength of co-existence and collaboration as one humanity respecting the diversity that makes life enriching and colorful. Swami Bharati spoke about the hidden common values in cultures that promote harmony and peace:

> I don't find the values differ, but the form differs. Ritual practices may vary. If you do fire ceremony called *Homa*, you use the herb here in India. Recently, I got incensed from Guatemala, the incense they use there for fire ceremonies. But the Spirit is the same, and the forms may differ at every step; I found reinforcement to the same view that there is a hidden harmony in life amid diversity of religious rituals and ceremonies and scriptures.

Swami Bharati associated hidden harmony with a unifying stream of consciousness hidden in different cultures and religions: "From my search and wide expansive search of the other religions and thought systems, I conviction that there is a stream of unifying consciousness in all different cultures, religions, and spiritualities." Being conscious of the hidden presence of the divine in various vicissitudes of life, the presence of *Sachi-dananda*, truth, consciousness and bliss, Swami Bharati acknowledged that his service to humanity was guided from within and relatively effortless: "One blessing when you live in the presence of God is that things work out effortlessly. You only make *Sankalpa* which means intention; you will find the hidden presence of the divine guiding and directing your steps." Through the daily practice of inner silence, Archbishop Flynn discovered his hidden wholeness even when he faced enormous challenges as a spiritual leader. He noted that he regular practice of meditation and adoration daily helped him clear his mind from the stress and strains of life and renew the freshness and discovery of the inner harmony beyond division and distress:

> I believe that spending time in silence daily and knowing that God loves me has made all the difference in the world; it has kept me balanced and peaceful within, it has kept me with a sense of humor, and it permitted me to face enormous challenges which every leader does. Indeed, every Bishop does. It gives a sense of being comfortable with self and peace and harmony within.

Ambassador Susan Johnson emphasized the need for striking a good balance between mind, body, and Spirit to enhance the quality of life and ministry. She noted, "In my circles, I am the balance doctor who maintains an outstanding balance of family, ministry, and public life." "I wrote a book "Rhythm of rest" to highlight the importance of discovering the harmony in life" Most of the women who began with me forty years ago have either died or left ministry since they did not keep the balance of life without knowing how to take a break from their active life. Looking back at his life, Palmer explained how he could see hidden harmony amid many broken moments in his life. Everything that was done or happened somehow made sense from a holistic perspective of life. The disposition of hidden wholeness did not happen overnight but painfully evolved, penetrating through life's illusions, embracing the strengths and weakness; light and shadows. As we grow in wisdom, we realize that Everything in life belongs to one another and Everything is interconnected beyond the seeming duality and separation. We see that life and death are not opposites. They do not cancel out one another; neither do goodness and badness. A journey towards the wholeness of life calls for a transition from *order* to *disorder* and finally to *reorder*. The realization of hidden wholeness does not replace the brokenness but aligns them to a unified whole without feeling divided.

> From the beginning, I have been sharing the hidden wholeness in me. I see in myself fundamental brokenness; golden boy being challenged in many ways, there are shadows, things swept under the rug. My view of myself is slowly evolved, painfully evolved. Beyond that sense, oh! I am a mess; there is this hidden wholeness. Both the strength and weakness and light and shadows, the hidden wholeness does not replace them but aligns them. We come to it by integrating two sides. An excellent catholic writer, Richard Rohr, has a book, *Everything Belongs*. This is one of his points that "everything belongs." I like that title. And it is a fantastic moment in life; a great passage in life, you begin to understand; Everything somehow done or happened somehow belongs. That is part of your wholeness; that is part of your hidden wholeness. And manifest that without being caught in the notion that things are separate. (Palmer)

Considering weaknesses or failures as a source and way of learning rather than denying them will help us manifest the hidden meaning. A disposition of authenticity and vulnerability is inevitable to embrace the shame of failures and the pain of dark moments in life to learn lessons that lead to inner awakening to a sense of wholeness in life. Treating failures as life-giving gifts is the way to manifest the hidden purposes of life. Then, in the second half of life, you are strong enough to hold the contradictions in yourself and others with compassion. Palmer described how his way of learning led him to manifest the hidden wholeness of life; its like seeing the light through the cracks:

> When I stop treating those episodes of being fired or failure at Spanish Harlem as things to be ashamed of or something to cast behind and be forgotten, I start treating them as sources of learning, learning about who I am, what the world is, and how the world works. I can dance with that, rather than more death-dealing. When I start doing that, I manifest hidden wholeness. If you talked to me 40 years ago, I wouldn't talk about my failures in Spanish Harlem, for it didn't belong to me; it didn't belong to the life I thought I wanted to live. Now I understand that it does belong, and it is part of me. If you had talked to me during the depression, Palmer, what is the life-giving role of depression? You are kidding; I am going to kill myself tonight. Now, I talk about it with the sense of serving others even more, fundamentally having learned about who I am through it. Oh, yes, you see the light through the cracks.

Cultivating contemplative eyes to see the hidden harmony in the world and ourselves will help us to reveal the deeper dimensions of our Being. The best practice of growing a contemplative eye is probably what Ken Wilber calls an "integral practice" In integral spiritual practice, we exercise all parts of ourselves daily regarding spiritual growth and wholeness. We do something for the body to keep it healthy (e.g., regular exercise, Yoga, walking, swimming); we do something for the emotions to keep it positive (e.g., therapy, dreamwork, emotional release); we do something for the mind to keep it afresh (e.g., reading, journaling) and we do something for the soul to keep it radiant (e.g., meditation) and feel the joy within. Palmer shared his conviction that each of us can trace the hidden wholeness, and by giving expression, we can enrich one another:

> I do believe that if we cultivate contemplative eyes to see the hidden in ourselves and the world, it gives us hope in doing this in whatever small way we are doing. We all have small ways to do things to reveal that wholeness. Bloom more fully and give expressions to that hidden wholeness in the world, for we are all inter-connected in different ways.

Swami Bharati was convinced that a hidden spiritual force within the body could be awakened with regular spiritual practice. The soul force can overcome the weakness of the body, and this unifying soul force can be awakened in those who pursue spiritual practices. Re-kindling the soul a pleasant place, mind joyful compassionate and friendly, and being indifferent to the negativities of life will help the leaders thrive and bring harmony in place of disharmony, light in places of darkness and peace in places of conflict. Thus, the mind achieves a state of homeostasis or steady mindedness to embrace the joyful and sorrowful experiences of life with deeper awareness and peaceful disposition. With breathwork and contemplative practices, the mind was disciplined, and the hidden soul force was awakened. With regular spiritual practices, the hidden powers of the soul such as love, peace, kindness, fortitude, and self-control will manifest inner freedom and hidden wholeness. Thus, the hidden spiritual power and energy of the soul quickened with daily mediation practices.

> The soul force and the *Prana* awaken your body. These people will tell you, there are times when I am lying down, and I think I won't get up anymore. But my master inside me says, is your work done? I reply, no, it's not done. Come on, get up; I taught you the *prana vidya*, the breathwork, use it; awaken yourself, get up; I do. I am not living by the force of the body but by the force of the soul. You see my five-compressed disk; still, I am sitting straight. It is proof of *Yoga* and its effectiveness of *Yoga*. (Swami Bharati)

Mutua recognized the hidden strength of the moral force to counter evil forces and asserted that moral force is more powerful than military force to bring lasting peace and unity. When the unprecedented Coronavirus pandemic of 2019 put the world at a stand still, it was evident that the countries with more unified decision-makers faced a threat more effectively than the countries where decision-makers are not united. The soul force or moral force is the hidden power present in humanity that needs to be awakened to counter the divisive forces of fear, polarization, violence, and war.

> I remember one time; the whole world was obsessed with the idea that the third world war was coming; terrible weapons like nuclear arms were created, and one of the weapons was AIDS itself. Because hundreds of people prayed that there never be such a war, there never was one. If enough people pray, we can stop even great disasters. Use the moral force and not the military force to win over evil. (Mutua)

The sacred texts of different cultures and religious traditions indicate hidden spiritual potential, and by awakening the inner power, the hidden harmony becomes manifest. A state of expanded consciousness is a developmental imperative; like Victor Frankl and Abraham Maslow, Pamela

Reed (2003) stated that self-transcendence is a natural and desired developmental stage that people must reach to be fulfilled and have a sense of wholeness. Swami Bharati testified to such an experience of self-transcendence that makes one whole. Swami Bharati had a profound experience of the spiritual luminosity and power when he visited famous places of pilgrimage across the globe irrespective of the different religions that held those places sacred. The following testimony reveals his heightened spiritual sensitivity and a sense of higher consciousness hidden in humanity:

> Mara (afflictive desires and forces in the form of evil) came to Buddha and offered the world's empires. But when something else becomes your reality, the kingdoms become nothing. You learn to be in the world but not of the world. An experience of transcendence makes you whole. You see the whole and act from the whole being to touch people lives meaningfully.
>
> When you go to that cave, electricity hits your head, and I had the same experience when I visited the shrine of the Black Madonna Church at Montserrat, Spain. I had the same experience in Laverna, Italy. Those are laces of awakened *Kundalini* (spiritual energy) whatever names you gave, Holy Ghost or others.

Leaders in the study spoke about the possibility of awakening the hidden potentiality of the soul, even though one might undergo severe discipline and external hardship. After having experienced severe persecutions and hardships at the hands of the colonialists, Mutua asserted with great confidence, "Even though your body is broken but your soul is not defeated. Our quest for wholeness is hearing this call to self-salvation for there is potential within." Thurston gained insight into her hidden consciousness through her painting and her own mystical experiences. She noted, "I got initiated in *Transcendental Meditation*, every day I did the meditation. Within six weeks I had my first transcendental experience through meditation other than through painting." She recalled that she gained the power of reconciling the opposites by discovering her spiritual potential. She embarked on the pursuit of fully exploring her spiritual consciousness:

> I had several other mystical experiences. One was an oral transmission where I quickly wrote insights down. It was a dissertation about the reconciliation of the opposites. Unity comes with the reconciliation of opposites. It was profound teaching which guided me into my wholeness. I continued my painting. As I was painting, I went into an altered state; a force in my

> body made me paint naturally, and I had a brush in both hands; I was ambidextrous. As soon as I finished painting, I looked at it, and I could not believe I had done it. It felt like somebody else painted it. After a few years, I became more interested in what was going on inside me; I wanted to understand the hidden consciousness; the Spirit was pulling me in that direction, and doing painting and selling was not interesting anymore.

Thurston's exploration of her hidden consciousness helped her experience her spiritual self with luminosity and grace. She recalled her extraordinary sense of heightened awareness. "But I was so held, so complete, and I was so happy. And every day a new lesson and a new grace, everything was grace-filled, my eyesight; Everything which I looked at was grace, filled with grace and beauty." Sri Sri explored the question of the polarity between form and formlessness to discover the hidden harmony in the universe. To gain inner freedom, the path of meditation to explore the depth of the inner Spirit, which is formless yet dynamic, has to be explored. The ability to make inner exploration will determine one's capacity to embrace the whole. He experienced inner harmony through his contemplative pursuit of the formless Spirit.

> Philosophically, I was asking whether God is with form or formless? One *sadhu* (ascetic) said differently, "You are both, with form and formlessness, then why not God be both." Even every human being is both form and formlessness. If you look into the mind, you don't see any forms. It is formless. Thus, realizing this polarity is very important for gaining inner freedom. I realized that the whole universe is in the form of God. The formless Spirit is in the universe. Divinity is both form and formless. Therefore, you can experience inner freedom and harmony through meditation on the formless Spirit. (Sri Sri)

Abbess Pema discovered the hidden dimension of life when she practiced *Zen* meditation and realized her inner capacity. "Something I tell you, which is very important in life. Since I became more contemplative, I have a great concentration in sitting meditation; after a few months, I could go into a place of deep peace and joy" (Abbess Pema). She expressed her ability to love unconditionally. "I became so certain of the other dimension of life by looking inside. I realized there is a capacity to love with no conditions." In the Buddhist tradition, discovering hidden wholeness is learning to live fully in the moment. Abbot Phap Son explored how a sense of mindfulness can help us to find the harmony and wholeness hidden in every moment of our life:

> In the Buddhist tradition, having inner harmony is to come to the stage where there is a certainty. And come to the point of no journey, just being in the present without the worries of the past and anxieties about the future. Mindfulness is the gift of being present in the moment. That may mean coming back to the breath and being still. Life moves from moment to moment. This moment contains the wholeness and harmony. That is the nourishment of mindfulness. Maybe you don't have to go 1,000 miles. Maybe being here and now is most important. Creating peace and harmony within oneself is a way to make peace and harmony in the world.

Surviving through the torments of the Rwandan genocide, Ilibagiza discovered her hidden wholeness and harmony by learning to forgive the killers from her heart. The deep hatred and a sense of revenge were far removed through her intense prayers and divine grace. "The feeling of hatred was the primary obstacle between the killers and me; now the hate is gone. It was pure grace. I know before I was in hell, but now I find myself almost in paradise." Sister Rosalind's prayer and meditation practice helped her discover hidden spiritual strength to deal with pain and suffering in her healing massage ministry and offer consolation to many. She recalled how she dealt with compassion fatigue: "If you learn to keep a detachment in prayer, you can be very compassionate without being burned out. We need to step back to step forward. Learning to do things with a sense of detachment is key to maintaining stability and grace under pressure. You experience the inner peace and maintain the calm disposition so that you are not caught up in dealing with the pain and suffering of people."

Pope (2022: 3) described the unitive stage, "This is the way of those who have their minds detached from temporal things, such that they enjoy great peace, and are not agitated by various desires, nor are they moved to any great extent selfish desires." Having been largely purged of these things, they have their minds on the spiritual dimension. It is called "unitive" since, at this stage, there is a "union" with the transcendent by love and the experience and exercise of that wholesome love that is universal and intimate at the same time. Cheng (2019) points out that there are three kinds of problematic human consciousness in Western culture. The first is anthropocentrism. Human beings are regarded as superior to other species, resulting in the alienation of human beings from other living creatures. The second developed in the Scientific Revolution of the seventeenth century and the eighteenth century, nature was treated as mechanical, controllable, and usable because people attained unprecedented confidence in human knowledge. This attitude gives rise to nothing but the alienation of human beings from nature. The third problematic type of consciousness is a limited perception of the reality of the self in modern society from a worldly point of view. The effort to ground the self through material means only leads to a sense of lack. This lack causes the alienation of a person from their true nature and consciousness. The accumulation of these three mindsets is behind today's alienation of nature from self, self from others, and self from the higher self. This division causes disharmony, and the cultivation of the "mind of sentient beings" brings an antidote to awaken the sense of interconnectedness and wholeness of life.

These leaders engaged in discovering their hidden wholeness by penetrating the broken surfaces with spiritual awareness. It was like a magnificent beaming light coming through the broken window glasses. As a result, they could find meaning and purpose even in turbulent times, cultivating a positive approach to life. Guided by the soul force, or moral power, they could find harmony and peace amid conflict and chaos. These leaders manifested their ability to live fully in the moment, discovering harmony, and wholeness hidden in every moment without grasping onto the past or being anxious about the future. Finding hidden wholeness amid brokenness made them live life to the full and help others do the same.

The leaders experienced their journey towards wholeness as a gradual unfolding of spiritual consciousness as the ultimate dimension of their Being. The practice of solitude and silence through meditation helped them penetrate through the superficial ego presentations and illusions at the surface of personality and unfold deeper dimensions of Being. The capacity for reflective awareness allowed them to practice mind-full living. The power of inner silence and presence in a world of turbulence and turmoil enabled them to penetrate through the illusions of life. The hidden wholeness of each leader manifested through existential struggles and crises like a light coming through the broken surface. The spiritual leaders knew that wholeness is not perfection but a journey towards greater harmony in life while embracing their shadows. They experienced a profound and iterative process of inner transformation that helped them move closer to a unified field of enlightened consciousness and leadership.

References

Amaro, A. (2019). Unshakeable well-Being: Is the Buddhist concept of enlightenment a meaningful possibility in the current age. *Mindfulness, 10*, 1952–1956. https://doi.org/10.1007/s12671-019-01179-7

Anālayo, B. (2021a). The four levels of awakening. *Mindfulness, 12*, 831–840. https://doi.org/10.1007/s12671-020-01530-3.

Anālayo, B. (2021b). The qualities pertinent to awakening: Bringing mindfulness home. *Mindfulness*. https://doi.org/10.1007/s12671-020-01398

Cheng, F. c. (2019). Human consciousness and its discontents: An ecological reading of *the Awakening of Faith* in the *Mahāyāna*. In A. K. Giri (Eds.), *Practical spirituality and human development*. Palgrave Macmillan. https://doi.org/10.1007/978-981-13-3687-4_23

Gordon, M. A. (2019). Awakening to wholeness: Aikido as an embodied praxis of intersubjectivity. In *Aikido as transformative and embodied pedagogy*. Palgrave Macmillan. https://doi.org/10.1007/978-3-030-23953-4_3

Gupta, A., & Reina, C. S. (2022). Leading through crisis: The role of mindfulness. In K. S. Dhiman & F. J. Marques (Eds.), *Leadership after COVID-19. Future of business and finance*. Springer. https://doi.org/10.1007/978-3-030-84867-5_16

Haynes, J. (1993). In a dark time, the eye begins to see. *Journal of Analytical Psychology, 38*, 137–154.

Jung, C. G. (2014). *Collected Works of CG Jung, Volume 9 (Part 2): Aion: Researches into the phenomenology of the self* (Vol. 56). Princeton University Press.

Leighton, T. (2003). *Faces of compassion: Classic bodhisattva archetypes and their modern expression*. Wisdom Publications.

Mix, L. J. (2018). Mechanism displaces the soul. In *Life concepts from Aristotle to Darwin*. Palgrave Macmillan. https://doi.org/10.1007/978-3-319-96047-0_12

Nissley, N. (2020, May). *Education & Training*. https://www.tcbusinessnews.com/our-finest-hour-the-power-of-recognizing-emerging-values-during-a-crisis/

Ostman, H. (2020). *The awakening*: Challenging authority and rewriting women's spirituality. In *Kate Chopin and Catholicism*. Palgrave Macmillan. https://doi.org/10.1007/978-3-030-44022-0_6

Pennachio, J. (1992). Gnostic inner illumination and Carl Jung's individuation. *Journal of Religion and Health, 31*, 237–245. https://doi.org/10.1007/BF00986275

Pope, C. (2022). *The purgative, illuminative, and unitive stages of spiritual life*. Retrieved on June 2022 from http://www.blog.adw.org.

Racionero A. (2018). The new leader as spiritual hero: The way of awakening. In J. Neal (Eds.), *Handbook of personal and organizational transformation*. Springer. https://doi.org/10.1007/978-3-319-66893-2_46. https://doi.org/10.1007/978-3-319-29587-9_46-1

Scharmer, O. (2009). *Theory U: Leading from the future as it emerges*. Berret-Koehler Publishers Inc.

Sirimane, Y. (2016). *Entering the stream to enlightenment, experience the stages of the Buddhist path in contemporary Sri Lanka*. Equinox Publishing.

Sreechinth, C. (2022, June). *Musings of Carl Jung*. https://www.google.com/books/edition/Musings_of_Carl_Jung/

The Yoga Sutras. (1997). *Translated by Swami Satchidananda*. Integral Yoga Publications.

Walsh, J. (Ed.). (1981). *The cloud of unknowing*. Paulist Press.

Woiwode, C., & Woiwode, N. (2019). Practical spirituality and the contemporary city: Awakening the transformative power for sustainable living. In A. K. Giri (Eds.), *Practical spirituality and human development*. Palgrave Macmillan. https://doi.org/10.1007/978-981-13-3687-4_9

Zenoff, D. B. (2013). Why organizations can endure for decades. In *The Soul of the Organization*. Apress. https://doi.org/10.1007/978-1-4302-4966-5_5

CHAPTER 6

Serving the Greater Goodness

The fourth essential theme from the research study, *serving the greater good*, is working ethically for the benefit of all concerned with a high level of awareness of oneself and the environment in which one lives. The theme describes the impact of leaders' awakened sense of co-responsibility and ethic of universal stewardship in their journey towards wholeness. Credo Mutua, an African Spiritual leader stated, "We are not who we think we are; we are not the owners of us but beings at the service of all." The phrase "beings at the service of all" indicates the transformed state of consciousness and enlightened actions to be of benefit to all sentient beings. In the similar vein, Swami Veda Bharati, a World spiritual leader in Yogic Meditation indicated his sensibility of being at the service of all, "To love all children as much as to love the children of my body; whoever comes in my presence should feel loved." Having experienced and made sense of many crises in their life and life of others, the leaders embraced the challenge and that led them towards an awakening of hidden wholeness. The intra-psycho-spiritual process of awareness, acceptance, and awakening led to offer themselves for the service of all.

This higher level of awareness and spiritual intelligence helped the leaders to see the interconnectedness of the world and embrace the Earth as one Family. A new sense of enlengthened leadership enabled them to commit their lives for serving the greater good. In addition, these

T. Thakadipuram, *Leadership Wholeness, Volume 1*,
Palgrave Studies in Workplace Spirituality and Fulfillment,
https://doi.org/10.1007/978-3-031-08053-1_6

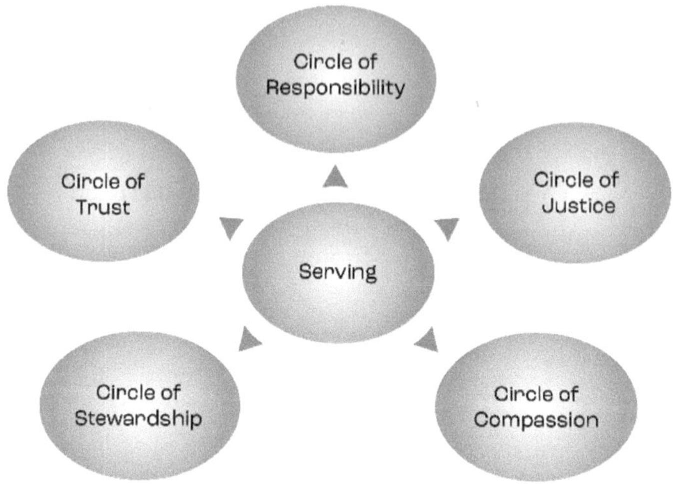

Fig. 6.1 Serving the greater good

inner dynamics of leadership wholeness helped them expand the sphere of their being into various other outer dimensions of life. The sub-themes of Serving the Greater Good: Circle of Trust (Personal Trust), Circle of Responsibility (Organizational Responsibility), Circle of Justice (Social Justice), Circle of Compassion (Global Compassion), and Circle of Stewardship (Environmental Stewardship) manifest the outer spheres of leadership wholeness as presented in Fig. 6.1. The circle of trust included the mentors, friends, and coaches who would help the leaders to see themselves clearly through authentic feedback and spiritual support. Having gained the trust of key support groups and colleagues, the leaders were able to exercise their leadership responsibilities with wisdom, compassion, and courage in the organization and beyond. They enabled the organizations to stand up for their immediate mission and the greater mission to serve the society especially for the least privileged. Some of them were global leaders extending compassionate service across the world. All the leaders were ecologically mindful and recognized the deepening crisis of the environment and the urgency of the need to care for the souls that included caring for the planet's soul.

Awareness of Interconnectedness

There is a deep connection among the living beings; everything is linked to everything else, sharing a common roof on the same planet. From this perspective of wholeness, the spirit of unity is emphasized to overcome division and separation manifested in the world. Mutua, an African spiritual leader, who traveled across the globe, noted a profound link between different cultures and traditions of humanity. He observed: "I found to my surprise that all of us everywhere share links, very deep links; in other words, we have more in common that binds us together than differences that divide us." A growing appreciation of the participatory nature of the universe enables one to rediscover the fact of relationality and interconnectedness. There is a deep connection between the self and nature, self and other-selves, and self and the higher self (Scharmer, 2007). The shared cosmic consciousness works as harmonizing link amid diversity and differences in the empirical world.

Realizing higher consciousness, Swami Bharati pointed out that realization of spiritual oneness and cosmic awareness is possible through an awakening of the mind: "The entire cosmos, all its galaxies, the particle of dust, all little waves and ripples in the ocean of consciousness everything becomes integrated. When you look deeply into your mind, you see nothing. Still, you also see everything deeply connected." From a spiritual point of view, these leaders traced a deep interconnectedness among cultures across the globe. Swami Bharati observed: "But the spirit is the same and the forms may differ at every step; I found a reinforcement to the same view in all my travels across cultures." Mutua expressed a similar view when he said: "I found that the world is one… all these differences are relative." Thurston recalled her experience of expanded, connected awareness from childhood onwards: "When many years later when I got into *Samadhi*, contemplation, I recognized it and remembered that when I was on the farm, it was the same state, a very expanded connected state. At this moment, there is no inside or outside." Thurston expressed the experience of interconnectedness as an experience of synchronicity. An understanding of expanded awareness through meditation and contemplation helped her see the world's interdependence and interconnectedness in her new field of consciousness (Jung, 1973). An endless path of synchronicity with the whole of creation marked her journey towards wholeness:

> My life has become an endless path of synchronicity. Everybody's life is like that, except they do not have enough expanded awareness to see all the pieces; they see life in a very linear fashion. For me, it is an all-encompassing, holistic experience. I can connect the dots in every direction. And I see inter-relationship between everything. And this is what you talk wholeness. Wholeness is just the collection of parts connected. It is the unity in diversity in the whole creation. In my place, you have zebra in the yard, and you can hear the roar of the lions; they are on the other side, for there is a reserve on the other side of the road.

A deep sense of belonging and connectedness was the core of Sri Sri's quest for wholeness. When a person gets enlightened, their awareness level expands, creating a sense of spiritual oneness and solidarity. Experience of the non-duality of nature and spirit was the bedrock of self-realization that reflected cosmic harmony and oneness. Sri Sri shared this enduring realization of the experience of oneness in his life: "I had this feeling from very childhood onwards that the whole world, everybody is part of me. Everybody belongs to me and no one is separate although distinct. The experience of oneness was quite natural for me." McBrayer, the chief flight control officer of one of the major Airlines, emphasized the fact that our understanding and awareness of the world is fast changing with technology, transportation, and communication revolution, and the ability to get connected globally enabled people to grow in a deeper appreciation of the world as an interconnected system:

> The world is a lot smaller place than it was fifty years ago. This is a globally connected world now. And I think you have to look at it with a global lens and be aware of the deep interconnectedness and global diversity. This new outlook makes us appreciate the hidden harmony of existence while honoring the genuine differences in our pursuit of collective well-being and the greater good. With this higher level of awareness, American Airlines has created interfaith chapels, prayer rooms, or meditation rooms at the busy airports such as Dallas in the USA and other places for people to relax, reflect, and find a moment of peace in their high stressed life of travel and business.

The revolution of the digitally connected world helps enlightened leaders balance the triple bottom line of people, profit, and planet in designing sustainable solutions for the future (Bronner et al., 2021). Archbishop Flynn emphasized the importance of exercising our responsibility to love our neighbor both personally and collectively across the globe: "Loving our neighbor is personal; one individual at one level; it also has a social dimension, our families, and communities; loving those we do not know, those living across the globe." He reiterated the responsibility to develop a sense of solidarity with racially and culturally different people: "All of us are called to develop a sense of solidarity with our neighbors who are racially and culturally distinct from us. We begin to live out the principle of unity in diversity, which is vital for our co-existence." The ethic of respect and co-responsibility for the other emerges from this deep sense of interconnectedness (Atenasio, 2019). This sense of co-responsibility assumes responsibility for common challenges and willingness to work together to advance the common good. Archbishop Flynn noted, "We must see that everyone is valued and respected and allow the marginalized their basic needs and rights." Similarly, Abbess Pema echoed the sentiments of love and responsibility in its personal and global dimensions:

> I grew up Christian, not so much with text but in spirit. My mother was imbued with the Christian principle of love your neighbor as you love yourself; no matter where people come from, what they speak, or how they live, just love them. As a Buddhist, I realize that this principle of love has both personal and global dimensions.

In search of his identity and meaning in life, Abbot Phap Son joined a voluntary association for environmental justice. From his social justice ventures and learning, Abbot Son realized that the whole of creation is interdependent and interconnected as he embraced the teaching of famous environmental scientists. "Satish Kumar, Frijitof Capra, and Vandana Siva were prominent teachers of the interconnectedness of reality and environmental justice advocating sustainable use of existing natural resources and advancement of remedial technologies. It was a deep experience cultivating a sense of solidarity with nature." Surviving tribal discrimination and genocide in Rwanda, Ilibagiza described how she was convinced of the oneness of humanity and the need to treat everyone as a human being forgoing hatred and divisions:

> My eyes just opened up. I knew this school. They have taught us about this war. But we did not want to talk about those days, how discriminated against we were at that time in the country. Forgetting about it, at least I was able to see people as human beings. Maybe they should have taught

> me; I should have told them when things were going bad. But I was completely trusting and believed that everyone was same as a tribe. That was the belief in my heart.

Zimpleman expressed the hope that more and more companies develop leadership and extend their sense of responsibility beyond just the business purpose: "You are seeing serious efforts by companies, large and small, particularly the larger companies began to take responsibility way beyond their business purpose. As leaders expand their understanding and perspective of the world as inter-related phenomena, they realize that they are serving not only their immediate organization but also the greater good of the society and its sustainable future. As a public company, we have responsibility to shareholders, but we have even a greater responsibility to society to ensure a sustainable future."

The leaders expressed their conviction of the inter-relatedness of all living beings on this planet and how it helped foster an ethic of co-responsibility. They have experienced a spiritual awakening and a realization that the entire cosmos and all living beings are interconnected. In turn, this conviction enabled them to promote co-responsibility, global solidarity, and universal Stewardship. Their shared experience of wholeness paves the way for an endless path of synchronicity and harmony despite apparent division, conflict, and disharmony in life. This higher level of awareness of the co-existence of reality comes as a critical antidote to the culture of division, polarization, exploitation, and mutual destruction. The leaders' understanding of the inter-connectedness of the world became the source and base for fostering a culture of co-responsibility in serving the greater good and guiding their organizations to a sustainable future.

Living with Deep Differences

A higher level of awareness of the interdependence and interconnection of the reality of existence enables one to maintain a deep respect for everything and everyone by acknowledging the differences that make a difference. The leaders were able to appreciate the world with an underlying sense of unity and harmony without undermining diversity's power and beauty. With an awareness of the commonality and differences, the leaders were engaged in promoting shared values that help unite humanity. They worked towards creating understanding and harmony among cultures and religions (Großmann et al., 2018). With this perspective, the globally diverse workforce was designed in many companies to keep up the principle of integration and differentiation. McBrayer led the teams of different cultures and religions in the globally diverse American Airlines to promote harmony, appreciation, and peace. Swami Bharati shared about his practice of respecting the different cultures by learning about them. That eagerness to understand and appreciate the wisdom of other cultures made him feel at home in any culture. While sense of unity helps one to seek common ground and appreciation of differences that makes difference helps one to expand the consciousness beyond one's limited perspectives. Swami Bharati made an effort to incorporate wisdom from different cultures and traditions in his teaching:

> I feel at home in any culture. But I must say that I can't give up the Indian Food. I went to China, and the temple gave me special honors. And when I go there, I do not begin with Upanishad, but I start with Lao-tzu and Taoism. Lao-tzu and Taoism are the epitome of holism and wholeness; and the best principles of self-governance. Upanishad gives testimony to the fact of the world as *Vasudaivakudumbakam, which means* "world as one family." (Ayamnijah paroveti ganana laghuchetasam udaracaritanamtu Vasudhaiva Kutumbakam (Maha Upanishad VI.71–73). This meaning of this verse means the narrow-minded people think of the world as high and low; me and the other, but the large-hearted consider the world as one family". (quoted in Seelan, 2015: 143)

Sri Sri recalled his disposition of a deep sense of respect, which was ingrained in him, helped to appreciate the goodness in everyone across the globe irrespective of race, religion, and culture when he reached out to 145 countries as a world spiritual leader. More than ever, diversity is such an important aspect on having a productive and healthy workplace, therefore respecting the diversity of your team and organization is just as important, allowing for people to feel accepted for being their authentic self. Respecting the dignity of the person is very fundamental to the spirituality and it results in how you can treat the other as your brother or sister. A deep appreciation of the other is the hall mark of a great leader who is always willing to learn from the other respecting them as a source of wisdom. Knowledge and wisdom as can come from many sources, so a sense of deep respect will help one listen and learn and appreciate the insight gained at every encounter. He noted:

> One thing is I used to respect everything and everybody. A sense of deep respect is part of my life. This is ingrained in me due to culture or education; I can't pinpoint it. Once, while traveling on a train from Delhi to Allahabad, I met an A/C (Air Conditioning) operator. The A/C operator was speaking with high knowledge and wisdom. I sense that knowledge and wisdom can come from the poorest of the poorest to the richest. Yes, the lord can come in any form. I met a nun in England; she used to say, if you can't see Jesus in the first person you see in the morning, you cannot meet him in the whole day; a sense of supernatural vision and conviction; ability to see the extraordinary dignity even in an ordinary person.

Archbishop Flynn manifested his deep respect for different religions and cultures in his words and actions. He believed that to be religious is to be inter-religious, and to be human is to be inter-human. Respecting the journey of each one paves the way for harmonious existence which prevents any form of bigotry, prejudice, and mutual destruction. When religion is politicized, it becomes dehumanized and loses its vital values of love, respect, fraternity, and collaborative existence. One who does not appreciate and learn to live with differences pave the way for self-destruction and the decline of the social harmony and peace. This holistic perspective of deep respect, acceptance, and love helped him demonstrate care for one another and their unique journey to wholeness. He observed that God loves everyone and that belief makes him respect people's differences. Trusting that each one has a unique story and perspective helps one promote joyful partnership based on authenticity and courageous participation, knowing that all are valued and respected. Archbishop Flynn noted that his deep respect for others and their different views brought about great success and joyfulness in his leadership team:

> Well, I think the respect for the other human person makes me reach out to the other. God loves everyone; we can't forget that. And the other person may live differently than I do, but that person's journey needs to be respected. So, I learn that when I am with others, I learn something from them; out of that respect for different religions and faiths. Honoring the significant differences promotes collaboration, team spirit, and happiness. This respect for others and born out of that respect was the collaboration…it is the key to collaboration. And you have gifts that I don't have, and I have gifts that you don't have; let's put them together and see what we can come up with. For example, the bishop has a council or a cabinet; it never bothered me if someone in that council said, pardon me, but I don't

know whether you are going in the right direction with this. Of course, I had people, and the people surrounding me were outstanding, with whom I worked and collaborated. And the result was a happy management team.

Having experienced the ordeal of apartheid in South Africa, Mutua was convinced that only a deep sense of respect and understanding for the differences in people and cultures could pave the way for harmony in life: South Africa has learned from its horrific past of racial discrimination and paved the way for truth and reconciliation to bring genuine racial harmony and national integration respecting the diversity of culture and race as a blessing rather than a burden. Believing naively in the goodness of people to love and care for one another initially, Mutua underestimated the power of evil forces that could undermine the basic goodness of humanity. Having lived through the horrors of racial bigotry and prejudice spread by the forces of Apartheid regime, he learned to appreciate more deeply the importance of respecting the diversity of life, culture, and civilizations to promote harmonious future of the society.

For a long time, I believed that if people understood each other, the world would be a better place. If people understand this man or that woman, what is it that he or she is afraid of? Whatever may be people's likes or dislikes, if we know that we can be good neighbors, we can live in harmony. The only way to live in peace is to understand and respect each other. The initiative of Truth and Reconciliation, directed by Archbishop Desmond Tutu and other enlightened leaders, promoted the idea of living with diversity and significant differences as a sine qua none of co-existence. It is essential to notice that Germany and South Africa have taken sustainable initiatives to preserve unity and diversity inspired by their horrendous past and cultural intolerance. But unfortunately, they were wrought about to protect cultural and racial hegemony. Hopefully, many nations will follow suit, reconciling the past and moving forward with remedial actions for a healthy and harmonious future in the post-digital age.

Palmer noted that he has a deep respect for different traditions and spiritualities. "One of the Eastern spiritual traditions I deeply admire and gain a lot of insights into is Taoism, which celebrates oneness in diversity, the ancient religion of China." One of the critical ways of honoring and living with the profound differences is by engaging in dialogue to promote understanding, making space for discussion and diversity in the workplace and beyond (McIntyre-Mills, 2019). It is not the differences that divide us, but in fact, it is our inability to recognize, value, and celebrate the genuine differences that divides us. The unity in diversity is maintained by convergent and divergent thinking. Abbess Pema indicated how respect is cultivated through dialogue and engagement of the other: "When I go to Benedictine Monastery, the Abbot says, 'we normally think, why not everyone thinks like me'? I realize that this thinking is not born out of respect." "It is not that you are not free to hold a different idea, but the decision-making is done in dialogue and understanding." That is the way to exercise authority by honoring unity in diversity and not by creating uniformity. Discovering common ground in the midst of obvious differences, Maya Angelou, in her celebrated poem, Human Family, stated, "I note the obvious differences between each sort and type, but we are more alike, my friends, than we are unlike" (Angelou, 2022: 1).

The capacity to honor and live with profound differences is born out of a deep awareness that each is unique and special in the galaxy of beings. This awareness manifested deep respect for genuine differences in views, cultures, religions, and races. Out of a deep sense of respect was born the willingness to learn, collaborate, and dialogue with each other to promote harmony and peace. The deep concern for the other is the antidote to the dynamic programming of control and manipulation in an inter-personal relationship, organizational leadership, and community living providing an antidote to prejudice, polarization, and politicization of civic life. These leaders were convinced that there is richness and beauty in honoring and living with the differences that make fundamental differences in life, serving the greater good.

Circle of Trust

On their road to wholeness, these leaders needed to find a few trustworthy relationships where they could be themselves and be honest. Through these authentic and transparent relationships, the leaders could explore themselves and discover their true selves. These relationships were safe, unconditional, and very supportive. Seeking personal and trustworthy relationships, they received guidance, affirmation, and strength to embrace the shadows and struggles of their lives. These leaders explored their authentic self through the circles of relational trust, unleashing joy and enthusiasm for life. Trust is the soul of a relationship, and it needs to be cultivated to grow and thrive as wholesome persons and leaders.

"Trust is the currency in the interdependent, collaborative world" (Covey, 2022: 2). Palmer observed that the circle of relational trust in which he explores his identity and integrity with utmost candidness is one of the most important relationships in his life:

> I think there are two critical things about the journey. First, I need to find at least one or two relationships where I am given that unconditional acceptance. You may be the president of something, but the relationship I am talking about is one where I don't have to be anything special. I don't have to be successful to win the other person's acceptance. All I need to do is to be myself. In this relationship, one can be honest with oneself and feel free to talk about where the confusion is happening, where the failures are happening, and what scares me. These things, as president, I am not going to say a word about in my role, lest people lose confidence in me. It is tough to get real in public, for there is judgment. We need, on our road to wholeness, those relationships in which we can speak honestly about our own life.

Palmer-created circles of trust to help people engage in honest speech and discover their souls. In a safe and confidential climate, when leaders can talk about their innermost struggles and thoughts, they can hear the most profound stirring of their souls. Palmer described the need to create circles of relational trust to be on the path towards wholeness. "And so, the number one factor on the road to wholeness is those opportunities where one can be honest with oneself and others." Palmer reiterated the need for such a reflective process when he noted, Nora Burton says, "the great task in our times is to hear each other into speech, into honest speech, true speech, and real speech." Similarly, Archbishop Flynn emphasized the need for a handful of trustworthy relationships where a person can be who they are without any reservation and can unburden their souls with unconditional acceptance:

> I need to have people in my life and count them on the one hand, the people in my life to whom I can go when I feel I messed something up. And have that person say to me, either with words or a look, that you are still okay. And sometimes, we do not take care of this; especially in leadership roles. We might have spouses, we might have families, but there are times when we can't even go to our spouses and tell our spouses how we messed things up. The complexity of the leadership role is such that we often make mistakes and decisions that are wrong. So, we need to have

> those few people, cultivated friends whom you can count on and have that person say, the sun will rise tomorrow, and you are still okay. It helps one to sort out, and it allows one to confirm one's decision, but it also helps us realize that even though we make a wrong decision, we are still precious people.

Swami Bharati reiterated the significance of maintaining relational trust between oneself and one's master to grow responsibly and be on the path towards wholeness: "One thing that happens in the *guru-shisha* relationship which is marked by deep trust, the disciple is always very critical of the guru in the beginning but remains transparent." Swami Bharati created a circle of trust among his spiritual aspirants called "Satsang" to engage in honest exchange and exploration of the inner self and divine consciousness. Mutua noted that when all his hopes of life were shattered by rejection and religious bigotry, the trustworthy African tribal men, who were traditional healers, saved him:

> And they took me to the Zulu land to my natural mother and grandfather. When Christian prayers failed, when white doctors did not know what was wrong with me, I found people who wore skins; I saw a woman wearing a skin skirt and smeared her body with red oak. I found to my surprise that this woman was my mother. These people, so-called heathens, were the ones who took me to my grandfather and saved me and helped me come back to sanity out from savages. I was trained in traditional wisdom and the path of Shaman, a Sangamon. I was part of the circle of wise men and women from Africa.

Mutua acknowledged that his most trustworthy friend and guide, John Dube, who was one of the founders of the African National Congress, mainly guided his life: "Dube believed in peace, and he believed in understanding. He worked for creating understanding between whites and blacks as one human family. He gave directions to my mind." Thurston was constantly conscious that she was in the circle of trust and guided by supernatural powers: "But I trusted the guidance, and I trusted the grace that is holding me very much." She also recalled that her most trustworthy teacher was instrumental in facilitating her spiritual awakening and finding wholeness in her life:

> I met my first teacher, Francis Sterns. She was a Jungian psychologist. I said I was supposed to be learning about the reconciliation of the opposites.

> She said I know about that because it is a Jungian thing. So, she taught me how to process my shadows and find the light within as a good friend and guide.

Sri Sri was grateful that he was in the close company of great teachers, friends, guides, and mentors as he was growing up. The foundational basis of spiritual life is laid down with the trusted people in your life whether they are teachers, parents, family circles, or business circles. Without this circle of trust worthy people, one cannot build one's life with confidence, clarity, and spiritual orientation. Trust is the center of every healthy relationship, when we think about the most critical relationships especially in our up brining, trust is the key factor, the glue that holds everything in relationship whether, family, business, community, and society at large. The fundamental significance of trust cannot be underestimated in building the wholesome life of leaders and business teams. Sri Sri noted that "Trust is the soul of sustainable business, and integrity is its limb." These circles of relational trust influenced him and helped him grow a universal vision of life:

> From the time I remember, I sat with my teachers. My teacher was the Thankamma teacher who was with Mahatma Gandhi for a long time. She was a spinster who dedicated her life to bringing everyone in the community together. She taught me prayer, values, and *Bhajans*. Similarly, Sudhakar Chaturvedi who was also with Mahatma Gandhi, taught me Sanskrit. He was a man of great trust and noble sentiments. So, I was fortunate to grow up in a circle of trustworthy and wise people.

Several leaders affirmed the critical role of trust played in their life and journey towards wholeness. Abbess Pema disclosed that she could place all her trust in that person when she found her teacher. "As I found a trustworthy spiritual master, it became easy for me to trust": "I felt safe enough to put my life in the hands of the teacher. Giving what is most precious, my life, I have to trust." Abbot Phap Son appreciated the climate of support and relational trust in his community where he could honestly process his life issues. "I can release the burden; I am not sure how to deal with it, but sharing it or making a joke about it." It is "the supporting climate and relational trust that makes the real difference in our life." Similarly, Sister Gefre said that she was fortunate to find sisters who were her ultimate support group: "When I look back now, I see how wonderfully God arranged that here I am today in this community of sisters which is my ultimate support group." She recalled, in turn, how she provided a climate of trust in her healing ministry: "I provide a safe climate of trust during the massage, and they would share their emotional burdens and leave changed people forever." Washburn established a network of CEOs to gather regularly and process their challenges in a trusting environment and teams to gain clarity and wisdom to excel as CEOs and caring leaders of the community. Nissley reiterated the need for developing a trustworthy relationship with ones on Board as well:

> Leaders are caregivers, caregivers to an organization. And you can ask that same question of who will care for the caregivers or who will care for the leaders. But there are very few people who care for the chief executive, you know, the only place that formally comes from is if you've got a caring board, you know, their job, often might be perceived as caring for the CEO. So as a leader, it is inevitable that you develop a circle of trust that keeps you honest and caring for the whole organization.

*The leaders emphasized the need for a circle of trust to grow in authenticity, accountability, and wholeness. They cultivated friends, teachers, mentors, and guides they deeply trusted and respected. The opportunity to explore honestly in a confidential, safe, and supportive climate of trust was critical for the leaders to discover their identity and integrity. Leaders' authentic engagement helped them expand the circle of trust and gain the organization's trust and credibility (*Kerse, 2021*). They learned to process their lives with utmost honesty and transparency through the Circles of Relational Trust. The leaders learned that relational trust is an inevitable ingredient to safely explore their inner selves, receive honest feedback, grow in an environment of wise discernment and thus cultivate an ethic of co-responsibility in their journey towards wholeness.*

Circle of Responsibility

The circle of responsibility for leaders in the study ranges from leading an organization or community of their own to inspiring worldwide audiences with their teaching and discourses. Teams of disciples and volunteers, assuming the responsibilities of managing and leading various networks, supported the leaders. The circle of responsibility centered on their respective roles in the organization as founders, executive leaders, and consultants. These leaders created and sustained organizational and institutional structures to carry out their missions with a great sense of accountability. In addition, they engaged in their sphere of work and responsibilities based on their calling, charisma, and vision. Palmer expanded his circle of responsibility by establishing the Center for Courage and Renewal to strengthen leaders. This center reaches out to working professionals across the nation to enhance their work by integrating who they are with what they do. Palmer noted, "As founder and senior partner of the Center for Courage and Renewal, I take great pride in how this small non-profit organization supports people in the serving professions." He explained how his center helps leaders renew their lives with responsibility and integrity:

> Good work is done with the heart, knowledge, and skill, done with a depth of commitment that brings integrity and courage to the workplace. But workplace culture can make it risky to reveal our hearts. So, we hide them – and sometimes lose them. By supporting teachers, medical professionals, clergy, and others who want to reclaim their hearts, we bring new life to them, their work, and the people they serve.

Abbate was mindful of the changing landscape of economy, politics and market and so relied on the power of networks to engage his management team to navigate the pandemic and the ensuing challenges in the hospitality industry with a higher sense of individual responsibility and organizational responsivity to support and build up the employees to serve the customers with a positive attitude and personal care (Condon, 2022). As a result, Abbate made a significant change in his understanding of the role and responsibility of the leader:

> As a leader, I used to go to restaurants that performed poorly, focusing on the process and results, and now I shifted my sense of responsivity to lift the energy and morale of the workers to assume responsibility and liability for their work and the work of others in the McDonald's chain of restaurants. With the shift, the focus is on implementing the servant, steward, and shepherd model of leadership.

Sri Sri was inspired to start *The Art of Living Foundation (AOL)* to increase the quality of life through spiritual excellence and human values. AOL is now the largest non-governmental organization globally, spread over 145 countries. Sri Sri observed: "An organization should be like a picture frame regarding organizational responsibilities. The frame should not eat away from the picture. Just as without a frame it is impossible to hold a picture, without an organization, any spiritual or social work cannot happen." At the same time, if the organization is too controlled, it is like the frame eating away at the picture, losing creativity and vitality. Sri Sri's organization has a loose structure, which allows freedom and creativity. The circle of responsibility envisaged by Sri Sri supports liberty and stability in organizations. Establishing meditation centers worldwide to train minds and cultivate spiritual consciousness, Swami Bharati expanded his circle of responsibility across the globe. He explained the transformation he underwent to leave the old responsibilities of being a professor at the university and take on a global spiritual mission serving humanity. Moving away from her career as a commercial artist with the new awakening, Thurston illustrated how she was destined to take responsibility as a spiritual teacher for the transformation of the mind. Thurston has a worldwide line of followers and disciples who carry the responsibility of helping people transform their ego-mind through spiritual training and retreats.

> I have been a schoolteacher; I was destined to be a teacher; I was an art teacher after leaving the school. I've been groomed to be a teacher for the transformation of the Ego. The courses I taught were how to process your shadow and dissolve the personality program, the difficult one, limiting, and getting in the way; in other words, the neurosis from childhood that makes up the shadow, I gave *Sakthi* for they would have the transcendent experience. I started the training called spiritual warrior training. They had to sign up for it was not open to the public. My organization is called *Core Light*, which focuses on helping people in spiritual awakening and transformation (Thurston).

Ilibagiza expanded the circle of her responsibility and service by establishing a foundation to help heal the victims of genocide. "Establishing the Ilibagiza Foundation to help others heal from the long-term effects of genocide and war" was her mission in life. Mutua was responsible for finding alternate cures for the menace of AIDS rampant in Africa, as his children were victims of this dreaded disease. Mutua described the enormous responsibility of the world community to combat AIDS. He insisted on the need to assume significant responsibility by concerted efforts to eliminate the disease of AIDS from the face of the earth. Playing his part, Mutua developed indigenous herbal medicine to combat AIDS:

> My heart is bleeding deep within me. I have children, and these children have many children of their own. AIDS has wiped some of my children out. Some of them are here, for I keep them alive with African herbs. African herbs can keep a person busy for many years. Even with full-blown AIDS, a person can be kept alive for 15 years. I wish God could give me the strength of a thousand lions so that we can fight against AIDS and stop it. I have proof among black and white people that we can beat aids with African herbs. If God would give me a thousand lives, it could be stopped. All you need is the power of character and a sense of responsibility to help others. Just as the light was brought to me as a blind person in a blind institution, so I swore I would bring light to others.

After having experienced many setbacks in her mission of doing healing ministry through massage therapy. Sister Gefre took up the responsibility of establishing healing massage therapy centers. Experiencing the power of healing from addictions, psychological trauma, and childhood wounds that blocked the flowering of wholeness in people, Sister Gefre took courage and strong determination to change the bad reputation of massage centers as prostitution parlors and established the pioneering massage center in United states for healing and recovery. She did the powerful healing massage for over fifty years. Today, it is well known that massage enhances blood circulation, increases the flow of oxygen to the tissues and organs, releases toxins, loosens and elongates tight muscles, and slows the heart rate, all of which serve to reduce stress and increase energy flow in the body. The overall effect for most people is a state of relaxation and an enhanced sense of well-being unfolding the healing power of the soul. She expanded her circle of responsibility by establishing many more healing massage therapy centers in many states overcoming the social stigma and turning America as the massage center of the world:

> When you look 40 years back, massage therapy was not well received because it was not received in the community and outside. People would call and complain to my community. I knew it was a beautiful gift, and it was ironic that people would look at this as prostitution. The community did not like it, but a handful of them supported me. I knew I had to change the image of massage. That firm conviction helped me to overcome all the odds and move forward. And interestingly, today, America has become the massage center of the world.

Many CEOs exercised their leadership by being mindful of corporate social responsibility and their duty to enhance the life of the community and society at large, addressing the less fortunate, and marginalized issues. Archbishop Flynn advocated that each of us has a sense of social responsibility to counter injustices in society, even though they might have occurred without our own: "The absence of personal fault for an evil does not absolve one of all responsibility. We must seek to resist and undo injustices we have not caused, lest we become bystanders who tacitly endorse evil, sharing guilt for it." Since the executive eldership decisions highly impact society, it is vital to have socially responsible leaders who champion the cause of social justice and sustainable development. Leadership is a significant antecedent to corporate social responsibility, and wholesome leadership expands the circle of responsibility to society (Ullah et al., 2022).

These distinguished leaders established circles of responsibility with their unique talents and life perspectives. They attracted others into their vision and expanded the circles of responsibility in the changing landscape of modern economy and markets to assume greater individual responsibility and organizational responsibility to serve the greater good. In addition, the leaders assumed moral responsibility to lead others with courage and confidence. The circles of responsibility focused mainly on respective teams in organizations and service networks that helped the leaders not only to engage in a meaningful and authentic journey towards wholeness but also hold them accountable and support others to do the same.

Circle of Justice

Although many leaders do not perceive themselves as champions of social justice, their sense of involvement and advocacy expanded the circle of justice where the cause of the most vulnerable is brought to the forefront of their care and leadership. Social justice is a central obligation of civil society, where the measure of the ethical integrity of a community is how it treats its most vulnerable members (Ross, 2020). The leaders in the study were well aware of social justice and how their perspective can influence and lead the organization to be an instrument of peace and justice in caring for the most vulnerable members. Their actions and policies affected people's thinking and changed the course of events to promote peace and justice across the world. These leaders influenced people by adopting proactive and creative ways of listening, accepting, and advocating for the cause of social justice and social progress. Except a few leaders who challenged the system of racial injustice and women's rights, there was no strong efforts to challenge the big and perversive unjust systems of in justice, poverty, hunger, and climate crisis as such. However, their spheres of influence ranged from the microcosm of their immediate families to the macrocosm of worldwide followers and organizations.

Archbishop Flynn talked about his circle of influence and justice and the people who inspired him profoundly to take up causes of justice in his area of concern: "I spend my life as a priest, bishop, and archbishop; I cannot but appreciate the unity and diversity of the people of faith and champions of the poor from Mother Theresa to Stanly Rother, who was martyred in Guatemala. They influenced me profoundly." He advocated dialogue and mutual learning as a way to integrate cultures and races: "Let us make this church welcoming and learning, a place of encounter and dialogue among peoples of all races and cultures." Combating the evil of racism and cultural prejudice, Archbishop Flynn took steps to influence the hearts and minds of people across races, cultures, and religions as a champion of justice and peace:

> At the archdiocesan level, I am committed to ensuring that people of color have a place at the table in the decision-making and leadership structures of the archdiocese. We will take affirmative steps to ensure that the values and vision of people of color helped shape our direction as a church. I called upon all of the educational institutions of the archdiocese to be especially alert to the issues of racial justice and victims' prejudice and to consciously strive to prepare students who are committed to racial tolerance and racial justice. Where appropriate, materials can be integrated into the curriculum so that students are equipped to understand and combat racism in both its individual and institutional forms.

Engaging in service projects and educational missions in the remote territory of Guyana, Swami Bharati described how he expanded the circle of justice and influence in the life of the people by creating educational institutions for the poor and marginalized: Education is the key to social progress and transformation of the unjust society to greater justice, equity, and freedom. Education was the best means to bring the people out of poverty and give them self-reliance. Swami Bharati noted, "These service initiatives helped the people in the margins come to the mainstream of life. I have absorbed these experiences into one complete whole in my life journey." Swami Bharati's influence spread across the globe through his role as a spiritual leader and his teaching and guidance despite challenging odds: "At that time, the doctor said, if this man sits in the airplane, he is dead; but since then, I have traveled across the world around 15 to 16 times, very busy traveling, giving lectures transforming minds through the practice of meditation." Taking moral responsibility to promote peace and justice, Swami Bharati established an ashram and a school in a remote farming community of Guyana to bring hope to their future and enable them to address the causes of poverty and injustice in the villages. While living under the oppressive regime of Apartheid, Mutua spoke about how he advocated the cause of justice for South Africans who were victims of colonialism to stand on their feet and break free of the clutches of domination and exploitation:

> I ask myself; how can I help people? Our people need help. Our people have no good leader except Mandela. Our people need help to rise on their feet and keep their heads high. Our people need help to break free from the clutches of apartheid, which is still hidden and prevalent. Our people cannot realize the fullness of their humanity until they realize their dignity and self-esteem. South Africa is still under the clutches of economic apartheid and exploitation. Despite colonial oppression, threats, and opposition, I formed alliances with native Zulus and Bushmen to defend our dignity, freedom, and age-old cultural wisdom. We still have a long road ahead of us.

Sri Sri explained how he was able from very early on to influence his peers as a peacemaker and gain respect from renowned as he embarked his mission to bring peace to the warn torn Iraq in 2007. In order to bring respite and peace to a nation disillusioned by years of bloodshed, Sri Sri Ravi Shankar visited Iraq from May 21–24, 2007. It was the first time that an Indian spiritual leader was officially invited by the Iraqi Prime Minister Nouri al-Maliki for a spiritual mission of peace and justice. The Iraqi Prime Minister emphasized the key role of humanitarian organizations like the Art of Living in rebuilding Iraq. He stated, "There are big powers who have big might, but they are not able to unite the hearts and minds of people. This work can be done only by a spiritual leader." When Al-Maliki invited Sri Sri's foundation to undertake its prison rehabilitation program in jails in Iraq. Sri Sri replied that he would like to extend The Art of Living's programs to all sections of Iraq's society, thereby benefitting a wider cross-section of citizens bringing a sense of relief to the unjust situation to the wounded humanity. He also expressed the view that every human being is a rare gift, and all should have a chance to make their mark on this earth: "Human life is a rare gift, and all people on this planet should have the chance to express their full potential." By reaching people who reach others, he influenced and directed people of different backgrounds and professions. Abbess Pema shared how she influenced people across the globe:

> Through an image of people who reach others, people in the western tradition would like to do something directly; that is why we have more people coming to Plum Village from worldwide, seeking guidance and inspiration. It is a ministry of presence and guidance. It is said that "the rose does not preach except by its fragrance." By cultivating peace within ourselves, we can create peace outside and promote justice in society.

Abbot Phap Son described how cross-cultural practices of sharing, holding spaces for the human spirit, and genuine dialogue influenced people across cultures and religions. The art of holding space means being present to the situation and people without any judgment, agenda or pre-calculation. It is an emotionally and spiritually freeing space of love and peace. A held space can then be a healing space, a loving space, a compassionate space that nurture and care for the person as he or she is. It is a space of potentiality, a creative space, a learning space. This is the presence that transforms. The old layers of ego patters dissolve in the presence of emerging higher consciousness. Being present to the collective consciousness in the interpersonal arena can bring about subtle and lasting transformation for the human psyche and its pathway towards healing and wholeness.

> Culturally, Vietnamese have a practice of drinking tea together. They find a lot of joy together. But the western person may not find so much fun in such tea sharing. So, everybody is holding the space for each other; it is so much an individual experience, but it is owned collectively and thus becomes a healing process; how do we assimilate experience is different for different cultures. For, the westerners hold space personally and individually. But here, it is stored more collectively, and the transformation of inner conflicts takes subtle ways. The dynamics of holding space collectively bring peace and harmony to a troubled situation.

Thurston described how she influenced the spiritual seekers with her discourses on meditation. "I had about a year of perfect freedom. Then I started to teach; Spirit would bring people; other people would come." She described in detail how intentional and consistent spiritual training and practices transmitted spiritual energy and awakened people's inner power to do greater good: "I went to different cities to train people in spiritual power and inner transformation. There were about 300 people who wanted to be initiated in the spiritual path of awakening initially and then many thousands came along to be initiated." Only a transformed mind can work towards changing society from injustice to justice, conflicts to peace, disharmony to harmony doing the greater good.

Having experienced miraculous healing, Sister Gefre indicated how she, in turn, became a source of healing for others: "Now that I am healed completely, that is what I want to do for others, be a healing agent. That is the motivation behind my starting the massage therapy clinics." Ilibagiza recalled how her family was influential in bringing people together in times of genocide and crisis: "I remember, after two days this war started, we had around 10,000 people in and around our home asking my parents what to do. My parents were people who were very much respected in the country." For Lim, a career turning point came through pro bono work. Lim became aware of the challenging situation faced by many women in Singapore after divorce or separation. One difficulty was finding somewhere to live. The majority of Singapore's 5.7 million people live in subsidized housing. Still, families who need two apartments after separation-one usually for mum and the kids, another for dad-found it is hard going to secure a second. Lim's transition into the field of women's advocacy in Singapore brought great fulfillment and passion for bringing about social transformation despite adversities. In 1990, Lim worked on legislation to help empower police to property investigate family violence. She is advocating for a career allowance, for cultural change so men take on more household and airing duties, and for the government to provide better facilities for the elderly:

> "The work I did for these women wholly changed me. My job paid me well, but it did not feed my soul. I was going through the motions. So, I felt sorry for myself. But, once I started doing this advocacy work for gender equality and championing the cause of violence against women, I thought that I was living my dream and doing greater good for the cause of women and gender justice. I have been doing Tai Chi for about five,

six years now. What is remarkable is your body becomes the energy. It's wonderful that you do it outside, so there are no mirrors. You are into yourself, but not self-conscious" Lim became AWARE executive director and set about using her professional skills to transform the organization by formalizing structures, expanding operations, and professional fundraising. There is much to do for the cause of justice and equality to accomplish the greater good in society.

As executive director of Singapore's Association of Women for Action and Research, Corinna Lim has worked to use her professional skills to transform the organization. "Often, we're told to shut up by men trolling us; they say we have no right to speak about national service because we haven't done it. There is so much weight put on this that we need to discuss it more" and "be our advocate for justice and fairness." Lim herself has been prominent last year, delivering the first round of the IPS-Nathan 2021 lectures in April and May, a series named in honor of former Singapore President S.R. Nathan. In the second of three lectures, Lim said that young women should be included in the two years of national service compulsory for all male citizens and permanent residents after they turn 18. She also wants national service extended to other occupations such as health and elderly care. She acknowledges her proposal is not popular: "Who wants to be conscripted, right? This is one of the highest-hanging fruits, but if we insist on compulsory national service, it should be open to men and women."

Lim's work in the not-for-profit sector resulted in a Fulbright scholarship that took her to New York. She studied for her master's in public administration at Columbia University in the late 1990s when dot.com fever was raging. She came back inspired and, in 2000, started her own tech company, called Bizibody, the nickname her mother had given her as a child because "I was so interested in everybody else's business." Unlike many companies of that era, Busybody still exists after morphing into a tech consultancy for the legal sector in Singapore. After about five years, Lim left, handing over the reins to Serena, who had started the business with her. After that, Lim became more involved with Aware. When the new guard made its move at the organization's annual general meeting in May 2009, she was heavily involved in the fightback as a leading national activist for the cause of justice and equality for women and children.

Empowering a Billion Women (EBW) Entrepreneurs, Vaderveldt and team enabled women to discover their inner potential, gain confidence to start business, and gain success to move out of poverty and marinization. In 2021, Inc. Magazine ranked EBW the #28 fastest growing private company in America. Vanderveldt found the courage and confidence to believe in something that is bigger than herself by understanding that there can be a lot of magic out there; "It was scary at the time and ridiculous, but I had a belief in it." She had to get over her limiting beliefs by finding mentors to help her bridge from the impossible to "the possible. It's about saying yes when everyone says no." Her first book, "Be the One: A BRIDGE to Make the Impossible, Possible" is released in September 2022. In manifold ways, Vanderveldt became the champion of women's empowerment and gain just place in workplace and beyond.

Leaders expanded the circle of justice by being advocates of social responsivity, equity, and fairness in the workplace and beyond. Several of these leaders were influential in bringing people together for service across the globe in times of humanitarian crises due to wars and disasters. They influenced people worldwide through their charisma, character, and selfless service. They lent voice to the poor and marginalized and engaged in building bridges across cultures and races. People were drawn to these leaders because of their presence, dialogue, and teaching. They expanded their circles of influence as champions of justice and equality to serve the greater good of humanity.

Circle of Compassion

Compassion is the quality of having the best intentions and genuine concern for others. Compassion in leadership creates stronger connections between people and expands the circles of concern, enhancing collaboration, trust, and loyalty. With the unfolding of the deeper dimension of being, the leaders expanded their circle of compassion and care. These leaders were deeply conscious of the pain and suffering rampant in the world and were moved with empathy and concern. The realization that *we are our brothers' keepers* helped them reach out with outstanding service to the less privileged in society. These leaders not only established charitable organizations to take care of the people in the margins but also encouraged their followers to reach out to others in genuine love and charity. Balancing compassion for your people effectively with getting the job done is not an easy task, but it is possible with greater self-awareness, courage, and wisdom (Hougaard & Carter, 2022). Thurston expressed her vision and conviction about the power of compassion: "I always have passion and compassion for the world. I never wanted to go somewhere else to find my pure spiritual self." While caring for the marginalized children in South Africa, Thurston described a fierce urgency to demonstrate authentic love in the world: "True love never divides; it always multiplies. I believe we are one human race. I believe we need to get to know each other and demonstrate our love. The world is stifling through the lack of love. It is all about love and compassion from the depth of our being."

Thurston described how she underwent a profound transformation of her ego-mind towards infinite compassion for everyone: "After three weeks of intense inner turmoil and spiritual processing, my heart was opened." I felt very close identification with the Goddess of compassion," *Kuan Yin,* which means *"one who hears the cry of the world"* is a Chinese Goddess of compassion. She is everywhere. I could easily identify with her and revive tremendous power of compassion." Similarly, Swami Bharati echoed his sense of expanded circles of compassion from his deeper spiritual awareness: "If all living beings are Atman (universal soul), how you can love one less and one more?" Swami Bharati was convinced that what makes people great is their selflessness and care for others. He reiterated that the greatness of leadership is embodied in compassion for others: Describing his life example of exercising compassion in the wake of aggression and violence, Swami Bharati explained how he cultivated an ethic of nonviolence and disposition of compassion to deal with negativity:

> What makes a person great? What stood out from the stories I read early on was a certain degree of expansion of one's area of thinking and selflessness. Even if it is Napoleon, he has to be selfless to take care of soldiers. His caring for his soldiers was matchless in history. That gave me the concept of leadership, how you handle others with kindness and respect. Gandhi emphasized the aspect of compassionate service when he said, "The best way to find yourself is to lose yourself in service." All the argument for nonviolence might not have worked with him when someone slapped you, and you just smiled, and that worked. He melted. That is the way. That was a moment of discovery: a discovery that the principle of nonviolence, the focus on forgiveness, and compassion only actually work in the real world. You can kill the negativity with a smile.

Archbishop Flynn emphasized that a sense of deep respect for others emerged from his spiritual consciousness and compassion. "Every person must be treated with a deep reverence and respect, for we are all sons and daughters of the one God, in whose sacredness we share." He emphasized the need for practicing love and compassion to help humanity live in harmony and peace: "God intends that we all live in harmony, that we practice a love that unites us and reflects our fundamental equality as human beings." Quoting Maya Angelou's famous line about compassionate leadership, "I have learned that people will forget what you said, people will forget what you did, but people will never forget how you made them feel," Archbishop Flynn reiterated the unfailing power of compassion to move the hearts of people to a culture of respect and nonviolence. Having received compassionate care from others as a blind person, Mutua observed how he is inspired to offer his love and care to others: "Just as the light was brought to me as a blind person in a blind institution, so I swore I will bring light to others." Finally, out of deep concern for the future of humanity, Mutua spoke about his vision of the world leaders coming together to stop wars and establishing genuine peace out of compassion for humanity and creating global peace:

> I wish, sir, a plate to be made, a plate of gold; on this plate would write a law that all wars in God's name should be outlawed. All wars in the name of national hegemony should be banned. All the world leaders, including the Pope himself, must sign this treaty because I see a great danger of the next war coming. It will be the biggest, the deadliest war, especially over the precious metal in South Africa, called Platinum. Platinum is the precious metal of the future needed to make airplanes. It will start in South Africa as the same tensions adhering to the Middle East in the name of resources such as oil are present here. People should forgive each other. They should sign a treaty, sir; why? If you look in history, wars fought by men who pretend to be fighting in the name of God are the deadliest and cruelest, destroying humanity.

Mutua expressed that today humanity needs to be ruled by a strong sense of compassion and unity: "If everybody is my people, I do not care whether you belong to this religion or that religion. There is only one religion; the religion of humanity." Mutua claimed that the spirit of compassion is the root of world peace and amity. "Today's main threat is not terrorism or global warming, but lack of understanding, respect, and compassion. No doubt nonviolence is the way to peace and prosperity."

He noted that the essence of the African word *Ubuntu* "I am because you are" is compassion and solidarity. The culture of Ubuntu indicates the fact of interdependence and seeing the other as the good neighbor.

From a leadership perspective, Ubuntu requires that leaders model the way for others. Ncube (2010: 79) states that as a role model, the leader legitimizes their leadership by committing to such universal values as honesty, sincerity, truthfulness, compassion, empathy, dignity, and respect for others. At Nelson Mandela's memorial, Obama (2013) spoke about Ubuntu, saying:

> There is a word in South Africa – Ubuntu – a word that captures Mandela's greatest gift: his recognition that we are all bound together in ways that are invisible to the eye; that there is a oneness to humanity; that we achieve ourselves by sharing ourselves with others, and caring for those around us. We can never know how much of this sense was innate in him or how much was shaped in a dark and solitary cell. But we remember the gestures, large and small – introducing his jailers as honored guests at his inauguration; taking a pitch in a Springbok uniform; turning his family's heartbreak into a call to confront HIV/AIDS – that revealed the depth of his empathy and his understanding. He embodied Ubuntu, but he also taught millions to find that truth within themselves.

Sri Sri described how he expanded his circle of compassion spontaneously while visiting Rome, offering peace and hope. A natural sense of compassion for people who suffer arise from a more profound spiritual consciousness of the oneness of reality and interconnectedness despite cultural difference and language barriers in the world. Spirituality is allowing compassion to flourish and grow across the universe to all people and all beings. Sri Sri exhorted, "Passion when you work, dispassion when you turn inward, and compassion at all times, this is the key to a fulfilled life." Dealing with negativity and anger is very important to cultivate a culture of compassion, understanding, and peaceful co-existence. "It is common to get angry and get upset about someone else mistakes. On the other hand, it takes a big heart to feel compassion and accommodate their wrong doings and give them a chance to change." Sri Sri described his encounter with a stranger and how he was able to transform the life by including him in the circle of his compassion.

> Another time in Rome, I was walking on a path. Suddenly, I felt like running up to a bush. I saw a man sitting in a bush. He cried for help; please help me; if you don't help me, I will end my life. I went there, and he looked at me. He did not know English. He came to me seeking blessings. He had no idea who I was, and I did not speak Italian either;

> with translators, we got connected. I blessed him, and he felt great peace. You can't put those things in logic. It does not make any logical sense. It is called providence; Nature puts you to such people. They get benefited. When I see them happy, it makes my heart sing.

Abbess Pema shared her practice of extending compassion to the universe: "I practice *Maitri (friendship)*meditation from my heart; Look at the person next to you, and then you can think of sending love to all. I realized that there is a capacity in me to love that has no conditions." The practice of mindfulness creates positive well-being for employees. It enhances their sense of compassionate engagement with the customers, thus enhancing the culture of compassion in the organization and beyond (Blewitt et al., 2015). Abbot Phap Son explained how he appreciates his master Thich Nhat Hanh's compassionate approach:

> Thai's [Thich Nhat Hanh] approach to relating to the Vietnam War was very compassionate. He did not see the Americans as enemies. He saw that they could suffer too. All suffer. His approach was not to break apart. You will see it in his writings a lot about such compassion. Without genuine kindness, you are creating an enemy; the enemy is outside and inside. A spirit of compassion helps you embrace the whole and see even the enemies as part of the whole. People in conflicts find Thai's approach to empathy and nonviolence very appealing. Even people from Palestine and Israel come here to get spiritually nourished. We have transformative practices in our community such as Beginning anew, deep listening, and compassionate listening. If you are open to love, you can feel the oneness in your heart.

Abbot Phap Son emphasized the importance of providing a compassionate environment in the community by citing an example from his master with the skill of deep listening and feeling the sufferings of the others and holding human space in the heart. Compassion means "to suffer with"—to be present to the suffering of another person, another living being or community. When there is a practice of compassion, it is not only feeling the suffering of the other but also awakening the feeling of inner warmth and kindness. What the world needs now to heal the brokenness in people's hearts is to provide a compassionate environment. He described such a decisive moment of healing in the presence of his Master Thich Nhat Hanh. His master gave the following mantra of compassionate presence:

> Darling, please know that I am here for you
> Darling, I know that you are here for me
> Darling, I know that you suffer; I am with you
> Darling, please know that I suffer, and please be with me.

Jemal et al. (2021) identified compassion and respectful care is an essential element to create positive environment and intimacy among healthcare professionals to bring about healing and wholeness. As the life experiences unfold with the practice of compassionate presence, the ability to know how other feel enable the person to enhance the quality of relationship. Making room for compassion seems to be a tall order in today's society especially when one is struggling to find compassion for oneself. Abbot Phap Son narrated the story of his Master providing compassionate environment by caring presence for a suffering woman and thereby bringing about healing and wholeness to her life:

> A lady who lost two children came to Thai's teaching session. One day during teaching, Thai understood her suffering and recognized it during his talks without her disclosing it to him. Thai may be able to do this because of the depth of his experience and infinite compassion in his heart. He said to one lady, "I know your suffering; I hold your suffering in my heart." At that time, she felt that she is healed and whole. The ideal is to provide that compassionate environment to every broken heart.

Palmer observed how he was able to influence his teenage children's lives with love and understanding. Practicing self-care enables the persons to be more compassionate with themselves and the other. A peaceful mind is a powerful mind and it can hold the agitations that come out of the other person with a proactive approach. Cultivating inner peace and kindness through mediation and spiritual practice enables one to be calm in the storm while communicating love, acceptance and compassion. The ability and willingness to hold space for the other even though you might have the correct answers in your head is critical to the holistic healing of relationships and manifestation of empathetic intelligence amid chaos and interpersonal tensions in the family between parents and teenage children.

> In our journey, there are all kinds of ways to be in the microcosm of our lives. Say I have a teenage child; as parents, we are often up in arms with the teenage child; there can be great transformation by learning to listen to the child and be more accepting of that child. Some of what that child

> is doing is resisting your resistance. When your resistance stops, then there is no need to resist. It doesn't happen overnight, and nothing happens ideally. It can be a movement in the right direction with yielding. It is not passivity or doing whatever you want. You continue to be present to them in a way that communicates love and gives that person space to work through. And there are very proactive ways to influence them.

The modern ways of manifesting our presence and dialogue, especially in the microcosm of our lives and work settings is of paramount importance to create a culture of compassion. However, in the macrocosm of our lives, Palmer insisted that it is all about the practice of nonviolence to create a better world. Koopmann-Holm and Tsai (2017) noted the cultural differences in the conception, experience, and expression of compassion across various nations and cultures. In American culture the more people avoid feeling negative, the more they feel positive in expressing compassion to the other especially when they are going through difficult circumstances where as in German culture, accepting of negative emotions is the way to express compassion and sympathy to the grieving ones. The feeling and expression of compassion at the microcosm of our lives gradually move to the culture of nonviolence and harmonious co-existence. Palmer stated:

> So, in the microcosm of our lives, the families, and neighborhood and work settings, it is presence and dialogue; this fantastic way of being present without being overbearing. And on a larger scale, I think it is all about nonviolence. It makes space for people to be who they are and walk with them in a gentle way; our way of keeping good company.

The capacity to love unconditionally is a way to become whole. Abbess Pema was convinced that she marked her journey to wholeness by all-embracing love: "Yes, I touch the pure land of Buddha sometime. It is the capacity to love the whole universe. Being whole is being in an all-embracing love." Similarly, Sister Gefre established healing centers to offer service out of compassion: "If you give up something to help someone, you will be rewarded in 100-fold, and the circle of compassion expands beyond your imagination." She was convinced that it is by small acts of kindness done with a magnanimity that one can expand the circle of compassion to a global level: "Doing small things with great love creates ripples of love and compassion all around." Ilibagiza spoke of the dire need for living from a heart of love and compassion to create a better world free of hatred and war:

> Every seed of hatred put there, misunderstanding put there, so that we can conquer, come out victorious, and never know how drastic the consequence will be. Rwandan genocide has shown that. But, at the same time, the seed of love we put there, we never know how big it will be. So we learn that we need to make decisions from the heart of love because they will follow us beyond measure. The love of a single heart can make a world of difference. So, I believe that we can heal Rwanda and our world by healing one heart at a time.

Forgiving from the heart is the way to expand the circle of compassion. With deep spiritual awareness, Ilibagiza noted how she was able to forgive the perpetrators of genocide: "All is possible, forgiving is possible; it brings you such a strong heart when you are put under fire, it makes you very strong beyond your imagination to forgive the ones who harmed you." Forgiveness and peacebuilding have become integral part of Ilibagiza's life that she began to organize the orphan children of war from the rival tribal groups in Rwanda to enhance their education and well being. Compassion is a basic human instinct and the more one intentionally exercises, the more humane the culture becomes. From a more profound spiritual consciousness, one can let go of the deep-seated negativity of emotions and pave the way for opening a new horizon of compassion and co-existence to serve the greater good of humanity.

Through their lives, teachings, and activities, leaders have demonstrated that expanding the circle of compassion can foster an ethic of co-responsibility. The circle of compassion is rooted in a spirit of concern for the suffering and empathy for the misery of the other. These leaders were empathetic in their hearts and extended their love to one and all beyond measure. They set great examples to show that every human being can live from a heart of compassion and help eliminate the culture of hatred, violence, and terror through deep listening, presence, and dialogue. The circle of compassion goes beyond the circle of responsibility, creating ripples of inspiration and acts of kindness and joy in the world. A sense of deep spiritual awareness and an awareness of the inter-connectedness of life helped these leaders to feel at one with humanity and empathize with the weak and suffering, making a significant difference in the lives of others.

Circle of Stewardship

Merriam Webster (2022) defines stewardship as "the careful and responsible management of something entrusted to one's care." The leaders exercised a more profound sense of Stewardship with people and communities based on their expanded spiritual awareness, interests in global issues, and universal perspectives. They believe that individuals are part of the larger whole and need to be interested in common affairs with broader views beyond their interests. They demonstrated that they could contribute to the welfare of the total and make a significant difference on the planet. Their circle of solidarity was based on an expanded awareness of the unity of humanity and the interconnection of the whole creation. For them, life is being authentic, considering the body, mind, and spirit are intertwined at the personal level, and human life is not apart from the creation.

The leaders advocated the need to go beyond the immediate concerns of charity to the deeper issues of justice, asking why there are escalating issues of injustice across the globe? Considering the world as one family, the leaders engaged in asking questions of justice, expanding their sense of solidarity with the human and the earth family. The engaged investors support and challenge the management to expand the circle of Stewardship to global issues and the common planet while focusing on the greater purpose and profit in business (Edmans, 2020). Vanderveldt, Award-Winning Entrepreneur, Investor, CEO and Founder of EBW Global Inc. and EBW Distributors, Former TV host, expressed her sense of global stewardship: "Getting behind the empowerment of women stimulates societies, entrepreneurs, job creation, accelerates revenue growth and develops inspiring and motivated leaders with a great sense of passion and stewardship." These leaders emphasized the need to learn to co-exist in the world as our life on the planet is at stake. Archbishop Flynn noted that the essence of having a sense of Stewardship and solidarity is to keep the principles of justice and charity as twin ingredients for the transformation of the world. He recommended, "We not only should be concerned about others' immediate needs but should ask a deeper question— why?" In a similar vein, he raised the following questions with a sense of universal solidarity:

> Why is it necessary for people in Mexico to come to the US in search of bread?
> Why racial disparity still exists even though we are all one human family?
> Why the fastest growing industry in the US is the prison industry?
> Why do we fail to invest in children across the globe?
> Why do we engage in multiplying weapons of destruction?
> Why don't we urgently care for our environmental stability?
> All these questions call for civil debate, and unless we ask these questions, we do not stand for God's kingdom? Is there a better way to live in solidarity with the less privileged?
> We must exist in the world and co-exist in the world in peace and harmony. I believe all of us are called to proclaim justice and work for the transformation of the world. We must keep one foot in front of the other, charity and justice. Keep social justice on the front burner, and we cannot but come forward with greater integrity, creating a sense of universal solidarity and universal Stewardship.

Thurston believed in spiritual solidarity and a sense of Stewardship to work for a better world: "Spirit chooses us what to do, when and how to do it, holding space for the transformation of the world." Swami Bharati expressed a similar sentiment when he said, "I shall not hesitate, I shall not step back, I shall not fear; I shall not enter nirvana until every being from a blade of grass to *Brahma* has liberated." Archbishop Flynn reiterated: "We must see that everyone is valued and allow the marginalized their basic needs and encourage the best for we are our brother's keeper." This sense of stewardship and solidarity is the need of the hour instead of being led by sheer greed and self-interest with profit motive alone to grow one's own company or organization with any cost. Palmer advocated the path of nonviolence to promote solidarity and Global Stewardship: "I must say that I am an aspiring pacifist for all things, including international relations." His ardent advocacy for dealing with global issues became evident in a non-violent and proactive way as he shared his views on war and peace. It is appalling to see that the spiral of war machine and violence hardly goes away without the collective goodwill and global collaboration:

> World War I was supposed to be the war that ended all wars. World War II was supposed to usher in a new era of peace. It has not just happened, and of course, it will not happen. Wars lead to more violence, and more

> violence leads to more violence. It was believed that World War II was necessary because of the holocaust. But it is reported that the holocaust did not start until the war was quite underway. The war provided Hitler with a protective cover to murder 6 million Jews. No one was there; the international community was not there, observing, listening, learning, and protesting. People who say, well, ultimately you have to turn into war, for it is the only way to solve the problem, really baffle me. I am hard-pressed by the issue of the war being sold. I am reading a fine book on nonviolence in world history, which is an unwritten history to a very great extent. Even all our history books celebrate violence. And on a larger scale, I think it is all about nonviolence. It makes space for people to be who they are and walk with them, not in a gentle way.

Sri Sri made his efforts to promote nonviolence and advocated solidarity to create peace in a violent world. Trusting the fundamental goodness of humanity and the soul's deep longing for peace and wholeness, Sri Sri made bold steps to reach out to the war-torn areas to bring about peace and harmony among the warring sections with his Art of living network. Exercising a greater sense of stewardship for the human family, seeing the role as a care taker for those who experience brokenness and crisis, the Art of living foundation reached out to the people across the world especially to the wounded people in times of war. He visited war-torn Iraq to champion peace and goodwill as a world spiritual leader despite opposition and international resistance:

> I went to Iraq in 2003 and told people: Why don't you give nonviolence a chance? Almost everybody welcomed me, including Nouri Al-Maliki, the current Prime Minister of Iraq. But one vice-chancellor of a University in Pakistan opposed it. He said, okay, your service activities are suitable. Do not stop people from their anger. If you are making them peaceful, they cannot take revenge, and they cannot finish every American on the planet. He said if you take away the anger from the people, that will not make them capable of handling the life of every American in the world. To take revenge for they are occupiers. There are people and extremists in every religion. They thrive in conflict. Perhaps they give us more jobs to do (laughing). That is why there is more work for us to promote nonviolence and universal solidarity.

Abbess Pema spoke of solidarity as cultivating peace within and peace outside: "I think as a community Plum Village has been called the village of peace. We cultivate peace within and peace without. Peace in the world and peace with nature. This peace creates a sense of cosmic solidarity." Sister Gefre spoke about the importance of mindful living to cultivate community stewardship: "I lived a life of simplicity and community being supportive and mindful of each other's well-being." Her experience of responsible stewardship emerged from her spiritual conviction: "And I became more conscious of the divinity in others and the dignity of all beings under the planet." Similarly, Sri Sri was convinced of a sense of spiritual solidarity: "There is no distinction in the divine as *mine or not mine* or to save someone and not some others; everybody belongs to the divine whether they are on the path or not." Sharing convictions about the interdependence of reality the need to cultivate deep sense of solidarity and caring stewardship among the people, Sri Sri noted, "Today is the day the wave remembers the ocean; where it was born. No waves can forget the fact that it is very much part and parcel of the ocean." The spiritual perspective of oneness brings about a sense of more profound harmony of co-existence just like the waves and the ocean. Sri Sri reiterated how spirituality could become a unifying force to create a greater understanding of solidarity among leaders and cultivate universal stewardship organizations:

> Whether people are in the industry or corporate or the professional world or organizations, we should not forget that they are all human beings. They all drink the same water for they are thirsty; they all eat the same grains for they are all hungry. They do not eat anything special; in the same way, spirituality is such an inner need in every soul. If it is presented in such a manner, which does not conflict with their systems of belief, it is received well. Without coming into conflict with systems of belief or prayer, then they have no problem. Spirituality can become a unifying force for humanity rather than a divisive one.

Having studied the ancient African beliefs and practices, Mutua asserted that there was a system of solidarity and togetherness in African culture long before the ethnic genocide in Darfur. The women in Darfur were strongly guided by such a sense of deep human solidarity. Solidarity is an awareness of shared interests, values, and sympathies that creates a psychological and spiritual sense of bond that ties them together as a cohesive group, family, or community. A sense of responsible stewardship emanates from this deeper awareness of human solidarity. Strong identification with one another with a deep bond of love and belongingness, the people of Darfur manifested exceptional feat of solidarity and stewardship to embrace the pain and suffering of the people The cultural practice of Ubuntu, "we are our brothers and sisters' keeper" found expression in amazing ways. Mutua noted:

> In Darfur, the ancient people created a system of togetherness (Ubuntu). In Darfur, known as the land of dawn, if one woman were to be killed by the *Janjawit* (militia), all the other women would just drop dead in solidarity. Why? Because it was believed that the ancient mother soul-built humanity, this mother soul was there long before a man thought that God was male. I found that the world is one. All these differences are illusory from a deeper perspective. A deep sense of solidarity and oneness needs to move the world from division to harmony and world peace.

Thurston exercised her sense of universal solidarity and stewardship by holding space for the transformation of the world by processing global issues. With an expanded awareness and a deep concern for the welfare of the world, Thurston and her team engaged in the work of processing current global issues with her spiritual practices and global initiatives. The circle of Stewardship is not limited to the human species alone but to the extended species of our planet. Honoring the animal kingdom for its role in maintaining the equilibrium of nature is essential to preserve the chain of life in the post-modern world of environmental destruction and decline of bio-diversity. Thurston said that she has the remarkable capacity to love animals and can communicate with animals creating a sense of cosmic solidarity with the animal kingdom. Thus, creating a deeper bond of solidarity and stewardship with the suffering humanity and the distressed animal kingdom, Thurston and group did the powerful practice of holding spiritual space and prayer vigils in time of crisis and turmoil:

> Spirit chooses us what to do, when, and how to do it; we do not have much recreation. But it is pretty much 24 hours a day, holding space for the transformation of the world. It is a full-time dedication; my staff, friends, and students are dedicated to the world and what is going on. For example, when the Tibetan uprising for freedom was breaking through, we were up all night processing the spiritual transformation of the world from conflict to peace. This is a spiritual practice to transform the world from within. On the other hand, I do animal communications. That was a gift given at the end of the cave experience. Because we have a lot of

> animals here, the wild animals of the world are under duress because the civilization is fast encroaching [sic] the animal world. That is why I have here a place to honor lions and animals to signify their role and importance for the world's stability and the natural harmony of sentient beings.

Mutua testified, in the similar vein, that one of the African women called Rebecca communicated with the plants: "Rebecca showed that human beings can communicate with plants, and the plants respond positively." The circle of solidarity expands to the vegetative kingdom, showing a deep link between humans and plants. They were deeply concerned about environmental issues, and they urged their followers to work in solidarity to find common solutions exercising a responsible environmental stewardship. Archbishop Flynn noted that leaders from all walks of life should work together for the regeneration of the environment:

> Some people ignore global warming because they feel a political party, they are not associated with has brought it up. And to me, that is not the issue. I think global warming is an urgent issue that needs to be addressed by scientists, politicians, and all the rest, putting their heads together and saying, this is what we must do to protect this Earth that God has given to us. But I don't know the answer; they have to develop a solution collectively. And the leaders must be aware of it. So today the most extraordinary solidarity should be seen in protecting our standard roof, the planet. That is the greater good we need to focus on to guarantee a sustainable future.

Mutua emphasized the need to work for the welfare of all rather than work for the benefit of a few. Serving the greater good is a way to a sustainable future. He cautioned that working in global solidarity and stewardship is the dire need of the hour as the peace and stability of the world are constantly threatened by greed and domination. In the short term, those who are led by a culture of greed can get ahead by exploiting people and extracting their wealth. But in the long run, businesses only succeed in the market by maintaining a strong moral culture that humanizes work, builds trust with customers, and orients workers towards creating value for greater good and serving the customer with excellence.

> Every country that is becoming very developed not in a healthy way and is looking for resources for unbridled consumption. What Gandhi said is

> true: "We have enough resources for our needs but not for our greed." Greed is the root cause of all evils. We are on the path of juggernauts. You know, sir, I ask myself, should one be the lion of fire, a dragon of flame, or should one be a voice in the darkness for peace and understanding in a world full of conflicts and divisions.

The leaders were deeply aware that there is massive injustice in the world. To alleviate the injustice, humanity needs to come together with a feeling of deep solidarity and stewardship for one another. "There is collective injustice in humanity today where the powerful exploits the weak" (Mutua). The spirit of stewardship urges the leaders to inspire the workforce to care for the greater good and become aware of the impending disasters of climate crisis and global disparity of wealth that threatens the very sustainable existence of the Planet and people. Swami Bharati reiterated the presence of massive injustice and environmental threats in the world and the need to combat it with an awakened spiritual consciousness, and responsible stewardship to transform the world:

> The challenges in the world, wars, and more than that, the massive collective injustice, nations to nations, rich to the poor in every country; India is a prime example of the injustice of the rich to the poor; powerful and the weak. Whatever I can write about it, I write it in little books; I say whatever I can say in lectures. I assess what I can do; the rest, I surrender to the divine forces and the forces of history. The entire cosmos, its galaxies, the particle of dust, all little waves and ripples in the ocean of consciousness, everything becomes integrated. Awakening to the spiritual consciousness and the responsible stewardship is a way to experience cosmic solidarity.

A sense of deep solidarity and Stewardship emerged from a deep awareness of these leaders' spiritual identity and interconnectedness with the wider world. The top leaders were engaged in social justice issues asking critical questions about the common good and collective responsibility. The presence of massive injustice and disparity in the world challenged them to find solutions and be proactive (UN, 2019). Advocating for the protection of the environment, animals, and bio-diversity, these top leaders expanded the circle of Stewardship. Ethics, values, and spirituality are foundational to understanding the preservation of global diversity and sustainability (Van Dyke & Lamb, 2020). They provide an excellent common ground to advocate a sense of global and cosmic Stewardship to transform the world and assure a better future for the planet serving the common good and the greater good.

Leaders practiced an ethic of co-responsibility and advocated collective responsibility in organizations across the globe to serve the greater good for a better future. Their growing awareness of the unified field of consciousness made them realize the co-existence of reality and interdependence of the beings on the planet. A sense of awakened consciousness of reality's interconnectedness helped these leaders deeply respect diversity and learn to live with differences. The ethic of co-responsibility is rooted in a culture of relational trust and mutuality. In their quest for wholeness, the leaders sought circles of relational trust to discover their identity and integrity, cultivating authentic dialogue and personal presence. Creating networks of responsibility and transformation, these leaders influenced the wider community and became catalysts for change. A broader view of life and a profound spiritual crisis experience helped these leaders empathize with others' suffering and pain. Expanding the circle of compassion not only to human beings but also to animals and the whole environment, these leaders expressed concern and care for all sentient beings. In a nutshell, the leaders promoted an authentic sense of responsibility and accountability in the workplace in serving the greater good. Leaders recognized their role in valuing every person and encouraged them to grow and bring out their very best facing the fire of crisis and overcoming resistance to change. A deep understanding of solidarity was practiced and encouraged at the global and cosmic level, especially in caring for the environment. Rooted deeply in the universal values of trust, respect, responsibility, compassion, and solidarity, the leaders nurtured and modeled an ethic of co-responsibility and universal Stewardship, serving the greater good in their quest for wholeness.

References

Angelou, M. (2022, June). *Human family*. http://googlesearch.com-humanf amily

Atenasio, D. (2019). Co-responsibility for individualists. *Res Publica, 25*, 511–530. https://doi.org/10.1007/s11158-018-09409

Blewitt, L., Wang, K., Nguyen, H., Johnson, A., Pidial, K., & Yu, N. (2015). Mindfulness: Creating the space for compassionate care. *Industrial and Organizational Psychology, 8*(4), 706–710. https://doi.org/10.1017/iop.201 5.104

Bronner, W., Gebauer, H., Lamprecht, C., & Wortmann, F. (2021). Sustainable AioT: How artificial intelligence and the internet of things affect profit, people, and planet. In O. Gassmann & F. Ferrandina (Eds.), *Connected business*. Springer. https://doi.org/10.1007/978-3-030-76897-3_8

Condon, R. (2022). *Network responsibility*. Cambridge University Press.

Covey, S. (2022, June). *The speed of trust*. https://www.speedoftrust.com/

Edmans, A. (2020). Stewardship: The value of engaged investors that both support and challenge management. In *Grow the pie: How great companies deliver both purpose and profit* (pp. 135–165). Cambridge University Press. https://doi.org/10.1017/9781108860093.010

Großmann, K., Alexandri, G., Budnik, M., Haase, A., Haid, C., Hedtke, C., & Shokry, G. (2018). Living with diversity or living with difference? International perspectives on everyday perceptions of the social composition of diverse neighborhoods. In S. Oosterlynck, G. Verschraegen, & R. Van Kempen (Eds.), *Divercities: Understanding super-diversity in deprived and mixed neighborhoods* (pp. 211–234). Bristol University Press. https://doi.org/10.46692/9781447338192.010

Hougaard, R., & Carter, J. (2022). *Compassionate leadership: How to do hard things in a human way*. Harvard Review Press.

Jemal, K., Hailu, D., Mekonnen, M., Telsfa, B., Bekele, K., & Kinati, T. (2021). The importance of compassion and respectful care for the health workforce: A mixed-methods study. *Journal of Public Health*. https://doi.org/10.1007/s10389-021-01495-0

Jung, K. (1973). *Synchronicity: An acausal connecting principle*. Princeton University Press.

Kerse, G. (2021). A leader indeed is a leader in deed: The relationship of ethical leadership, person-organization fit, organizational trust, and extra-role service behavior. *Journal of Management & Organization, 27*(3), 601–620. https://doi.org/10.1017/jmo.2019

Koopmann-Holm, B., & Tsai, J. L. (2017). The cultural shaping of compassion. In E. M. Seppälä, E. Simon Thomas, S. L. Brown, M. C. Worline, C. D. Cameron, & J. R. Doty (Eds.), *The Oxford handbook of compassion science* (pp. 273–285). Oxford University Press.

McIntyre-Mills, J. (2019). Maintaining space for dialogue and diversity. In J. McIntyre-Mills & N. Romm (Eds.), *Mixed methods and cross-disciplinary research: Contemporary systems thinking*. Springer. https://doi.org/10.1007/978-3-030-04993-5_3

Merriam-Webster. (2022, May). Stewardship. In Merriam-Webster.comdictionary. https://www.merriam-webster.com/dictionary/stewardship

Ncube, L. (2010). Ubuntu: Transformative leadership philosophy. *Journal of Leadership Studies, 4*(3), 77–82.

Obama, B. (2013, May). *Tribute to Nelson Mandela at memorial service* (businessinsider.com). www.businessinsider.com

Ross, D. (2020). Social justice. In S. Idowu, R. Schmidpeter, N. Capaldi, L. Zu, M. Del Baldo, & R. Abreu (Eds.), *Encyclopedia of sustainable management*. Springer. https://doi.org/10.1007/978-3-030-02006-4_186-1

Scharmer, C. O. (2007). *Theory U: Leading from the future as it emerges*. Society for Organizational Learning.

Seelan, R. (2015). *Deconstructing global citizenship* (p. 143) (H. Bashir & P. Gray, Eds.). Routledge. ISBN 978–1498502580.

Ullah, I., Hameed, R., Kayani, N., & Fazal, Y. (2022). CEO ethical leadership and corporate social responsibility: Examining the mediating role of organizational ethical culture and intellectual capital. *Journal of Management & Organization, 28*(1), 99–119. https://doi.org/10.1017/jmo.2019.48

United Nations. (2019). *Universal Declaration of Human Rights*. http://www.un.org/en/universal-declaration-human-rights/. Accessed 6 March 2019.

Van Dyke, F., & Lamb, R. L. (2020). *Values and ethics in conservation*. Springer. https://doi.org/10.1007/978-3-030-39534-6_10

CHAPTER 7

Conclusion

The goal of this book was to summarize the insights from the lived experience of wholeness interviewing leaders across the globe. More research is needed to explore the various implications of the idea of wholeness and spiritual intelligence in leadership and management as emerging topics of research and scholarship. I hope this book provides insight, inspiration, and practical wisdom for leaders, scholars, practitioners, and anyone interested in a more profound spiritual journey to wholeness and contributes to the greater wholeness of life.

This book presented the key findings of the research on leadership wholeness as a model of spiritual intelligence. The focus was on the key aspects of wholeness: sensing crisis, embracing crisis, awakening hidden wholeness, and serving the greater good. These are the inner dimensions of the leadership journey's existential, learning, moral and spiritual aspects, along with the outer dimensions of personal, organizational, social, global, and environmental wholeness. This work has several implications for scholars, leaders, and practitioners interested in better understating leadership wholeness from the perspective of spiritual intelligence.

T. Thakadipuram, *Leadership Wholeness, Volume 1*,
Palgrave Studies in Workplace Spirituality and Fulfillment,
https://doi.org/10.1007/978-3-031-08053-1_7

Wholeness: A Model of Spiritual Intelligence

Chapter 2, Wholeness: A Spiritual Intelligence Model, outlined the intrinsic and extrinsic dimensions of wholeness in relationship to leadership. *Spiritual Intelligence* is defined as the higher consciousness and the innate ability to respond with wisdom, compassion, and courage while maintaining equanimity. An in-depth inquiry into the lived experience of the phenomena of wholeness manifested in top leaders of both profit and non-profit sectors across the globe resulted in the discovery of critical insights that helped to construct a model of spiritual intelligence. Many conceptualizations of spiritual intelligence have emerged in the past two decades (Atroszko et al., 2021; Emmons, 2000; Griffiths, 2017; Sisk, 2019; Wigglesworth, 2012; Wilber, 2006; Zohar & Marshall, 2004) as a result of the growing body of research in the fields of psychology, neuroscience, spirituality, and management. Spiritual intelligence (SQ) manifests with higher consciousness and more profound awareness embracing rational intelligence (IQ), emotional intelligence (EQ), and other multiple intelligences. This definition of SQ assumes an adaptive, perceptive, and meta-cognitive capacity with several abilities and skills that may be part of one's leadership competency relevant to problem-solving situations. Thus, spiritual intelligence can be described as holistic Intelligence. Spiritual intelligence is based on self-awareness, contextual awareness, universal awareness, and holistic presence.

The four essential themes that emerged from this research are *Sensing Crisis, Embracing Crisis, Awakening Consciousness, and Serving the Greater Good*. Analysis of these four themes formed the basis of the creation of this model of spiritual intelligence. First, this model describes the inner dynamics of leaders' journey towards wholeness (see Fig. 2.1). The four quadrants of the *Sensing, Embracing, Awakening, and Serving* process indicate an intense path of progressive self-realization, exploration, and higher consciousness leading to greater wholeness of life. These four processes envelop the existential, learning, spiritual, moral, and ethical dimensions of leadership that flow into life's personal, organizational, social, global, and environmental dimensions.

Wholeness: A Spiritual Intelligence Model-Inner Dimension

The leaders in the study demonstrated the ability to sense and recognize existential crises either in themselves or in others around them. Sensing is the "moment we redirect our attention from the objects to the source" (Scharmer, 2022: 3). Our perceptions expand and remain open to what is happening outside and inside us. We begin to see from a different perspective, which leads to recognizing the crisis within and assessing its manifestations. A new way of seeing, learning, and doing is inevitable to discover wholeness amid brokenness and crisis. The crisis experience becomes crucibles of new ways of seeing, sensing, and learning. After encountering the initial trauma of the crisis, the leaders moved into a deeper place of exploration that led to embracing the crisis as a challenge. Instead of seeing the crisis in life as a problem, it challenged the leaders to a deeper place of recognition and acceptance after the initial trauma of shock and awe, denial, and disbelief. Most profound acceptance enabled them to discover the hidden strengths and shadows or blind spots with a new lens of attention and intention. Accepting the crisis as a challenge opened a new door of possibilities both inside and outside. Failures become the catalyst for new solutions and discoveries, a greater sense of authenticity and audacity grew within the person penetrating through the illusions of life, and the leaders began to match their leadership role with the deeper purpose of the soul and society.

Embracing the crisis as a challenge urged the soul to search for more profound and higher dimensions of consciousness that led to an awakening of hidden wholeness. This spiritual awakening began with regular spiritual practice creating inner silence, solitude, and serenity. A firm commitment and dedication to regular spiritual practices such as meditation, reflection, and inspirational dialogue with enlightened friends and support groups created the ambiance of receptivity and reciprocity to experience wholeness within. The Self is moved to a deeper place of spiritual consciousness and the oneness of the universe. The awakened leader with a higher sense of consciousness experiences inner harmony, peace, and bliss, and the reality of the inner connectedness of the world as a family. This realization of the world as a family does not emerge without more profound wisdom, tenacity, and compassion, the salient characteristics of spiritual intelligence. This spiritual awakening of wholeness resulted in a realization of the world as one family, where everything is connected to everything else. It enabled the leaders to dedicate their life serving the greater good in the world. Offering life in service to contribute to the collective well-being of the world is a hallmark of a life of wholeness and spiritual intelligence. This led to the various outer dimensions of wholeness/spiritual intelligence: Leadership Development, Organization Development, Work Life-Fulfillment, Corporate Social Responsibility, and Environmental Stewardship.

Wholeness: A Spiritual Intelligence Model-Outer Dimension

The awakening of hidden wholeness led to deeper explorations of holistic Intelligence and made the leaders feel greater responsibility for their own life and the world's. A selfless spirit of service with a new sense of co-responsibility is demonstrated at five levels: Personal Trust, Organizational Responsibility, Social Justice, Global Compassion, and Environmental Stewardship (see Fig. 2.2). The trajectory of this leadership journey is non-linear, after the infinity loop pattern, similar to breathing in and breathing out the process of progressive evolution. It is a more profound transformational process of learning, growth, and adaptability, enabling the leaders to be resilient in times of volatility, ubiquity, complexity, and ambiguity in the business environment (Krause & Balasescu, 2022; Sternberg, 2020; Tafoya & Poeth, 2021). While the inner dynamics that contained the four processes of sensing, embracing, awakening, and serving centered on the *being* of the leader, the outer dynamics of Personal Trust, Organizational Responsibility, Social Justice, Global Compassion, and Environmental Stewardship emanated from the *doing* of the leader. These five dimensions of engagement with the followers, community, and the larger world depended upon the level of consciousness cultivated and sustained by the leaders. The quest for leadership wholeness was expressed in these practical ways of co-responsibility and many global initiatives of the top leaders. Their ethic of co-responsibility flowed from their sense of moral values and the obligation to the whole universe as they became aware of the deep connection between the individual Self and their universal or cosmic Self. This enlightened spiritual consciousness was the platform from which their sense of universal compassion, responsibility, solidarity, and stewardship emerged. Thus, the leader's quest for wholeness revealed the inner dynamics of wholeness and spiritual intelligence that emphasized the importance of learning from the crises by embracing them and awakening the hidden wholeness of being to express themselves in the outer dimension in selfless service to the organization, society, and the world at large.

This spiritual intelligence model focuses on the existential, learning, spiritual, moral, and ethical dimensions of leadership wholeness applied in leadership development, organization development, workplace-life fulfillment, corporate social responsibility, and environmental stewardship. The previous literature on spirituality intelligence looked at spirituality as an extrinsic component organizational leadership, whereas this model looks at spirituality as an integral part of leadership and whole system transformation (Atroszko et al., 2021). The essential themes depicted in this book are present across gender, cultures, organizations, and spiritual traditions. The spiritual intelligence model, described in this book, can be used for holistic leadership development focused on the whole Self in current organizational contexts. As the organization becomes global, the workplace becomes more multi-cultural; the findings in this study provide insights for developing global leaders with spiritual intelligence and a sense of wholeness. This model enriches the research on workplace spirituality and spiritual leadership with new insights into wholeness and spiritual intelligence (Altman et al., 2022; Dhiman, 2017; Dhiman & Kriger, 2018; Fry, 2007; Gull & Doh, 2004; Singh & Singh, 2022). Connecting leadership wholeness and spiritual intelligence from a broader perspective of corporate spiritual responsibility and environmental stewardship, this model could strengthen the emerging leaders in the wake of rising global ethical challenges and escalating ecological crises. Chapters 3–6 outlined the four aspects of the leaders' journey towards wholeness: Sensing Crisis, Embracing Crisis, Awakening Wholeness, and Serving the Greater Good through inner explorations and practicing the ethic of co-responsibility.

Sensing Crisis

Chapter 3 discussed a crucial part of leaders' journey towards wholeness: their deep awareness and recognition of the various kinds and levels of crises happening in their world, their organizational contexts, and the life of the world. Here, the word "crisis" does not imply an impending catastrophe but is considered a crucible for transformation, a catalyst for change. Cambridge Dictionary defines "sensing as to feel or experience something without being able to explain exactly how." The word "sensing" means "the moment we redirect our attention from the external object to the internal source" (Scharmer, 2022: 3). Hence, "sensing" is understood as the ability to recognize the situation and discern the deeper meaning of it. A spiritual crisis is defined as a "crucial episode of life in which fundamental questions about the meaning and purpose of life are raised" (American Dictionary of Psychology, 2022: 1). The experience of the spiritual crisis can be categorized into two major types: the internal crisis and the external crisis. The internal crisis manifested as Identity Crisis, Value Crisis, and Spiritual Crisis, and the various aspects of external crisis manifested as Social Crisis and Ecological Crisis (see Fig. 2.1). For leaders in this study, the experience of these crises provoked questions of meaning and purpose at the internal level and questions of justice, freedom, and responsibility at the external level. The manifestation of existential spiritual crisis such as identity crises, value crises, the meaning crisis on the inner side, and social and environmental crises on the outer side results in massive disruptions. Alienation of Self and other (sociological crisis), alienation of Self from nature (ecological crisis), and alienation of Self from the higher Self (ethical crisis) result in brokenness (Scharmer, 2022). Those experiences informed the leaders' spirituality and leadership perspective. The external crises flow from the internal crisis, and both reinforce each other, making the situation worse. By its very nature, a crisis is chaotic and complex, and thus it can provoke danger or trigger opportunities for growth and transformation. A new way of seeing and sensing is needed to move from brokenness to the wholeness of life. Leaders experience existential spiritual crises in different ways depending on the context of their lives and business environment. The internal crises manifested in the form of identity crises, value crises, and meaning crises.

The leaders demonstrated the ability to sense the spiritual crisis that presented itself as alienation from Self and nature (ecological crisis), alienation from Self and the other (social crisis) alienation from Self and the higher Self (ethical crisis). These leaders experienced this brokenness as a spiritual, social, and ecological crisis. Their lives were shaken for some time by intense psychological and emotional turmoil leading to traumatic experiences, both personal, social, and collective traumas (Linstroth, 2022). These necessary and critical life experiences have shaped their journey towards wholeness and outlook on leadership and Spirituality. They described their experiences as crucibles of learning. The process of sensing or pre-cognition of crises manifests deeper Intelligence and awareness that helps leaders take a bold stand of conceiving and embracing the challenge with a positive and constructive attitude. Lastly, these prominent leaders manifested how they learned from these crises by embracing them as a challenge rather than problems to discover critical insights in their journey towards wholeness through Lenz of spiritual intelligence.

Chapter 3 showed how the leaders could sense and identify various dimensions of their spiritual crisis from an identity crisis, value crisis, spiritual crisis, social crisis, and ecological crisis. From their ability to sense crisis, they embraced the crisis as a challenge with tenacity, courage, and confidence, turning them into opportunities for awakening the hidden wholeness of life.

Embracing Crisis

The leaders in the study embraced their spiritual crisis as a challenge turning them into an alchemy of transformation. Engaging in self-exploration rather than self-denial and projection, the leaders turned the negative experiences into a catalyst for change and growth. People who refused to embrace the crisis as a challenge either perished or remained in their brokenness. The ability to embrace crisis as an opportunity made the leaders challenge their assumptions and discover their inner capacity for higher consciousness and innate ability to respond to the situation with greater wisdom, compassion, and courage, maintaining a sense of equanimity regardless of the situation. The five aspects of the process of embracing the crisis are: *Awareness of strengths and weaknesses, Self-acceptance, Failure as a learning experience, Growing in authenticity, and Matching soul and role* (see Fig. 4.1). The qualities of deep awareness, deep acceptance, learning, and integration helped them to grow as authentic, creative, wise, and courageous leaders. The supportive network of resources and trustworthy mentors helped the leaders to grow in resilience, grit, and grace to embrace the crisis as an opportunity for growth and transformation. The creativity of crisis emerges from integrating polarities and forging a new path for change and growth. Leaders learned to integrate and create a synthesis of people, process, quality, productivity, profit, and planet (Hollnagel, 2022) to realize more remarkable life's wholeness.

In embracing crisis, the leaders demonstrated the deepest level of self-acceptance, learning from their failures and weaknesses and turning them into the alchemy of inner transformation. They realized that wholeness is not just in success alone, but weakness and shadows are part and parcel of their journey towards wholeness. They were demonstrating the ability to hold the paradox of light and shadow, which resulted in a profound shift in consciousness, broadening the base of their life and deepening the roots of understanding. Living a life of authenticity and integrity helped leaders embrace life fully and integrate who they are with what they do. These leaders showed the remarkable resilience of spirit in embracing the whole of their life with its light and shadow, which resulted in the experience of incredible vibrancy, harmony, and integration.

Awakening Hidden Wholeness

Chapter 5's third essential theme, Awakening Hidden Wholeness, describes the leaders' profound inner transformation, self-discovery, and self-realization process. The sub-themes present the various aspects of the leader's inner journey are presented in Fig. 4.1. The spiritual awakening process begins with the *cultivation of spiritual practices* leading to *inner silence* and *inner transformation*. Then, the discovery of the pure potential emerges as the soul *keeps moving towards the light of consciousness*, penetrating through the illusions and touching reality. This spiritual awakening to wholeness culminates in the experience of *inner harmony, bliss, and profound inner peace*. Tolle (quoted in Kieves, 2018: 46) said, "That is real spiritual awakening when something emerges from within you that is deeper than who you thought you were. So, the person is still there, but one could almost say that something more powerful shines through the person." This spiritual awakening process helps the person to embrace the whole Self. This realization led the leaders to a deeper experience of self, "I am not living by the force of the body but the force of the soul" noted Swami Bharati. The consistent spiritual practices enabled the leaders to experience spiritual awakening to wholeness and maintain a deeper sense of awareness, acceptance, awakening, and dedicate their lives for the service for the greater good.

Serving the Greater Goodness

In Chapter 6, the fourth essential theme, *Serving the Greater Good*, is described as working ethically for the benefit of all concerned with a higher awareness of responsibility for serving the common good and greater good. This theme shows the impact of leaders' awakened sense of co-responsibility and ethic of universal stewardship for the care of the soul and the care of the planet. The phrase "being at the service of all" indicates the transformed state of consciousness and the enlightened actions to benefit all sentient beings."We are not who we think we are; we are not the owners of us but beings at the service of all." Having experienced the spiritual crisis in their life and others, these leaders embraced crisis as a challenge that led them to an awakening of hidden wholeness. An awareness of interconnectedness acknowledges a deep connection among living beings sharing a common bond and roof on the same planet. From this perspective of wholeness, the spirit of unity is emphasized to overcome division and alienation manifested in the world. This higher awareness of the co-existence of reality is an antidote to the culture of division, polarization, exploitation, and mutual destruction. The capacity to honor and live with deep differences is born out of a great awareness that each one is unique and special in the galaxy of beings. This conviction presented as a deep respect for genuine differences in views, cultures, religions, spiritualities, and races and challenges one to expand and grow. From this sense of deep respect for diversity comes the willingness to learn, dialogue, and collaborate to promote harmony and well-being. The leaders' understanding of the interconnectedness of the world became the source and base for fostering the ethic of co-responsibility in serving the greater good and guiding organizations to a sustainable future. The subthemes of Serving the Greater Good: Circle of Trust (Personal Trust), Circle of Responsibility (Organizational Responsibility), Circle of Justice (Social Justice), Circle of Compassion (Global Compassion), and Circle of Stewardship (Environmental Stewardship) manifest the outer sphere of leadership wholeness as presented in Fig. 6.1.

Leaders' awakened sense of consciousness and wholeness resulted in the growing awareness of the co-existence of reality and the interdependence of beings on the planet. They practiced an ethic of co-responsibility and advocated collective responsibility in organizations across the globe to serve the greater good for a better future. A deep respect for diversity helped them to live with differences that make a difference. The ethic of co-responsibility is rooted in a culture of trust and mutuality. The leaders sought circles of relational trust to discover their identity and integrity, cultivating authentic dialogue and discernment. They influenced the broader community as a catalyst for change by creating networks of responsibility and transformation in their organizations. A holistic view of life and experience of profound spiritual crisis helped these leaders empathize with others' suffering and pain and create a circle of compassion not only for human beings but also for animals and the whole environment with concern and care for all sentient beings. In a nutshell, the leaders promoted an authentic sense of responsibility and accountability in the workplace in serving the greater good. Valuing every person encouraging them to grow and bring out their very best, facing the fire of crisis, and overcoming resistance to change, these leaders modeled the way of workplace wholeness. A deep sense of solidarity was practiced and encouraged at the global and cosmic level, especially in caring for the soul and the planet's soul. Rooted deeply in the universal values of trust, respect, responsibility, compassion, and solidarity, the leaders nurtured and modeled an ethic of co-responsibility and universal stewardship, serving the greater good in their quest for wholeness.

The spiritual intelligence model presented here helps explore the existential, learning, spiritual and ethical dimensions of leaders' inner Self and the outer dimensions of leaders' personal, organizational, social, global, and environmental Self. Through the lived experience of leaders, this model unfolds the deeper dimensions of being and doing as a whole self. This deeper and broader framework helps us discover ourselves, develop ourselves, and place ourselves where we can make the most significant contributions to organizations, communities, and the world.

In conclusion, wholeness/spiritual intelligence is a fascinating topic that has triggered my curiosity and inspired my research for over a decade. Some scholars have applied this model in their study and reported generating further interest from leaders and practitioners in applying the insights from the model in their workplace, theory, and practice. Laurie Brummit from the department of Educational Innovations, University of North Carolina at Chapel Hill, USA, had applied the wholeness model presented in this book in her research with leaders in 2021. She noted:

> It's a fascinating framework. I did use your model. I have written a manuscript from my thesis that I will be presenting on. I enjoyed learning about the concepts. When I presented at conferences, many audience members had more questions and were interested in its application in their workplace. I recall one professional that ran a hospital. She was very intrigued by the model. She specifically was looking for ways to coach and mentor doctors through the challenges/crises they experience in their jobs. I remember her being more focused on coaching new doctors, but she was not limited to that group. She wanted to know more about how the model could be used to help her work through problems with them. Or give them the model they could personally implement when necessary.

The goal of this book was to summarize the insights from the lived experience of leaders across the globe. More research is needed to explore the various implications of the idea of wholeness and spiritual intelligence as emerging topics of research and scholarship. I hope this book provides insight, inspiration, and practical wisdom for leaders, scholars, practitioners, and anyone interested in a more profound spiritual journey to wholeness and contributes to the greater goodness of life.

References

American Dictionary of Psychology, Existential Crisis, Apa.org. (2022).

Altman, Y., Neal, J., & Mayrhofer, W. (2022). *Workplace spirituality: Making a difference, Boston*. De Gruyter.

Atroszko, P. A., Skrzypińska, K., & Balcerowska, J. M. (2021). Is there a general factor of spiritual intelligence? Factorial validity of the polish adaptation of spiritual intelligence self-report inventory. *Journal of Religion and Health, 60*(5), 3591–3605. https://doi.org/10.1007/s10943-021-01350-2

Dhiman, S. (2017). On becoming a holistic leader. In *Holistic leadership*. Palgrave Macmillan. https://doi.org/10.1057/978-1-137-55571-7_1

Dhiman, S., & Kriger, M. (2018). Eastern approaches to organizational well-being: Ontological levels of leadership in Hinduism, Buddhism, and Taoism. In S. Dhiman, G. Roberts, & J. Crossman (Eds.), *The Palgrave handbook of workplace spirituality and fulfillment*. Palgrave Macmillan. https://doi.org/10.1007/978-3-319-61929-3_2-1

Emmons, R. A. (2000). Is Spirituality an intelligence? Motivation, cognition, and the psychology of ultimate concern. *The International Journal for the Psychology of Religion, 10*(1), 3–26.

Fry, L. W. (2007). Spiritual leadership: State-of-the-art and future directions for theory, research, and practice. In J. Biberman & L. Tishman (Eds.), *Spirituality in business: Theory, practice, and future directions* (pp. 133–140). Palgrave Publishers.

Griffiths, R. (2017, September). *Spiritual intelligence paradigm*. https://www.academia.edu/3854094/The_Spiritual_Intelligence_Paradigm

Gull, G. A., & Doh, J. (2004). The transmutation of the organization: Toward a more spiritual workplace. *Journal of Management Inquiry, 13*(2), 128–140.

Hollnagel, E. (2022). Systemic potentials for resilient performance. In F. Matos, P. M. Selig, & E. Henriqson (Eds.), *Resilience in a digital age. Contributions to management science*. Springer. https://doi.org/10.1007/978-3-030-85954-1_2

Kieves, T. (2018). *Thriving through uncertainly: Moving through the fear of the unknown and making change work for you*. Penguin Random House LLC.

Krause, W., & Balasescu, A. (2022). Engagement as leadership-practice for today's global wicked problems: Leadership learning for artificial Intelligence.

In G. Meiselwitz (Eds.), *Social computing and social media: Design, user experience, and impact*. HCII 2022. Lecture Notes in Computer Science, Vol. 13315. Springer. https://doi.org/10.1007/978-3-031-05061-9_41

Linstroth, J. P. (2022). Racial trauma and racism. In *Politics and racism beyond nations*. Palgrave Macmillan. https://doi.org/10.1007/978-3-030-91720-3_5

Scharmer, O. (2022, June). *The essentials of Theory U*. https://www.leadershipnow.com/leadingblog/2018/04/the_essentials_of_theory_u.html

Singh, R. K., & Singh, S. (2022). Spirituality in the workplace: A systematic review. *Management Decision, 60*(5), 1296–1325. https://doi.org/10.1108/MD-11-2020-1466

Sisk, D. A. (2019). Spiritual intelligence: Developing higher consciousness. In B. Wallace, D. A. Sisk, & J. Senior (Eds.), *The SAGE handbook of gifted and talented education*. Sage.

Sternberg, R. J. (2020). Transformational giftedness: Rethinking our paradigm of gifted education. *Roeper Review, 42*(4), 230–240.

Tafoya, D. W., & Poeth, L. (2021). From events to crises, catastrophes, and disaster: Before the collapse. In *Healthcare leadership in times of crisis*. Palgrave Macmillan. https://doi.org/10.1007/978-3-030-75965-0_3

Wigglesworth, C. (2012). *SQ21: The 21 skills of spiritual intelligence*. Selected Book.

Wilber, K. (2006). *Integral spirituality*. Shambhala Publication.

Zohar, D., & Marshall, I. (2004). *Spiritual capital: The wealth we can live by*. Berrett-Koehler Publishers.

Appendix A

Name	*Title*	*Age*	*Organization*	*Education*	*Years of experience*	*Nationality*
Sri Sri Ravishankar	Founder President	66	Art of Living International	PhD	44	India
Ingrid Vanderveldtt	Founder CEO	51	Empowering Billion Women	MBA	30	USA
Ambassador Susan Johnson	Founder President	65	Empowering Black Women International	PhD	40	USA
John Abbatte	CEO	55	McDonald Franchise, California	MBA	30	USA
Parker Palmer	Founder President	80	Center for Courage and Renewal	PhD	50	USA
Larry Zimpleman	CEO	70	Principal Insurance	MBA	40	USA
Immaculee Illibagiza	Founder President	45	Ilibagiza Foundation	PhD	20	Rwanda/USA
Tom Mahoney	CEO	66	Chairman ITA Group Holding	MBA	40	USA
Steve Lacey	CEO	68	Meredith Corporation	MBA	35	USA
Greg McBrayer	Chief Fight Controller	65	Major Airline	MBA	40	USA
Corrina Lim	CEO	58	AWARE-Singapore	MBA	30	Singapore

(continued)

T. Thakadipuram, *Leadership Wholeness, Volume 1*, Palgrave Studies in Workplace Spirituality and Fulfillment, https://doi.org/10.1007/978-3-031-08053-1

(continued)

Name	*Title*	*Age*	*Organization*	*Education*	*Years of experience*	*Nationality*
Archbishop Harry J. Flynn	Archbishop	–	Archdiocse of St. Paul& Minneapolis	PhD	50	USA
Thurston Temple	Founder President	70	Core Light	MA	40	South Arica/USA
William Jarema	Founder President	67	Mercy Center for Counselling	MSC	35	UKRAINE/USA
Gary Selman	Founder CEO	72	First Call Leadership Consulting Firm	MBA	40	USA
Carolyn Washburn	Chief Editor	58	Des Moines Register/Cincinnati Tribune	MA	35	USA
Nick Nissley	President	56	Michigan Community College	PhD	30	USA
Andy Anderson	EPHA Chief	70	EPA, USA	LLB PhD	40	USA
Swami Veda Bharathi	Founder President	–	Himalayan Meditation Center	PhD	55	India
Credo Mutua	Chief Zulu Shaman	–	African Renaissance Center	PhD	45	South Africa
Abbot Phap Son	Abbot	59	Plum Village Buddhist Monastery	MA	25	Spain
[a]Abbess Pema Kuang	Abbess	75	Buddhist Monastery	MA	40	Ireland
Sr. Rosalind Gefre	Founder President	–	Gefre Massage Therapy Clinic	MA	40	USA

[a]Pseudonym is used for those participants who did not wish to be identified

Appendix B: Interview Questionnaire

"Tell me about the key moments or situations encountered in your journey towards wholeness." Exploratory probes included:

- "How did the situation come about?"
- "How did you engage in the situation?"
- "What did you feel?"
- "What was the impact of the situation?"
- "What made the experiences part of your journey towards wholeness?"

The same exploratory probes will be used for the different situations or moments of the experience of the journey towards wholeness identified by each leader participant.

T. Thakadipuram, *Leadership Wholeness, Volume 1*,
Palgrave Studies in Workplace Spirituality and Fulfillment,
https://doi.org/10.1007/978-3-031-08053-1

Index

T. Thakadipuram, *Leadership Wholeness, Volume 1*,
Palgrave Studies in Workplace Spirituality and Fulfillment,
https://doi.org/10.1007/978-3-031-08053-1

Y

MIX
Papier | Fördert gute Waldnutzung
FSC® C083411

Kolibri 360 GmbH
Ferdinand-Jühlke-Straße 7
99095 Erfurt, Deutschland
produktsicherheit@kolibri360.de